T0305061

Corruption and Criminal Justice

Corruption and Criminal Justice

Bridging Economic and Legal Perspectives

Tina Søreide

Professor, Norwegian School of Economics (NHH), Norway

Edward Elgar
PUBLISHING

Cheltenham, UK • Northampton, MA, USA

Published by
Edward Elgar Publishing Limited
The Lypiatts
15 Lansdown Road
Cheltenham
Glos GL50 2JA
UK

Edward Elgar Publishing, Inc.
William Pratt House
9 Dewey Court
Northampton
Massachusetts 01060
USA

A catalogue record for this book
is available from the British Library

Library of Congress Control Number: 2015952685

This book is available electronically in the **Elgar**online
Law subject collection
DOI 10.4337/9781784715984

ISBN 978 1 78471 597 7 (cased)
ISBN 978 1 78471 598 4 (eBook)

Typeset by Columns Design XML Ltd, Reading
Printed and bound by CPI Group (UK) Ltd, Croydon, CR0 4YY

Contents

Preface and acknowledgements

Since the beginning of this century – a century that seems no less corrupt than the ones that preceded it – I have had the opportunity to observe corruption in many of its forms. I have studied the problem in different countries, both rich and poor, at different levels of governance, and in different industries and sectors. Equipped with a variety of analytical tools, I have tried to understand the mechanisms of bribery, the inner life of public institutions, and the political economy of governance in the most challenged societies. As a policy-oriented researcher and 'governance expert' – for a period employed by a large development partner – I have sought to come up with recommendations for governments and state institutions that want to do battle with corruption.

For a dozen years, while I thought my work was meaningful, some questions kept nagging at me, and left me feeling incapable of understanding the very problems I was expected to solve: Why is it so difficult to hold these gangsters accountable for their corruption? Why are those politicians and officials who are known to steal from state coffers not removed from public office? Why are firms allowed to continue their practices despite being widely suspected of offering bribes? How can civil servants extort clients for bribes undisturbed by law enforcement? I had approached corruption from many different angles, but not from a legal perspective, and I became increasingly aware that criminal law was the key to many of the problems I wanted to solve. After all, criminal law is the ultimate reaction to harmful acts in a society, and when this reaction cannot be relied on to hold offenders accountable, other integrity mechanisms – 'international best practice good governance' among them – seem to fail as well.

By a fortunate coincidence, as I came to this conclusion I was invited by the Faculty of Law at the University of Bergen, Norway (where I happen to live) to do a postdoctoral project on the economics of criminal law. The project, which is part of a research program called 'Theory in Practice: Risks and Responses in the Modern Criminal Law,' is financed by the Norwegian Research Council. The program managers are Jørn Jacobsen and Linda Gröning, to whom I am forever grateful, not 'only' for the three-year stay at their faculty, but also for our many lively debates about criminal law and society. I am also very grateful to the faculty's criminal law research group, who had never before let an economist be part of their team. My handicap as a novice in law was graciously endured, and I was allowed to learn from my colleagues, who did not necessarily expect me to educate them about economics in return. What I *was* asked to do was to write something about what those involved in criminal law could learn from my experiences with various forms of governance dysfunctions, discuss some of the current criminal law challenges in the slippery world of corruption, and consider solutions from the perspective of both law and economics. Which is how this book began.

Much of the intersection between law and economics, I found, is *terra incognita*, a land largely unexplored despite the literature called 'law and economics.' The mere question of what constitutes an efficient criminal law response to corruption is usually understood very differently in these two camps. But by combining their different approaches to, and critiques of, criminal justice responses of corruption, it becomes easier to see what a well-performing criminal justice system might look like. In terms of developing sustainable strategies to combat corruption, the combined reasoning is greater than the sum of its parts.

Without direct and indirect support from colleagues, friends, managers and mentors, this book project would never reach its completion. In my studies of corruption, development and law enforcement, I have had the benefit of generous advice from more experienced researchers in the field. Especially, I want to thank Susan Rose-Ackerman, Kalle Moene, and Mark Pieth. Moreover, the book draws on insights generated over years engaged in the development community, and I am grateful for numerous useful debates with former colleagues at the Chr. Michelsen Institute (CMI) and the World Bank. The book project was encouraged by colleagues at the Faculty of Law, University of Bergen. Especially I am grateful to Linda Gröning, Jørn Jacobsen and Ernst Nordtveit. Also, a deep thank you goes to the Norwegian School of Economics (NHH), Department of Auditing, Accounting and Law, where I now work, for generously securing the opportunity to complete this book project – and encouraging continued research in the law and economics of corruption.

Many of the messages in the book are studied in greater detail in research projects conducted with co-authors on various papers over the past three years, including Emmanuelle Auriol, Kjetil Bjorvatn, Linda Gröning, Erling Hjelmeng, Kalle Moene, Susan Rose-Ackerman, Arne Tostensen, Ingvild Aagedal Skage, Rasmus Wandall and Aled Williams. In addition, the book has benefited from useful dialogue with Jennifer

Arlen, Jan Fridthjof Bernt, Nicola Bonnuci, Marianne Djupesland, Pascale Dubois, Birthe Eriksen, Antonio Estache, Frank Fariello, Siri Gloppen, Charles Kenny, Drago Kos, Michael Kramer, Nuno Garoupa, Alon Harel, Charles Kenny, Gert Johan Kjelby, Ivar Kolstad, Helge Kvamme, Paul Lagunes, Abiola Makinwa, Yasutomo Morigiwa, Guttorm Schjelderup, Elin Skaar, Guro Slettemark, Peter Solmssen, Bertil Tungodden, Ørnulf Øyen, and José Ugaz. Research assistance from Elias Braunfels, Emilie Hornfelt Paulsen, and Jan Tore Remøy has been greatly acknowledged, and my son, Eirik, kindly helped to find references to philosophers in the past.

Finally, I want to give a big thank you to those who have kept on with me through the writing process. Nigel Quinney advised me on all parts of the book. He pointed out weak arguments and did what he could to bring my dull drafts up to a readable level (any remaining errors and boring passages are totally my fault). Edward Elgar endorsed this project even before it started, and that has been an enormous support and motivation. Especially, I want to thank Tara Gorvine, Stephen Gutierrez and Victoria Litherland. I am also grateful to my husband Olav, who bore with me – never fed up seeing me lost in the laptop over the summer.

Tina Søreide
Bergen, 15 August 2015

PART I

The problem and its consequences

The problem and its consequences

1. Introduction

The term 'corruption' means 'impairment of integrity, virtue, or moral principle,' according to *Merriam-Webster's Dictionary*,[1] and comes from the Latin *com*, meaning 'with, together,' and *rumpere*, meaning 'to break.' It is often used to mean that something is rotten, in a depraved state, unsound, putrefied. Today, the word is associated with the illegitimate use of authority for personal gain, most commonly pertaining to the authority administered by government institutions. Corrupt individuals entrusted with protecting and promoting social values breach their duties and sell government decisions that should not be for sale. In general, those who demand and buy the decisions through bribery are equally culpable. Widespread corruption undermines the basis for state authority and the foundations for development. Such far-reaching consequences make corruption a serious form of crime.

How fit is the criminal justice system to deal with the challenge of corruption? This book approaches that question by exploring the nature and impact of corruption, examining current criminal law responses, analyzing the obstacles to more effective control of corruption, and suggesting ways of overcoming those obstacles. Written for practitioners, policymakers, and scholars, this book draws on both conceptual insights and empirical evidence to help understand why and where corruption thrives and what might be done to combat it more strategically.

Corruption as both a concept to be analyzed and a practical problem to be tackled has attracted the attention of scholars from many fields, especially law, economics, anthropology, and political science. Members of these disciplines have had much to say about corruption, but less to say to one another. This book is intended to stimulate scholarly dialogue, if not between all four disciplines, then at least between law and economics. Their lack of appreciation of the other disciplines' reasoning denies legal scholars and economists the opportunity to make use of interpretive tools that could yield a richer understanding of the problem that both disciplines strive to unravel but neither adequately understands.

---

[1] Merriam-Webster: http://www.merriam-webster.com/dictionary/corruption (retrieved 5 August 2015).

Most economists, for instance, continue to pay far too little attention to the moral dimension of corruption, blinkered by their view of corrupt officials as profoundly rational actors. For their part, many legal scholars remain reluctant to embrace economic solutions – on settlements, leniency, corporate criminal liability, and more – that could help curb the scourge of corruption. If economists and legal scholars are more open to borrowing ideas and insights from one another, they will be better placed to provide policymakers with anticorruption strategies that work far more efficiently.

1.1   THE SCOPE OF THIS BOOK

This book began life as a study of criminal law responses to the problem of corruption. The study took an economic perspective, yet was conducted in a Nordic law faculty where I was frequently reminded of legal principles and values. Setting out with a notion of criminal justice systems as penalty-imposing entities, I came to realize that there are in fact multiple objectives associated with these institutions, and that if basic state-society foundations are recognized, criminal justice systems may function as catalysts for norm-shaping processes in their societies.

What constitutes an efficient criminal law response and sanctioning in corruption cases, however, must be investigated from several angles, and if insights are to have practical implications, it helps if experts of both law and economy understand and recognize the same conclusions and strive to understand each other's concepts. But then, as one often discovers in cross-disciplinary environments, even a seemingly precise word such as 'corruption' encompasses too many meanings and is subject to such disparate analytical approaches to permit mutual understanding. Despite sharing a common technical language because of similarities in law enforcement approaches across countries, a legal scholar and an economist may well come to very different conclusions about the nature and implementation of strategic solutions to corruption. By distilling down real world complexities, as well as sophisticated economic analyses and legal arguments, it might be easier to see where legal scholars and economists agree and where they disagree.

The book contributes to the ongoing international debate about what we do and should do to control corruption – a debate in which numerous researchers, government decision-makers, and policy advisers participate, each contributing a different set of perspectives, arguments, examples, and opinions. One of the arguments that this book brings to the debate is that criminal justice systems play a decisive role for the performance of integrity mechanisms in a society, and that this role is too often ignored or misunderstood by those who promote good governance more generally. Anticorruption refers to a whole lot of initiatives beyond the scope of criminal law, initiatives that in different ways raise the level of integrity in a society, in the sense of promoting adherence to moral and ethical codes, preventing the theft of common resources, and reducing unfair decision-making. The criminal justice system should not replace other critically important governance integrity mechanisms; instead, it is the backbone that secures their performance. For a criminal justice system to play this role, its laws and sanctions must be supported by the society of which it is a part. The more embedded this system is in society, the less repressive it has to be and the fewer the resources that have to be spent on law enforcement. The system will not be seen as legitimate unless it convincingly contributes to preventing crime, operates with fair procedures, and allocates its resources cost-efficiently. Given these aims, I argue, law enforcement can benefit substantially from an economic understanding of efficiency, which refers to a state where resources are allocated depending on what has the best effect in society while avoiding waste. The challenge is to determine how trade-offs can be made between core legal principles and pragmatic solutions without sacrificing the former or undercutting the latter.

In terms of practical proposals for law enforcement improvements, I argue that there is still much to gain from harmonized legal definitions, especially of criminal negligence. Responsibility should be extended to include those who benefit indirectly from corruption or condone the facts even if they are in a position to react against the crime. Private sector players, which depend on society's recognition of a legal framework within which profits can be made, should not be allowed to do business unless they provide the most essential information necessary for efficient law enforcement and have basic corporate compliance systems in place. Current law enforcement challenges, combined with a weaker position of states vis-à-vis powerful multinational corporations, can only be met if corporate liability rules are enforced, recognizing the substantial differences between the regulation of organizations involved in crime and the regulation of criminally liable individuals. The principles of duty-based sanctions regimes, which increasingly guide the criminal justice regulation of corporate crime in the private sector, should be used in the regulation of state institutions as well, albeit with a different set of sanctions than those used for the private sector. When it comes to processing cases of corporate liability, I argue that negotiated settlements enhance the prosecutor's flexibility and that all countries should formally introduce such settlements into their law enforcement systems, yet there are challenging trade-offs that must be understood and addressed. When it comes to criminal sanctions, I discuss principles for '*efficient sanctions*' – a phrase that implies that sanctions should not be more repressive than they need to be, although determining need is difficult in this context. I also argue that debarment of suppliers for public contracts should be taken out of the hands of the government agencies that manage public procurement and added to the arsenal of sanctions that can be imposed by the criminal law system. In addition, I emphasize that many activities – such as lobbyism and crony capitalism – occupy a gray zone of corruption and are difficult to investigate and prosecute from a criminal law perspective. Efficient strategies, therefore, require coordination between a variety of law enforcement institutions that observe the problem from different perspectives, including tax authorities, competition authorities, and organized crime units.

The book is organized into two parts. The problem of corruption, its consequences, and practical law enforcement difficulties are presented in part 1. The practical value of principles and conceptual solutions depend of course on how they match the characteristics of the problem. This is a difficulty when it comes to corruption because it is not only a multi-faceted problem; there is also huge variation across countries in the problem's extent, and its underlying causes are difficult to determine. Part 2 discusses solutions. With their methodological tools for assessing challenges in society and theoretical frameworks for analyzing efficiency, economists offer illuminating perspectives on the problem of corruption and ideas about efficient law enforcement. These conceptual solutions encounter difficulties in implementation, mostly due to an apparent reluctance among legal scholars to reassess their principles and traditional solutions in light of the law enforcement benefits that pragmatic anticorruption approaches can yield.

This introductory chapter sets the stage for the rest of the book by describing and defining key concepts, terms, and relationships. The following section, section 2, introduces corruption as a concept and a complex phenomenon that takes different forms. Section 3 comments on different academic understandings of the corruption phenomenon, and highlights distinctive approaches in law and economics that are especially relevant for arguments presented in this book. Section 4 explains what I understand by *anticorruption strategies* and *integrity systems*, while section 5 provides a brief overview of criminal law responses to corruption, and points at the difficulty of defining *efficiency* in a criminal law context. These introductory clarifications, standpoints, and perspectives are built upon throughout the book.

1.2 CORRUPTION: A MANY-HEADED MONSTER

1.2.1 The Law Enforcement Difficulty

We know quite a lot about the mechanisms of corruption and the various forms it can take, but that does not necessarily mean that we are well equipped to deter, detect, police, and prosecute it. The obstacles preventing effective law enforcement are numerous and often daunting.

While this book addresses corruption at all levels of governance, the problems involving the higher levels of governance are the most challenging. I will not keep referring to Latin terms, but the much cited proverb from ancient Greece, *corruptio optimi pessima* – which means 'the corruption of the best is the worst' – seems to indicate that this fact has been understood for as long as there have been governments.[2]

Corruption at elevated political levels is typically as hard to combat as it is destructive of a government's legitimacy and even of a country's internal stability. When citizens see their deceitful leaders acting with impunity and thwarting constitutional checks and balances, the resulting anger and frustration can generate sympathy and recruits for guerrilla groups and rebellions. The Arab Spring that started in December 2010 in Tunisia and Algeria, for instance, was fueled in part by popular anger at regimes that were not only autocratic but also corrupt.[3] What was pushing people over the edge, according to Sarah Chayes (2015:70) 'wasn't just poverty or misfortune in general – it was poverty in combination with acute injustice: the visible, daily contrast between ordinary people's privations and the ostentatious display of lavish wealth corruptly siphoned off by ruling cliques from what was broadly understood to be public resources.' Furthermore, as Louise Shelley (2014) explains, political corruption is one of the reasons why terrorist groups and crime syndicates from Chechnya to the Middle East to Brazil manage to recruit followers prepared to undertake operations that could cost them their lives.

This readiness to take up arms reflects a widespread sense of powerlessness among ordinary citizens who know corruption is not confined to a handful of national leaders, but permeates domestic elites and is tolerated or even encouraged by powerful international actors. High-level

---

[2]   Merriam-Webster: http://www.merriam-webster.com/dictionary/corruptio%20optimi%20pessima (retrieved on 5 August 2015). According to Hume and Beauchamp (2007:141), the phrase may have its origin in Aristotle's *Nichomachean Ethics*.

[3]   Nucifora, Churchill and Rijkers (2015).

corruption, such as the systematic demands for bribes associated with Indonesia's Suharto regime; the large-scale 'grabbing' in Kenya by Presidents Kenyatta, arap Moi, and Kibaki; and the strategic manipulation of state institutions by President Fujimori in Peru, cannot take place unless the central players in a regime have a powerful group of followers. Domestic corporate elites also hold a huge part of the responsibility in such cases, because they have accepted political corruption in return for favorable industry regulation and the willingness of law enforcement officials to turn a blind eye to corporate misdeeds. For their part, many foreign corporations have gladly paid bribes to avoid competitive pressures and secure inflated contract payments.

Corruption at political levels is hard to combat through law enforcement systems, in part because it can take place without the formal involvement of government representatives or elected political leaders, and therefore, it is difficult to hold them criminally liable. Informally, representatives of the executive may allow their family members or their allies to occupy a position from where they can control entry into a market, the allocation of subsidies, or other framework conditions. They can use this control to manipulate the market in exchange for bribes, yet their activities are largely hidden from the view of law enforcers, especially enforcers from other countries. Bribe transactions are difficult to verify, especially when masquerading as apparently reasonable consultancy payments or smuggled within legitimate deals. The recipient may bank the bribes in secret bank accounts, accept them and keep them in the form of cash, or competently launder them. Criminal law investigators often have a difficult, if not impossible, job to identify illegal parts of apparently legal operations and separate those who should be held liable from those who are most likely honest. On top of these difficulties, investigators may not know for certain whom in their own ranks they can trust. Corrupt networks may cut across politics, state administration, and the private sector, and in some cases obstacles to investigation and prosecution come from inside the prosecuting authorities.

The more a society suffers because of corruption, the more visible the international community's shortcomings typically are in terms of providing the kind of assistance or bringing to bear the kind of pressure that might have helped the society follow a less corrupt and a more development-friendly path. Pressures and sanctions imposed by foreign or international bodies are not impotent, but they are much less powerful than effective law enforcement within the country where the corruption occurs. A court case in the United States or northwestern Europe involving firms involved in bribery in, say, Libya, will not solve Libya's corruption problems, even if it raises the risks faced by multinational corporations that conduct business in those countries. The problem of corruption cannot be solved outside the societies where it occurs, but unquestionably, it provides a helping hand if international players involved in the crime are held liable abroad.[4]

As Transparency International has pointed out, the risks of political corruption are not confined to poor and middle-income countries. Many of the 427 foreign bribery cases reported by the Organisation for Economic Co-operation and Development (OECD) (2014) involve corruption in countries scoring high on the United Nations Human Development Index. In the most developed societies, some forms of undue influence might go unnoticed due to their unclear legal status or because law enforcers simply do not search for corruption in their countries' government institutions. But there are good reasons to keep an eye on close ties between politicians and firms, among them the lure of protectionist policies, subsidies, and market-share enhancing mergers, all of which high-ranking government representatives might control. A case that helped dispel the naïvety that until recently blinded many Europeans was the French Elf Aquitaine case, associated with what is now Total – an oil company with a network of allies in French politics.[5] The oil producer, which had obtained lucrative contracts by greasing the palms of the leaders of African natural resource-rich economies, was used by its executives as a private bank account for buying political favors, mistresses, fine art, apartments, and other luxuries. The case, described by *The Guardian* (on 12 November 2007) as 'the biggest fraud inquiry in Europe since the Second World War,' was investigated under the leadership of magistrate Eva Joly. Not only did she encounter substantial resistance from leaders of several French state institutions, she also received death threats and had to be protected by security guards during the whole criminal justice process (Joly, 2003).

The global financial crisis that started in 2007 when the US housing bubble burst, which in turn had been created by the irresponsible supply of mortgages, is another reminder of how corporate cronyism can challenge any democracy. Weak government regulation allowed or encouraged questionable trading practices, compensation structures that encouraged short-term deal flow over long-term value creation, and a lack of adequate capital holdings from banks and insurance companies to back the financial commitments they were making. Despite the huge

---

[4] For a taxonomy of 'international players' and their role in causing and curbing corruption, see discussions in Rose-Ackerman and Carrington (2013).

[5] The oil producer *Elf Aquitaine* was partly privatized in 1994, merged into *TotalFinaElf* in 2000, and since 2003 it has been operating under the name *Total*.

losses sustained by national economies, major financial organizations, and millions of families, hardly any business leaders were held criminally liable for creating the conditions that precipitated the global economic crisis, and suspicions grew that their influential friends in government had protected them from prosecution.[6] In recent years, it has become evident that weaknesses in the most developed countries' financial regulation harm economic development across the globe. Cases have emerged in which the largest banks in Europe and the United States were involved in money laundering, collaboration with the Mafia, tax evasion, helping clients break UN imposed sanctions, and negligence when it comes to reporting other forms of highly suspect transactions. Evidently, financial secrecy and tax avoidance are no longer concerns associated primarily with Caribbean islands.[7] The LuxLeaks scandal, which broke in December 2014 with the disclosure of a large number of secret tax agreements in Luxembourg, leaves no doubt that multinational corporations – such as Pepsi, IKEA, AIG, Coach, Deutsche Bank, and around 330 others in this case – exploit the lack of financial regulatory coordination for highly unethical tax planning and for hiding whatever transactions they may have reason to hide.[8]

Criminal justice systems are important components in the fight against corruption. But whether they are the most important institutions is difficult to say. Peter Eigen, the founding father of Transparency International, once told me that 'criminal law is the least interesting [topic] you can study if you want to control corruption!'[9] His point was to emphasize the importance of a holistic approach, where a broad set of integrity mechanisms are put in place and the government is adequately controlled with checks and balances. Eigen has also underscored the need

---

[6]   See McCarty, Poole, and Rosenthal (2013) and Cargill (2014).

[7]   Banks found to have been involved in one or several of these offenses include KPMG, ABN AMRO Bank, Citigroup, Barclays, Bank of America, Riggs Bank, UBS, HSBC, the Royal Bank of Scotland, and the Bank of New York, among others. For a useful introduction to the problem of financial secrecy, see Shaxson (2011), NOU (2009) and the websites of civil society organizations working for financial transparency, including Tax Justice Network, Global Financial Integrity, Global Witness and Publish What You Pay.

[8]   The confidential tax agreements were identified through investigative journalism by ICIJ, The International Consortium of Investigative Journalists, see http://www.icij.org/ – in particular on LuxLeaks: http://www.icij.org/project/luxembourg-leaks.

[9]   Conversation with the author in Trondheim, Norway, on 7 February 2015. See Eigen (2003) for an account of how he established Transparency International and his views on how to control corruption.

to confront corruption from many angles with the involvement of various types of actors, including civil society, the private sector, and government institutions.

A holistic approach is indeed essential, but it does not render the criminal justice system irrelevant. To the contrary, the corruption-controlling effect of a holistic approach will rely largely on the presence of a criminal justice system. A spectrum of mechanisms can enhance integrity in various institutions, but criminal justice institutions form the bedrock upon which a government's efforts to control harmful acts must be based. Unless the criminal justice system functions well, other integrity systems may fail to function as intended.

But what, exactly, does it mean for the criminal justice systems to 'function well?' The detection of and reaction against corruption can assume many forms, serve different objectives, and be coordinated in various ways with other anticorruption forces in a society. In addition, the criminal justice system's rigid institutional structures can make it difficult to imagine alternative ways of approaching and controlling crime. These systems are replete with principles established to protect legal values, many of which operate on the basis of case law that stretches back hundreds of years, and they are usually not environments in which reformist perspectives are strongly encouraged. Furthermore, corruption poses challenges of a sort that many current systems are not designed to handle. Most criminal justice systems are developed to tackle simpler forms of crime, in which one or more individuals are responsible for a clearly defined crime and are identified through investigation, their guilt is clearly established in court, and they cannot escape clear-cut sanctions such as fines or incarceration imposed by a judge. Complex cases of corruption present much sterner challenges. A network of allies, often spread across multiple jurisdictions, may have a variety of ambiguous, shadowy responsibilities for the crime. It might be clear that they draw benefits from the corruption, and yet it may be extremely difficult to hold them criminally liable. The crime may be hidden in complex organizations or behind informal power structures that trump formal government hierarchies. What should the criminal justice response be when corruption undermines government institutions, subverts legal systems, and, as it happens in some countries, threatens the very existence of the state?

From a pragmatic point of view it is clear that we cannot allow corruption to destroy societies simply because the problem does not fit with the organization and design of our criminal justice systems and jurisdictions. Thus, we should determine what constitutes an efficient criminal law response, and then adjust our systems accordingly. From a more conservative perspective, however, there are obvious risks associated with a departure from the procedures associated with a predictable well-developed and value-based criminal justice system. When challenged with new forms of crime, ad hoc modifications are tempting. The problem is that there will always be new forms of crime – as society develops, whereas the qualities associated with a stable system – well embedded in society and based on long traditions – could be exactly what we need to stand against new forms of crime. While a narrow approach to the problem would make it easier to find solutions, it is necessary to take into account this duality if we want to develop coherent strategies for more efficient criminal justice responses to corruption and other complex forms of crime.

1.2.2   The Concept of Corruption and Corrupt Acts

Before we can determine the role the criminal justice system should play in the fight against corruption, we first need a clear notion of the corruption phenomenon. Without clarifying what needs to be combated, we cannot hope to prevail. Corrupt players will easily navigate around law enforcement measures, while governments may be able to look as though they are tackling the problem while in reality getting nowhere. A nuanced typology of corruption's diverse forms, combined with knowledge about its extent, is necessary to craft a targeted response and to evaluate how anticorruption measures work in practice.

Corruption is difficult to place within a legal definition. The 'corruption' refers to depravity and grave immorality, and how one pretends to be loyal while betraying the institution one represents and the values one is supposed to protect. In her book about the concept, Laura Underkuffler (2014) describes corruption as a 'dispositional concept,' meaning that it may refer to a state of mind rather than to an act. The word 'corrupt' is often used to describe what a person has become or the absence of integrity in an institution, and as such, the problem is difficult to regulate through criminal law. In addition, if we take 'corruption' to refer to 'something rotten,' we need to have some idea of the required extent of the rottenness for an act to qualify as 'corrupt.' The everyday greed with which most of us struggle, including propensities to exploit positions, circumstances, and even friends for personal gain of some sort, is not necessarily sufficient to qualify as corruption. The misuse of authority and influence must be of a certain scale. This is why legal definitions often refer to *undue* influence, as if the word 'undue' is clarifying. Apparently, *some* influence peddling is fine, but at a certain level, it is simply not acceptable. That level will depend on a society's ideals, moral standards, experiences, and cultural norms, and is plainly a matter of perspective. Enforcing a law against corruption therefore requires a principle for drawing the line between the acceptable and the unacceptable.

Such a principle must be associated with the protection of the integrity that is necessary for state structures to function. State administration involves the application of a complex set of norms. Bureaucracy implies delegation of authority. Their efficient performance requires space for discretionary judgment. The performance of the state therefore depends on each representative's loyalty to government objectives, which are usually seen as steps toward further development of society as a whole. Corruption is a departure from this premise. Corrupt decision-makers offer choices that deviate from the formal aims of the institutions they represent. The corrupt decision-maker's 'costs' associated with such choices are compensated for by personal benefits of various sorts, usually in the form of monetary bribes but sometimes involving changes in status, position, or power, or some uncertain benefits to be acquired in the future. Given this compensational aspect, it makes sense to think of corruption as a *trade in decisions that should not be for sale.* Those who are willing to provide decision-makers with benefits, directly or in terms of some subtle support, expect something in return. They would not provide a decision-maker with those benefits unless they can obtain (or increase their chances of obtaining) something that would otherwise be unobtainable or at least harder to obtain. The compensation for the moral costs and risks associated with the self-serving decisions, breach of public duties, and deceit of common values is a *price,* often a negotiable price.[10] To categorize an act as corruption, it is therefore useful to search for the element of a bargain around decisions that should not be traded, including failed negotiations to reach such a bargain.

The identification of what appears to be a corrupt bargain is not sufficient for placing criminal liability, but it is a useful way to distinguish cases that call for further investigation from those where the term 'corruption' is less applicable, despite some apparently unfair allocation of benefits.

---

[10] Political theft of state revenues on a grand scale is often described as 'corruption,' which fits well with the notion of 'something rotten.' Given the importance of a nuanced approach, however, I refer to such acts as 'theft.' Nonetheless, as many cases show, the theft rarely goes on without some clear-cut corruption as well, and thus, grand-scale theft is associated with political corruption.

1.2.3 Forms of Corruption

Its indistinct content has led the term 'corruption' to be used to
encompass a range of acts, allocations, and bargains. In addition to the
word 'corruption,' the facets of the problem most frequently referred to in
this book are 'extortion,' 'bribery,' 'collusion,' and 'negligence.'

In this book, *extortion* (or *extortive corruption*) refers to situations in
which an individual or firm is exposed to pressure to pay a bribe.
Typically, this pressure takes the form of a government representative
demanding a bribe in exchange for a decision regarding a service,
license, or approval otherwise offered free of charge or at low cost.
'Extortion' can also refer to the act of demanding a bribe in exchange for
the 'opportunity' to avoid an undeserved disadvantage, such as paying a
fine, even if no offense has been committed. In these cases, it should be
noted, the bargaining powers between those negotiating a corrupt deal are
asymmetrically allocated, which means one side of the deal feel pressed
to be involved.[11]

Bribery is the offer or transfer of bribes, and is thus more act-specific
than the more character-describing 'corruption.' Bribery is often associated with the attempt to influence a government decision.[12] Cases of
bribery often involve a middleman, or in other forms, a third party. From
a legal perspective, where the aim might be to determine liability, the
question of bribery will often depend on who knew or should have
known what. From an economic perspective, from which the question is
why players make what choices, the question is rather what transactions
were made in exchange for what and to whose benefit.

Collusion (or *collusive corruption*) refers to collaboration for the joint
benefit of the collaborators at the expense of society. A bribe is offered
and willingly transferred to facilitate a service, alter a decision, or

---

[11]   Normally we think of the extorting player as the one holding a government
position. There are also cases, however, where a civil servant, a judge or
politician is exposed to extortion from clients. Facing the demands from a mafia
organization, for example, the 'bribe' can take the form of 'absence of violence'
and result in a biased decision that might be difficult to distinguish from the
circumstance where these decision-makers accept or by extortion demand a
monetary bribe.

[12]   In this book, however, I do not use the terms 'active' and 'passive' bribery
or corruption. These terms are often applied in the legal literature (including in
legal definitions), with 'active' denoting the one who pays a bribe, while the
recipient is referred to as 'passive.' I consider these concepts misleading, because
the 'passive' is often the most active and, in my view, the one who most clearly,
or actively, violates his or her duties.

influence a government strategy (for example, on taxation or protectionist policies). A business leader might negotiate industry regulation as an exchange of benefits with a minister. A school manager might collaborate with a government oversight representative to embezzle funds allocated for education. Collusive corruption is subtle and often inhabits a gray zone, where it may be hidden behind campaign finance or compensated board positions. At its simplest, it may involve a naïve willingness among high-ranking officials or politicians to support their good friends. In contrast to 'extortion,' 'collusive corruption' refers to a genuine agreement between those involved, both or all of whom benefit from the crime. The bargaining powers between those involved in the deal are now allocated more symmetrically, which means, both parties can influence the contents of the deal and none is forced to take part.

Negligence is rarely used in the corruption literature but is indeed relevant. A well-established concept in criminal law, 'negligence' holds that a person can be held criminally liable for the failure to foresee an avoidable danger and so allow it to manifest. The degree of assumed culpability is denoted with overlapping terms: 'negligence,' 'gross negligence,' and 'recklessness.' The most serious form is recklessness, usually described as a 'malfeasance,' where a defendant knowingly exposes another to the risk of injury. When it comes to criminal negligence, the 'crime' is the absence of foresight as to the prohibited consequences. Even though the failure to act responsibly may have caused enormous damage, and even though the accused was aware of the risks, there may have been no criminal intent, and therefore no culpability. In corruption contexts, negligence can be associated with business leaders who fail to take sufficient precautions to prevent their firm's involvement in corruption, or public sector managers who skip control and compliance checks on services and investments. Knowledge of corruption risks should lead to caution, and responsible players should be expected to make the necessary enquiries. Negligence is a form of criminal culpability, yet the criminal justice response is weaker compared to crimes committed with intent. In Norway, for example, driving at high speed on ice in the middle of the night implies a risk of being held criminally liable for unintentional murder if a pedestrian is hit and killed by the car. However, even if no one is hit, the act may also result in a penalty, though with a far milder sanction – typically an administrative fine. A pertinent question is whether the decision to operate in the world's most corruption-prone societies should add to the risk of being held liable for criminal negligence, even for operations that are common in countries where corruption problems are relatively rare.

A term that could easily be associated with criminal negligence is 'corruption-fueling activities,' which refers to transfers made to governments or state institutions despite a clear risk of corruption and without the necessary external controls on spending of the transferred amounts. The label is relevant for some development loans or aid transfers, as well as for transfers made by the private sector – for example, in relation to the privatization of state-owned entities or the taxes paid in connection with production and export of nonrenewable natural resources. The negligence in these cases will rarely, if ever, lead to criminal liability, although the negligence is closely associated with the causes of corruption.

Like 'corruption-fueling activities,' a number of terms are associated with corruption, although the acts that they describe are not only legal but also legitimate. 'Lobbyism,' for example, refers to acts of attempting to influence decisions made by officials in the government, especially the legislature, without concern for the consequences for other groups in society if the desired decisions are taken. When combined with payments to political parties, such influence is called 'campaign finance' and moves a step closer to the acquisition of decisions 'that should not be for sale,' especially when the payer's identity is kept confidential and voters left unable to judge the potential impact on political decisions. Although it is a democratic right for citizens to influence government decisions, these acts are often associated with corruption and are sometimes used as a cover for corrupt transactions. 'Capital flight' and 'tax avoidance' are associated with complex cases of corruption as well as grand-scale theft. The players involved are usually powerful, typically with a row of well-paid lawyers who help them find legal loopholes, create cover operations that make illegal transactions appear legal, and defend those acts in court, if necessary.

Some other terms associated with corruption are 'crony capitalism,' 'embezzlement,' 'kleptocracy,' 'state capture,' 'regulatory capture,' 'facilitation payments,' 'tender-corruption,' 'queue-corruption,' 'kickbacks,' 'patronage,' and 'rent-seeking.'[13] Several of these concepts and practices are explained later in the book. When the legal status of specific acts cannot be confirmed, I sometimes avoid using the word 'corruption,' and instead use the term 'grabbing,' referring to the act of acquiring more benefits than one is entitled to while imposing costs on other members of society.[14]

---

[13]   These terms are listed with definitions in Søreide (2014:2).

[14]   In the edited volume *Corruption, Grabbing, and Development* this was a recurrent solution for authors referring to the details of corruption cases that had not been brought to court, see Søreide and Williams (2014).

Eventually, the connection between entrenched corruption and government dysfunctions makes it relevant to address the question of 'government legitimacy' and which acts or institutions are 'legitimate.' In this book, '*not* legitimate' can be understood as regimes or government institutions that allow political theft and bureaucratic corruption to go on at the expense of the supply of basic state services and law enforcement. *Legitimacy* thus is not used with reference to a country's specific constitutional stipulations, but rather to conditions that are commonly associated with well-functioning state-society relationships.

1.3 COMPETING UNDERSTANDINGS OF THE PROBLEM

As the abundant terminology demonstrates, corruption is a many-sided phenomenon. At its core, corruption is trade in decisions that should not be for sale. But the mechanisms at play, who achieves what, and the consequences for society all depend on the decision in question, the allocation of bargaining power between those involved, and the counterfactuals (that is, what would have been the case if the corruption had not taken place). Endeavors to understand the problem lead to layers of explanatory factors. The individuals involved are part of organizations, institutions that have their own unique histories, cultures, and other qualities, and that, to varying extents, reflect the histories and cultures of the wider economic sectors and the countries to which they belong. Those involved in corruption are subject to various forms of pressures, expectations, regulations, and risks, the latter including not only the formal and informal consequences if caught in the crime, but also sometimes the consequences associated with deciding *not* to exploit the opportunities for corruption.

1.3.1 Corruption in Social Science

Not surprisingly, given the complex set of factors that must be assessed in order to understand corruption, a variety of analytical perspectives have been brought to bear on the phenomenon. As noted earlier, the disciplines most represented in the academic literature on corruption are anthropology, political science, economics, and law, while sociology has contributed importantly on crime more generally. There are few clear boundaries between these disciplines. They overlap because researchers use one another's concepts and methodologies and draw on some of the same insights from history, psychology, sociology, and philosophy. Some features found in explanations of corruption are nonetheless associated with the different disciplines.

Anthropology offers theories on how framework conditions and history shape cultural norms and individual assessments of right and wrong. Anthropologists have sometimes been criticized for being too understanding of corruption, as if such transactions can be forgiven simply by noting the presence of exogenous forces, such as an international expansion of capital or a restructuring of the state driven by foreign pressures and elite interests. Even so, many of the authors in this field see corruption as a serious obstacle to development that cannot be excused by norms and culture. What they seem to agree on, according to Sandy Robertson (2006), is that corruption must be understood as a by-product of the formal rules that seek to separate individuals from the offices they hold. Despite the obvious need for state administration, and for government representatives who act as neutrally as they can, the required institutional frameworks are constructs that regulate power and privileges on a grand scale. When judgments are heavily affected by the personal interests of the individuals involved, it is easier from a criminal law perspective to blame the individuals rather than the institutions – even if the institutions have been designed on premises accepted only by a minority of the society.[15]

Sociology approaches crime with the view to explaining the social context in which behaviors are committed. An individual's deviance from formal laws or accepted norms develops as the result of such factors as group pressures, life experiences, network of contacts, social class, opportunities in life, and familiarity with crime. While sociologists have contributed importantly to explain crime, their imprint in theories on corruption and strategies against the problem is less evident. It was nevertheless the sociologist Edwin H. Sutherland who coined the term 'white-collar crime' – as 'crime committed by a person of respectability and high social status in the course of his occupation.'[16] Sutherland (1945) emphasized the importance of *not excluding* crime committed by business leaders and the wealthy from crime definitions, and thus contributed importantly to generating support for criminal law regulation of corruption and other forms of business related crime. His arguments

---

[15]   What Robertson (2006) also underscores is the discipline's methodological advantages in studying organizations as constructs – for example, how corporations can be a construct for allocating wealth to a group of individuals at the cost of others.

[16]   Laid out in speech on 27 December 1939 to the American Sociological Association, titled *The White Collar Criminal.*

significantly influenced sociologists' understanding of crime, but as Michael L. Benson and Sally S. Simpson (2015:71–73) point out, the discipline has reached no clear consensus on theoretical approaches to explaining white-collar crime, including corruption.

Political scientists seek to explain corruption as the result of the mechanics of a larger governance system, including functional weaknesses in constitutional checks and balances and various power games. The discipline describes the formal and informal institutions and practices that shape a country's distribution of power and resources, and is a constant reminder that corruption must be seen in light of the state's position in society – that is, in light of the extent to which the social contract between citizens and state is well-formulated and respected. A corruption problem will have different solutions when rooted in a weak state – where informal loyalty to decision-makers and family matters more than formal institutions and rules – compared to a de facto dictatorship with authoritarian control of all parts of society. Bo Rothstein (2011) and Alina Mungiu-Pippidi (2015) describe how anticorruption successes are the result of how a society manages to provoke multiple forces against the problem, and claim that it cannot be fully understood by investigating individual choices.

Legal scholars approach corruption by studying legal systems and the ways in which rules can help regulate acts of corruption and the reactions against the problem. A central question for legal scholars is how to balance individuals' right to be protected from state controls, interventions, and various state-imposed burdens (such as reporting requirements and restrictions on roles and ownership) against the need to give the law enforcement system the tools it needs to respond to corruption and protect society against its consequences. The legal literature also explores numerous associated issues, including legal definitions of corruption, whether corruption should be regulated by criminal law or administrative law, who should be held responsible for corruption in a given setting, which sanctions they deserve, and how to enforce anticorruption regulations and harmonize them with other rules, institutional structures, and legal systems.

Economists consider decisions, including acts of corruption, as the result of rational individual cost-benefit assessments. Choices are assumed to be optimized according to the personal preferences of agents (meaning members of society) and information available to agents about the likely outcome of alternative options. Corruption is predicted if the individual's net benefit of committing such crime exceeds the perceived benefits associated with honest alternatives. Economic analysis of legal responses and the justice system forms a separate field of research known

as 'law and economics' and is conducted primarily by economists yet
often commented on by legal scholars. The analytical endeavors of most
relevance to the discussions in this book seek to explain how individuals
and corporations can be *incentivized* to comply with the law and report
incidents of corruption. The economic discipline also offers principles for
the allocation of scarce law enforcement resources, criteria for maintaining well-functioning checks and balances, and proposals on how to
organize state bureaucracy so as to mitigate corruption.[17]

1.3.2 Law and Economics

The 'law and economics' term easily gives an impression of harmony
between the two disciplines, or at least of a sturdy bridge between them
over which scholars can ferry complementary contributions to the fight
against corruption. In the law and economics academic discourse, however, harmony can be hard to find and bridges, where they exist, can
seem fairly unstable. In Europe especially, but also in the United States,
economists and legal scholars frequently disagree on the validity and
practical value of different theories. No single view can be categorically
associated with either discipline, but each discipline is associated with a
certain criticism of the other. Many legal scholars frown on economists'
reputation for ignoring legal principles and moral aspects, which are the
points of departure for most legal analysis. And whereas the legal
discipline stresses the importance of procedures, especially in criminal
law (where much attention is devoted to questions such as: 'Are the
offender's rights protected?'), economists are far more outcome-oriented
(and ask questions such as: 'What are the consequences of this sanction
or procedure for society at large?'). This difference explains why
economists are typically interested in the deterrent effect of sanctions
(that is, 'To what extent will harsher punishment prevent crime in the
future?'), whereas legal scholars are more likely to embrace a more
retributivist perspective (that is, 'Punishment is desirable in response to
crime irrespective of its consequences').[18] The distance between the
disciplines is further widened by their use of different methodologies.
Economists apply abstract mathematical analyses based on what outsiders often consider to be oversimplified assumptions about reality,
while the legal discipline searches for answers in philosophy, ethics, and
former court cases.

---

[17] Chapter 4 provides a review of important results in this literature.
[18] Alon Harel (2014) explains in simple words the differences between
retributivist views and classic economics.

A more fundamental difference relates to how the different disciplines tend to understand criminal acts. The classic law and economics literature (that is, economic theories of law enforcement) explains the extent of corruption in society as the aggregated result of rational choices given trade-offs between honest and illegal gains and the risk of being detected and the consequences thereof. Conceptually, deciding whether or not to commit a corrupt act is not too different from deciding whether to buy a product or a service based on its price; the decision depends on the size of the values at stake. Despite the fact that corruption is to a large extent the result of some moral judgment, classic economics has offered little room for assessing it as such. The law and economics literature accepts that rational agents can have a high moral cost for committing such crime, but the moral aspect is considered a one-dimensional character-istic, as just one among several costs in an act-consequentialist structure of reasoning. The explanatory value of classic law and economics theory is reduced to pointing out trade-offs considered by agents with suffi-ciently 'low moral costs'; the theory tells us little about the variety and relative weight of factors behind agents' moral judgments, or where those judgments come from.

The law and economics literature has generated a slew of policy recommendations that have had a significant influence on legal systems, especially in the United States, where collaboration across law and economics is common in universities. In Europe, however, there is a notable resistance to accepting such policy recommendations, which are considered too pragmatic for the protection of justice and fairness – values that are expected to have indirect impacts on moral development in society.

The divides between the two disciplines, while real, are not unbridge-able, however. Indeed, intrepid scholars have been trying to build bridges for several decades. Within law, there are those who support the classic economic understanding of law enforcement – the defining statement of this school of thought being Gary Becker's (1968) cost-benefit analysis – and among both economists and legal scholars there are skeptics who recognize weaknesses in this approach. The skeptics' main problem with the classic economic approach primarily boils down to its normative implications, especially for legal sanctions. The theory postulates that individual decision-making can be regulated by adjustments to the risk of detection and the repression level, as if the choice to commit crime can be controlled primarily by imposing higher risks (that is, higher costs) on an individual. The main purpose of criminal sanctions, therefore, is considered to be their impact on *potential* offenders, others than the offender who is subject to sanctions. Implicitly, in the case of corruption, the theory reduces the criminal justice system to an institution whose job it is to maintain a level of threats adequate to deter those who might otherwise be tempted to accept or offer bribes. A central question posed in this book – which may help to bring the disciplines together – is whether this threat-based strategy is a reliable strategy for promoting principled decision-making and for developing the moral caliber of members of society. Could it be that in our eagerness to regulate we might have drawn too ambitious normative conclusions from our very simple descriptive models of crime?

The choice of committing crime, corruption included, obviously depends on a complex set of factors; it cannot easily be 'regulated.' The integrity that keeps decision-makers from exploiting opportunities for corruption may well be the result of a mixture of rule-consequentialism, nonconsequentialist reasoning, and group rationality – if at all the result of predictable rational judgment. For many individuals, involvement in corruption is simply not an option; in their everyday life, they do not assess the trade-offs related to various crimes, such as robbing the local bank, murdering their mother-in-law, or exploiting opportunities to reap corrupt benefits. Such a stand against corruption is too important to be treated analytically as a one-dimensional cost-variable that follows exogenously from individuals' expected ranking of personal preferences. Economists are now starting to accept that an individual's subjective space for acting is more limited by his or her moral barriers than has often been assumed in the past.[19] Where these moral barriers come from is relevant for the development of efficient anticorruption solutions. As neither economists nor legal scholars have a complete answer, this is a uniting challenge – regarding which each discipline has to look beyond its traditional approaches.

1.4 ANTICORRUPTION APPROACHES AND INTEGRITY SYSTEMS

However we understand the mechanisms of corruption, there is broad consensus that governments need to keep in place barriers against it. There will always be a mix of motivations behind the decisions made by high-ranking government officials and politicians, ranging from the most selfless and benevolent ambitions to a thirst for power and personal

---

[19] This concern is not only addressed by economists. See, for example, Rose and Heywood (2013), who note a dearth of studies of integrity in the political science literature.

enrichment. Corruption leads to benefits for narrow groups at the expense of society as a whole, and the temptation of accepting just some of these benefits is the reason why this problem is widespread.[20] Despite a proclaimed commitment to anticorruption, some governments restrict markets to benefit a few, offer subsidies or tax cuts for those who can manage well without them, deviate from regulatory principles, or let their allies take over state-owned entities. Regardless of their readiness to sign anticorruption conventions, some governments condone or even contribute to financial secrecy, permitting powerful individuals and firms to use structures designed to hide corruption, evade taxes, and avoid responsibility for other forms of crime. For these different reasons, all countries need to have solid *integrity systems* in place to control procedures, assess the results of government decisions, and observe inefficiencies in state administration.

1.4.1 Detection and Prevention Beyond Criminal Law

Non-criminal strategies against corruption include a broad range of formal and informal measures, and their effect depends on the dynamics and coordination between them, as well as institutional competencies and independence. Most countries across the world have similar formal integrity systems, although their performance varies greatly. Some structures within these systems are intended to disclose rule violation, while others have primarily preventive effects.[21]

Examples of integrity mechanisms intended to *prevent* corruption are the various impartiality requirements commonly applied in state administration as well as access-to-information laws, both of which are expected to reduce the inclination for biased decision-making. Conflict-of-interest regulation is highly relevant for avoiding corrupt decisions, yet different countries define it differently in accordance with their own views on discretion, their own problems with corruption, and the structures they already have in place to prevent biased decision-making.[22]

At the political level, the most important disciplinary effect comes from democratic elections that abide by rules designed to ensure that the

---

[20] All such biases are not a result of corruption; they can be motivated by political power games, revolving-door career ambitions, or short-sighted populist campaigns.
[21] Because the risk of being detected is preventive, the distinction between disclosure and prevention may appear artificial, but in light of the function of integrity mechanisms, it makes sense to categorize them along these lines.
[22] For discussion, see Rose-Ackerman (2014).

process is free and fair. Hearing procedures are commonly employed when high-profile decisions are about to be made, so that highly skewed proposals can be rejected or amended before the decisions are made. Many countries have a public lobby register, ownership rules, and registration of ownership interests.[23] In addition, regulatory agencies – such as those that regulate utilities and exercise financial control – are often placed at arm's length from their respective government departments with the aim of preventing corrupt or populist officials from overruling their regulatory decisions.[24] To prevent corruption in markets as well as the manipulation of sector regulation and control, there are competition law, procurement rules, and employer liability rules. As part of procurement law, suppliers (firms and individuals) can be debarred from participation in future tenders if they have been involved in corruption. Disqualification for professional activities is an option in criminal law as well, albeit one rarely applied. The fact that corruption is also criminalized is expected, over the long term, to affect norms in society and raise the risks associated with corrupt acts.

State-organized integrity mechanisms intended to *disclose* corruption include various monitoring and investigation efforts as part of the law enforcement system, auditing requirements, taxation, measures to protect and reward whistle-blowers, lenient criminal law treatment upon self-reporting, and various transparency mechanisms. Other institutions in place to react on observed acts of corruption include financial intelligence units, public procurement units, competition authorities, and even foreign embassies (the latter being especially relevant in cases of cross-border bribery), although a 2014 OECD review of investigated bribery cases concluded that these four categories of institutions are notably deficient in fulfilling their anticorruption responsibilities (OECD, 2014:33). At the political level, a national audit institution usually oversees the government's administration of the state, including the details of its spending and the extent to which value for state money is secured. The role of these institutions has been steadily enforced in many developing countries, especially since the early 2000s, making high-level corruption more difficult to conduct unnoticed.[25] Outside the formal state

---

[23] For a comparative perspective on the status regarding such rules and registers, see OECD (2014).

[24] For a brief introduction to the problem and relevant literature on power hunts and corruption in the regulation of utilities, see Benitez, Estache, and Søreide (2010).

[25] The strengthened position of national audit institutions came well to impression in a comparative study of fraud in state administration conducted in

structures, other institutions such as the press and watchdogs are key players in promoting integrity. They disclose corruption and inspire formal systems to react to it, yet their role depends on the extent to which they enjoy access to information and the right to free speech.

1.4.2 Evaluation of Integrity Systems

The performance of integrity systems is subject to frequent evaluation and public debate in most countries, and some countries collaborate to secure independent evaluation of how the systems work. Internationally, the most comprehensive collaboration for such evaluation is the *Group of States against Corruption* (GRECO), an initiative from 1999 established by the Council of Europe.[26] GRECO assesses each member state's anticorruption mechanisms and presents a public report that describes their strengths and weaknesses. Upon the release of the reports, governments are given a deadline to make the required institutional adjustments. The extent to which the revealed weaknesses are acted on varies, but at least these reports make it more difficult for governments to ignore the need for sturdy integrity structures.

No less important are the assessments conducted by civil society organizations, which often reveal severe weaknesses in countries' integrity systems. Examples of such work are the National Integrity Studies (NIS) conducted by *Transparency International* chapters around the globe. Their summary of findings in Europe pointed at severe weaknesses in the barriers against political corruption. *Global Integrity*, another civil society organization, reports on a large number of integrity mechanisms for countries all over the globe, while the *World Justice Project* presents cross-country statistics on how well legal systems function, including the risks of corruption. *Reporters Without Borders* publishes a yearly index that ranks countries according to civil society's and media's opportunity to act as watchdogs. Reporters Without Borders also keeps track of the number of journalists killed because of their job.

The problem is that many corrupt decision-makers whose activities have been detected and exposed by integrity structures are likely to continue their involvement in crime unless the revealed corruption leads to hard-hitting consequences for them. Sadly, many of them will have

---

Tanzania, Malawi, and Ethiopia, a study where I was involved myself, see Søreide, Skage and Tostensen (2012).

[26] For an introduction to the Council of Europe, see: http://www.coe.int/en/web/about-us/who-we-are, and for information about GRECO, see http://www.coe.int/t/dghl/monitoring/greco/general/3.%20What%20is%20GRECO_en.asp.

reason to believe that critical voices will often abate, while investors, voters, and development partners are all pleased if integrity mechanisms are formally introduced, even though they are toothless in practice.[27] Some law enforcement initiatives run the risk of becoming *façades* behind which decision-makers can grab even more than before, while silencing critics who want to see the anticorruption laws enforced.[28] Integrity systems are therefore a necessary but insufficient barrier to corruption. Non-criminal measures can more easily be manipulated, ignored, or overruled, which is why a country also needs a system that holds those involved in corruption responsible for their crimes, whatever their position in the government hierarchy and however well connected they are to powerful private sector players. This system is the criminal justice system.

1.5 CRIMINAL JUSTICE RESPONSE

A country's criminal justice system is expected to distinguish between acts that are acceptable to society and those that are unambiguously objectionable, and then to sanction acts categorized as crime. By enforcing its criminal law, the state protects citizens not only from other citizens' crime, but also from excessive use of power by state institutions. What is the role of these functions in the context of corruption? This section clarifies what is meant by 'criminal law regulation' as this is much applied later in the book.

1.5.1 Crime and Criminal Law Regulation

References to the 'criminal justice system' usually mean criminal law and the institutional structure for enforcing this law. The term 'criminal law' denotes both the processes of developing laws (for example, drafting and revising a law, conducting some form of consultation on the proposed law's merits, approving the law by the constitutionally defined legislative institution, and publishing the law) and the resulting legislation. The institutional structure for criminal law enforcement includes police forces, prosecutorial units, courts, prisons, and correctional services. The

---

[27] Frequent failure to enforce laws against corruption led the international anticorruption watchdog, Transparency International, to choose strategies against impunity as one of their main focus areas.

[28] The concept of 'good governance façades' (for grabbing), studied by Moene and Søreide (2015), will be further addressed in Chapter 6.

enforcement process that takes place in this system, 'the criminal justice value chain,' typically includes the following steps:

(1) having a case disclosed or suspicion reported;
(2) conducting an investigation by collecting evidence and hearing testimonies from the accused and witnesses;
(3) charging the perpetrator or settling the case by some (formal or informal) plea bargaining;
(4) holding a trial at which the evidence is weighed up by a jury or judge (not if the case is solved outside of court);
(5) determining the nature and extent of the criminal justice reaction (for example, a fine, imprisonment, victim compensation); and, eventually,
(6) returning the offender to society and/or seeking to reduce the likelihood of a repeat offense.

Across countries there are huge similarities in which acts are considered to be crimes, and thus subject to criminal justice rules and institutions. One of the reasons why there still are differences is the fact that there are alternative legal approaches for the regulation of undesired acts in society. Tort law, for example, seeks to ensure that individuals and firms are held responsible for the damage they cause. Tort law is also intended to deter individuals and firms from causing damage in the first place, just as criminal law is expected to have a preventive effect.[29] Administrative law serves the purpose of correcting behavior, and administrative fines are reactions against insufficient compliance with the law.[30] Criminal law is different because it provides the legal basis for a sharper reaction against acts that are totally unacceptable, and therefore, the standard of proof is generally higher than for other offenses. Criminal law regulation, with the use of imprisonment as a possible sanction, is reserved for the most serious forms of undesired acts, and, compared to other areas of law, such regulation conveys a clearer message about what is intolerable. In the case of criminally defined acts, an absolute standard holds: we will not allow *some* corruption, *some* assault, or *some* money laundering, because these acts are considered damaging no matter what the extent.

The acts categorized as crime are usually of a sort that society as a whole is thought to have an interest in preventing, irrespective of the victims' identities. Criminal acts will often cause outrage followed by

---

[29] See Arlen (2013) for economic analyses and perspectives on tort law.
[30] For a collection of corruption-relevant articles on administrative law, see Rose-Ackerman and Lindseth (2010).

demands for retribution. The problems associated with vengeful victims (or their families and friends) mistaking the offender's identity and escalating violence have resulted in special procedures for criminal law. The government is normally responsible for overseeing and financing criminal law enforcement, controlling investigation and prosecution, ensuring careful assessment of the offender's liability, and making sure that sanctions are determined by impartial judges and set within agreed-upon limits.[31] Too harsh a reaction would be cruel and brutalize society, while a failure to react would fail to deter crime, deviate from a sense of fairness, and encourage private retribution.

Its obligations to uphold justice and offer protection make the criminal justice system something more than a penalty-imposing unit. Its responsibilities in defining, controlling, and sanctioning crime give the system the capacity to influence citizens' principled judgments. When the system functions well, it has the potential of catalyzing the development of norms, which affect the *moral cost* of committing corruption and other forms of crime. Although the broad range of integrity mechanisms mentioned above also contribute to the process of raising the moral cost of crime, it is the criminal justice system that makes the definitive judgment of an act, and by reacting when crime is disclosed, it upholds the other integrity mechanisms.

1.5.2 Corruption as Crime

Most countries in the world regulate corruption as crime, as defined by their criminal law. While acts of corruption have been found damaging and punishable as long as there have been government structures, only very recently have we seen international collaboration on what to include in the criminal justice definition of crime. Upon a process that started in the 1970s with non-binding international government agreements, The United Nations Convention against Corruption (UNCAC), signed in 2003, and (by the end of 2014) implemented by some 170 countries, blazed a trail toward legal harmonization that in turn opened the door for expanded collaboration on investigation, prosecution, and asset recovery.[32] Another, earlier milestone was erected by the OECD. The OECD Anti-Bribery Convention was signed in 1997, entered into force in 1999, and was followed by a comprehensive process of evaluating the

---

[31] Bowles, Faure, and Garoupa (2008) explain economic perspectives on the scope of criminal law and criminal sanctions.

[32] As of November 2014, there were 173 signatory parties, including 170 UN member states, the Cook Islands, the State of Palestine, and the European Union.

law enforcement performance and progress by each signatory state.[33] As these conventions have been signed by countries and implemented in their law enforcement systems, the rules regulating corruption have on many points become more harmonized.

The two conventions emerged out of a process kick-started by the United States, with its Foreign Corrupt Practices Act (FCPA) of 1977 (amended in 1988). The OECD convention was developed in large part because of pressure from the United States, which found that the FCPA was inefficient and damaging to the US export industry as long as other countries did not abide by similar regulations. The work of the OECD was slow in the beginning, not least because corruption in foreign jurisdictions was tacitly accepted by many European leaders, despite the fact that such acts were forbidden in the countries where they occurred. Indeed, several European countries offered tax deductions for bribes paid abroad, regardless of domestic criminal law regulations. The signing of the conventions signified a step away from a political climate in which actions that could undermine foreign societies' criminal law regulation were largely tolerated (as if bank robbery was perfectly acceptable as long as it happened in another country). After fifteen years of pressure from the United States, the OECD introduced its Anti-Bribery Recommendation of 1994,[34] which was the first OECD instrument that urged member governments to take steps against foreign bribery. That document served as an important starting point for further legal developments in this arena, with the Council of Europe and the then newly established Transparency International adding their weight to the push for further action. Other important instruments for the regulation of corruption as crime include the 1996 Inter-American Convention against Corruption of the Organization of American States, the 1996 EU Protocol to the Convention on the Protection of the European Communities' Financial Interests, the 1997 EU Convention on the Fight against Corruption, the Council of Europe's 1999 Criminal Law Convention and 1999 Civil Law Convention, and the 2003 African Union Convention on Preventing and Combating Corruption.

The international collaboration behind these different conventions has established an invaluable platform for enforcement of anticorruption law both within national jurisdictions and across borders. In practice, however, as will be described in Chapter 3, many obstacles still obstruct the

---

[33]   The full official name is *The Convention on Combating Bribery of Foreign Public Officials in International Business Transactions.*

[34]   Formally, 'Revised Recommendation of the Council on Combating Bribery in International Business Transactions' (OECD, C(97)123/FINAL).

implementation and efficient enforcement of these conventions. Simply to fill the many loopholes of the OECD convention, for example, the member governments had to agree on a set of additional recommendations, the 2009 Anti-Bribery Recommendation.[35] Acts of corruption are still regulated differently by the European Union, the Council of Europe Convention, the UNCAC, and the OECD convention, and when it comes to implementation at the national level, many countries appear to have *created* loopholes for corruption when they have adapted the conventions to their own criminal law and criminal justice system. As Radha Ivory (2014:13–17) explains, the last fifteen years' anticorruption treaties are 'suppression conventions' – as they 'encourage and oblige their signatories to take steps to criminalize transnational criminal conduct' and 'envisage that crime will be investigated, tried, and punished under domestic law, typically through collaboration between states in criminal matters' (Radha, 2014:14).[36]

The international collaboration toward harmonized criminal law regulation of corruption breaks with the notion of a criminal law that develops as part of the society it regulates. From a pragmatic perspective, this is not a problem if only the contents of the laws can be justified. Full international harmonization cannot be expected, however, because institutional structures and constitutional principles differ across countries. For leaders who wish to keep opportunities for corruption, despite the pressure for reform, such differences legitimize a call for recognition of a country's culture and norms – then sometimes used to disguise or justify a lenient political attitude on corruption.[37] Examples of areas where law enforcement is impeded by inadequate criminal law regulation include the specific definition of the criminal act, the description of players to be held responsible for corrupt acts, the regulation of corporate criminal liability, the statutes of limitations, a lack of whistle-blower protection laws, and commitments on the mutual assistance necessary for providing evidence during investigations.

Criminal sanctions for corruption usually take the form of monetary fines and imprisonment. The repression level varies significantly across countries. In some countries, a low repression level is associated with a

---

[35] This is a formal agreement made by the OECD Working Group on Bribery. For details, see the OECD website: http://www.oecd.org/investment/anti-bribery/anti-briberyconvention/oecdantibriberyrecommendation2009.htm.

[36] Radha (2014) provides a comprehensive review of international treaties and international soft law norms on corruption, and addresses specifically the legal basis for asset recovery and the protection of property under this legislation.

[37] This claim is substantiated in Chapter 3.

generally lenient attitude to corruption, while in others, such as the Nordic countries, a relatively low repression level is the result of a criminal law tradition with limited faith in the efficacy of hard reactions. The United States, however, applies particularly severe sanctions, which it defends with reference to their expected deterrent effects. In China, where the government has felt it necessary to take a clear stand against corruption, the most extreme cases of bribery can be punished with the death penalty. Across countries, government representatives who accept bribes are generally sanctioned more severely than the private individuals who offer bribes, and where private-private corruption is criminalized, sanctions on such acts are generally milder than for corruption in state administration and government.

1.6 EFFICIENT CRIMINAL JUSTICE RESPONSE

Substantial progress has been achieved in anticorruption over the past two to three decades, especially if considering law-related activities. Despite the problem of political corruption, governments across the world increasingly enforce their integrity systems and express commitment in numerous initiatives intended to improve law enforcement. In November 2014, for instance, the G20 leaders agreed to recognize the damage caused by corruption, as well as loosely formulated anticorruption commitments.[38] In parallel with government efforts, researchers, civil society actors, and policy analysts are working to measure and explain the corruption problem. What all committed players seem to agree on is that corruption should be targeted *efficiently*. But how, exactly, to define 'efficient' in this context is not so clear.[39]

The complex set of factors that determine corruption in a society is one reason for this lack of definitional clarity. Even if we keep the discussion

---

[38] See Chapter 2 for details.

[39] According to the dictionary Merriam-Webster, 'efficiency' means 'the ability to do something or produce something without wasting materials, time, or energy' while 'effectiveness' refers to 'producing a result that is wanted: having an intended effect' (http://www.merriam-webster.com/). In terms of 'doing the right thing' and the question of strategic law enforcement responses to corruption, I prefer the term 'efficiency' – as describing the best allocation of resources, given well-defined goals, while avoiding waste. System efficiency will take all important goals into account, and not merely sub-goals, like the number of cases or the speed with which cases are processed. The obvious problem with the word is its lack of accuracy when goals that we want to reach 'efficiently' are inadequately defined.

of definitions to terms used within the criminal justice system, it is still difficult to say precisely what the word 'efficient' means. The criminal justice system's role in controlling crime defies exact measurement; the system evolves as part of a society and a larger system of government, making it difficult to identify causal connections between the system's different components and the extent of corruption. Furthermore, aside from the problems of disentangling complex organic systems, it is difficult from a conceptual perspective to establish what constitutes efficient criminal justice response to corruption. Should we gauge efficiency by a rise in the number of corruption cases solved and offenders punished? If so, should we count the 'important' corruption cases differently than the less important cases, and if so, how should we determine level of importance? Should efficiency depend on the relationship between the perceived extent of corruption in a society and the number of cases processed?[40] If this relationship is difficult to establish, then perhaps 'efficiency' could refer to the impact of criminal law enforcement on the integrity in decision-making or the value for money in public spending? But the answer is no, because such features are determined by a number of factors. And so, the discussion can go on and on, heading in numerous directions simultaneously but never reaching a conclusive destination. In policy debates, we refer to 'criminal justice efficiency' as if it is a common goal, but once we try to be precise about what this means in relation to corruption, a hazy fog clouds our conversation.

Legal scholars have tended to associate the word 'efficiency' with some specific quantifiable effect: the number of cases, for example, or the speed of reaction. And in the literature, they have often reminded policymakers that efficiency should be balanced against other important concerns, such as fairness and a legitimate criminal law process. For economists, 'efficiency' means to optimize strategies to attain a certain objective, given available resources and constraints. As such, efficiency means to achieve 'a desired reduction in crime using a minimum of resources and given other constraints.' If fairness is deemed to be relevant to this understanding of efficiency, it is incorporated in the optimization of policy strategies. Different aims can either be given different weights (that is, ranked) when defining an overall objective, or a strategy toward one overall objective (for example, reduced crime) can be subject to other

---

[40]   If so, what should the interpretation be of the ten times more citizens in United States prisons compared to Europe? See International Centre for Prison Studies – http://www.prisonstudies.org/highest-to-lowest/prison-population-total.

aims, which are then treated as absolute constraints (for example, due process). These features of the economic approach make the methodology applicable for identifying optimal – or 'efficient' – solutions.

Even so, this is no more than the application of a technique whose results depend on the elements put into it. The approach itself tells us little about *the concept of efficiency* in criminal law, because, with reference to this economic understanding of efficiency, the 'desired reduction in crime' can in fact be understood in many different ways and is also subject to political views. The definition's reference to a 'minimum of resources' glosses over or invites political trade-offs between short-term and long-term costs, as well as direct and indirect effects; savings in the short run may imply more problems later. Moreover, the phrase 'given constraints' requires some level of agreement in society on what are considered more or less absolute constraints in terms of, for example, acceptable sanctions or the use of state revenues. To what extent is the protection of human rights considered a law enforcement constraint, for example? Traditionally, economic analyses of law enforcement have concentrated on very narrow objectives, especially the direct deterrent effect on marginal offenders, and have only recently started to consider the importance of various indirect consequences. When it comes to corruption, meaning that *something is rotten* in the governance of a society, these indirect consequences of the criminal justice system may matter the most.

2. The causes and consequences of corruption

We need to know the consequences of corruption for several important reasons. In the first place, knowledge about the damage caused by corruption motivates action against the problem. Second, details about what forms of corruption cause what kinds of damage enable us to set policy priorities that match the scale of the problem, with the more damaging forms receiving the most urgent attention. Third, knowledge about the extent of the problem over time allows us to better understand the mechanisms at play and to more accurately assess the impact of anticorruption strategies. We need facts to know if our anticorruption strategies work.

When it comes to the world of criminal justice systems, information about corruption's consequences is seen by legal scholars as necessary to determine an appropriate criminal law reaction. From a legal perspective, the scale of the damage caused by different corrupt acts should be reflected in the decision to criminalize some of those acts but not others. Similarly, from a retributive perspective, the damage caused should guide the judgment of a reasonable sanction. If the consequences of a corrupt act are unclear, a judge will typically be cautious not to sanction the offender too heavily. By the same token, if the consequences are thought to be more severe than they actually are, the offender will likely face a more severe reaction than what is appropriate given the consequences of the act. An unnecessarily severe reaction (assuming some societal agreement about what is necessary to meet sanctioning objectives) is not only costly to society; it is also an excessive use of state force and authority vis-à-vis a citizen, which should obviously be avoided by a government that represents the people. In short, knowledge about the damage caused by corruption is vital to set a sanction 'correctly' – and hence, such knowledge is an essential condition for *efficient* law enforcement.

Unfortunately, the required information about corruption's impact is often in short supply or of questionable reliability. The problem we face is how to obtain reliable estimates of the corruption problem – in its many forms and facets – and how to interpret correctly the information we do have. The extreme vagueness of the general understanding of the phenomenon – 'something is rotten' or 'power is misused for personal benefit' – does not make it any easier to collect precise data. Nonetheless, we should not abandon hope of obtaining empirically verified insights. Even if it is very difficult to determine and measure corruption's exact impact, we do know a lot about how corruption hurts states and societies, and where and how it thrives, and we are getting better at determining its extent and frequency.

This chapter explains what we know (and what we don't know) about corruption's consequences, in the process identifying the kinds of conditions in which corruption thrives. The first section of the chapter explores the relationship between corruption and economic development. The second section explains why the consequences depend on the factors that drive the corruption. The following section highlights the problem of corruption in deeply dysfunctional states, where the consequences of corruption are hard to disentangle from the consequences of a yet more deep-seated problem: constitutional failure, if not complete government breakdown. The fourth section explains where we stand in terms of accurately assessing the extent and impact of corruption; this section provides a brief overview of empirical achievements and challenges in determining corruption's scope and consequences. The chapter's main messages are summarized in a concluding section.

2.1 CORRUPTION HINDERS ECONOMIC DEVELOPMENT

Despite the difficulties of estimating the extent of corruption, we do have a lot of approximate information, especially from perceptions-based corruption indices, randomized household surveys, and extensive business surveys conducted with a consistent methodology over many years in a row. What can these data tell us about the relationship between corruption and economic development?

2.1.1 Corruption, Income Levels, and GDP Growth

One of the clearest macroeconomic findings about corruption is that the perceived magnitude of the problem in a given country correlates with that country's income level. No country is free of corruption, nor of the responsibility for finding international solutions to it, but the problem is generally far more widespread in poor countries than in wealthier ones. Numerous studies using different corruption estimates have confirmed this relationship between level of income and scale of corruption,[1] and Transparency International's map of perceived corruption (see Figure 2.1) across the world illustrates the relationship in striking fashion.[2]

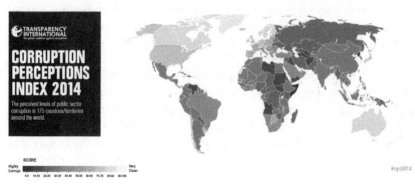

Source: http://www.transparency.org/cpi.

Figure 2.1   Transparency international's corruption perception map

The correlation between estimated corruption and economic growth is more difficult to confirm, especially because a country's gross domestic product (GDP) reflects economic activity but does not distinguish between corrupt and noncorrupt contract allocations. A large infrastructure project adds to GDP growth even if a significant proportion of the project's financing is siphoned off by corrupt politicians. Spain and Angola, for example, are countries that have been commended by the World Bank and other observers for their infrastructure investments, despite the suspicion that many contracts go to firms owned by those countries' political elite. Regardless of how unnecessary, poorly constructed, or badly maintained the projects are (a hospital in Luanda, for example, was built with so many defects that it could not be put into service), they still bring about GDP growth. GDP is boosted, first, by the construction of a new building; second, by the process of demolishing the building; and third, by the construction of a replacement building. Germà Bel, Antonio Estache, and Renaud Foucart explain how Spain overinvests

---

[1]   For reviews of data sources and results, see Olken and Pande (2012), Lambsdorff (2007), Treisman (2007), and Svensson (2005).

[2]   The map is available on Transparency International's website at http://www.transparency.org/cpi2014. The darker the color of a country, the higher level of perceived corruption in that country. The darker countries are typically also poor countries.

in infrastructure as the result of an 'intense and somewhat incestuous relationship between the political power (of all colors) and the construction industry' (Bel et al., 2014:134). The country's now famous 'ghost airport' – built at tremendous cost but then left unused – is just one example of a notorious problem.[3]

The growth-corruption correlation must also be understood in light of how economic growth depends on a broad range of economic factors apart from GDP, such as markets, political stability, natural resources, and foreign direct investment. While corruption typically reduces growth, so that it is below what it would have been without corruption, a country's economy may still experience positive economic growth even though it suffers from corruption.[4]

Despite the GDP inclusion of corrupt activities and the complex set of factors influencing economic activity, numerous statistical studies have confirmed a significant negative relationship between GDP growth and estimates of perceived corruption.[5] After screening more than one thousand analyses of this relationship, Mehmet Ugur and Nandini Dasgupta (2011) conducted a meta-analysis of the 115 most robust ones. Based on this aggregated material, they estimated the impact of corruption on GDP growth for low-income countries and higher-income countries. For the low-income countries, they found a 0.59 percentage point decrease in growth for each unit increase on a corruption perception index. For the complete sample of countries, they found a 0.91 percentage point decline per unit increase of perceived corruption.[6]

The negative correlation between economic development and corruption is confirmed in the graph below. Figure 2.2, prepared for this book, shows four graphs, all with the GDP growth per capita on the vertical axis and an estimate of the absence of corruption on the horizontal axis. The graphs show estimates for the absence of corruption (a) overall;

---

[3] See *The Financial Times* on 17 July 2015: 'Spanish ghost airport costing €1bn attracts offer of just €10,000.'

[4] The difficulty of understanding *how much* corruption hampers growth is debated by Svensson (2005) and Treisman (2007).

[5] The relationship was identified by Mauro (1995), who conducted one of the most often cited macrolevel analyses of corruption, the result of which has since been continually confirmed using higher-quality data and more nuanced contextual analysis.

[6] For a review of results and discussion about correlations between corruption and growth, see OECD, 'Issues Paper on Corruption and Economic Growth,' prepared in 2013 for the G20 leaders' meeting in St. Petersburg, http://www.oecd.org/g20/topics/anti-corruption/Issue-Paper-Corruption-and-Economic-Growth.pdf.

(b) in the judicial system; (c) in the civil justice system; and (d) in the criminal justice system. The corruption estimates are produced by the World Justice Project, and are calculated using surveys in which experts are presented with certain scenarios and asked, for each of those scenarios, what the typical law enforcement outcome would be, what the government's response would be, and how likely and how soon a solution would be found. These responses are put into a dataset, with each country's capacities regarding a number of law enforcement activities characterized with scores, and thus quantified. The estimate on corruption is therefore calculated somewhat differently than other estimates, but the GDP-corruption relationship is similar to what has been found using other data. In other words, Figure 2.2 largely confirms a rough relationship between corruption and both income levels and growth per capita.

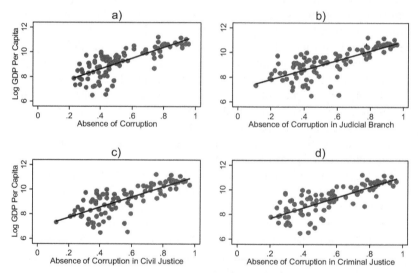

Note: The graphs show clear positive correlations between development and the absence of corruption across countries. Development is measured by the natural logarithm of GDP per capita (Penn World Table). The slopes in the four figures are as follows: (a) 4.40, (b) 3.84, (c) 4.09, and (d) 4.23. A similar picture emerges for corruption as measured by the Worldwide Governance Indicators and the International Country Risk Guide. *Note:* For more details about the data used, see the World Justice Project at: http://worldjusticeproject.org/rule-of-law-index; the World Bank's Worldwide Governance Indicators at: http://info.worldbank.org/governance/wgi/index.aspx#home; and the International Country Risk Guide prepared by Political Risk Services at: https://www.prsgroup.com/about-us/our-two-methodologies/icrg.

Figure 2.2   The relationship between perceived corruption and economic development

These statistical correlations are important in terms of confirming the problem at the macro-level – namely, that corruption is strongly associated with development obstacles – and they should help spur governments to take steps to control such a clear-cut and damaging problem. But in terms of interpreting the problem and understanding *what steps* must be taken to address it, the correlations are not so useful. They do not tell a story about the causalities and dynamics, and therefore, they offer few insights into how corruption hinders economic activity or how low income levels lead to more corruption.

From a policy perspective, the main problem in making use of these correlations is the difficulty of understanding exactly what problems they reflect. Several studies have sought to identify the main explanatory factors. Johan Graf Lambsdorff (2007) provides a review of such results, and points at the relationship between investment levels and GDP as particularly important. Jakob Svensson (2005) identifies human development as a factor strongly associated with the corruption-GDP growth relationship. As these authors underscore, however, corruption is highly context-specific. It takes many forms, and plays out differently at different levels of governance, in different regions, and across different sectors. Usually, corruption is just one of many problems – such as a lack of resources or low levels of administrative competence – that bedevil developing societies and generate or perpetuate governance dysfunctions. Rough correlations between corruption and income levels or growth levels do not help us distinguish the problem of corruption from other problems in society. Different problems require different solutions, and cost-efficient strategies imply targeted approaches. Box 2.1, for example, describes the complex challenge of elephant poaching on the African continent, which is undoubtedly something corrupt and rotten, but whose fundamental causes and multiple direct and indirect consequences are impossible to determine. The extent of the problem of elephant poaching can never be fully captured by a graph or a corruption index, and highlighting the growth-corruption relationship is not of much help to us in finding solutions.

Moreover, many scholars have pointed out how corruption may take more subtle forms in societies with better-performing integrity systems (which tend to be in higher-income countries), and thus the problem's true extent in the wealthier world may be underestimated. A study by Emmanuelle Auriol (2014), for instance, uses results from the World Bank's Business Climate Survey and finds that, while extortive corruption is higher in countries with lower income levels, the relationship with income levels is more uncertain when it comes to collusive corruption.

Also, Lambsdorff warns that the corruption captured by various data-collecting exercises may not be the most harmful: 'corruption between the political elite and the business community in form of cronyism, preferential access to government contracts or freedom from prosecution may be fundamentally more important and much harder to measure' (Lambsdorff, 2015:101). This aspect of the problem is understudied, both analytically and empirically. Ray Fisman, who has examined the economic value of political connections, nevertheless finds clearer evidence for such connections to be a problem in countries with both lower income levels *and* weaker institutions.[7] The exact causality between institutions and economic activity is still difficult to verify because what affects good institutions will also affect development. Daron Acemoglu, Simon Johnson and James Robinson tried to disentangle the problem by tracking the historical roots of bad institutions, seeking to understand the role of colonial settlers in current developing countries. Their findings largely confirmed that weak development follows from bad institutions and corruption. Moreover, corruption at political levels, these researchers conclude, is particularly damaging because politicians exercise de facto control over resources that are essential for development (Acemoglu et al., 2001, 2005).

These different avenues of research confirm that it is right to associate corruption with impediments to development, despite the problems of determining the role of institutions and the difficulties of assessing corruption at political levels.[8] Efficient strategies against the problem, however, require a far more nuanced understanding. Ideally, we should be able to distinguish causes from consequences, cultural from economic factors, and long-term, indirect effects from the immediate, direct impact. In pursuit of such an understanding, we need a framework for understanding at least the direct consequences of corrupt acts, a subject to which we now turn.

2.1.2   The Direct Damage Caused by Corrupt Acts

How can we determine the direct consequences of individual acts of corruption? The deadly chemical explosion that shook the Chinese city of Tianjin in the evening on 12 August 2015 – claiming more than 100 lives, injuring around 700, and damaging 17 000 homes – was quickly suspected to be a consequence of corruption. Major shareholders of the

---

[7]   See Fisman and Miguel (2010) and Fisman (2015).

[8]   This problem is what appears to have motivated Acemoglu et al.'s (2001) famous study of poverty, corruption, and the root causes of weak institutions.

company that owns the chemical storage facilities had unduly influenced their political connections to circumvent safety regulations.[9] While it only rarely leads to explosions, corruption increases *the risk* that such tragedies can happen – and this is a problem that must be addressed, regardless of how decisive the corruption is in combination with other factors.

The consequences of any individual act will depend on the circumstances in which that act was committed and on what choices and government decisions were altered as a result of the act. What would the government decision have been if it had not been 'sold' – in other words, what is *the counterfactual*? The results of decisions made by an honest but very incompetent decision-maker, or by one who is too lazy to assess alternative options, are not necessarily superior to the results of a bought decision. Corruption is, therefore, one among several factors that systematically distort decisions, taking them further away from the optimal options that could have been chosen. Nonetheless, even though corruption might be only one of several distorting factors, insofar as it contributes to decisions that deviate from the goals of state institutions, it harms society.

2.1.2.1 Categorizing the distortions of corruption

The direct harm can best be understood by considering how corruption distorts the allocation of benefits and/or increases costs. All forms of corruption can be categorized in this way. The idea of categorizing consequences according to their effect on costs and allocations originated with Susan Rose-Ackerman, who was the first economist to develop a comprehensive set of analytical tools for understanding the mechanisms of corrupt decision-making.[10] According to her approach, we must understand the price mechanism of bribery in order to see bribery's consequences. The more that the prices for various benefits to which one is entitled increase because a bribe has been paid, the higher the costs. Corruption will typically steer benefits toward those who pay bribes, instead of those who are formally entitled to the benefits, which suggests that corruption distorts the assessment of who qualifies for the benefits.

---

[9]   See Foreign Policy on 19 August 2015: 'Massive Tianjin blast highlights flaws in China's governance model' (by Thomas Kellogg and Kevin Slaten). See also *New York Times* on the same day – 'Chinese report details role of political connections in Tianjin blasts' (by Dan Levin). Both newspapers cite Chinese sources.

[10]   These analyses are presented in Rose-Ackerman (1978) and later applied in Rose-Ackerman (1999).

The consequences of these distortions will depend on how abundant or scarce the benefits in question are; typically, the scarcer they are, the more valuable the decisions are about who receives the benefits. The higher the willingness to pay bribes to obtain the benefits, the more attractive is the corruption for decision-makers. Table 2.1 presents a framework for placing corrupt decisions into four different categories, with examples given for each category.

Table 2.1   A framework for categorizing corrupt distortions

		TYPE OF ALLOCATION	
		QUALIFICATION-STEERED	AVAILABLE FOR ALL
DEGREE OF SCARCITY	LIMITED	**Category A** *Examples*: Public procurement contracts Building permits in a city Surgery involving organ transplants Government-appointed positions	**Category B** *Examples*: Tickets for public transport Routine public hospital services Public parking (such as berths for boats in a city-administered port) Vaccination programs
	PLENTY	**Category C** *Examples*: Customs clearance Tax benefits Drivers' licenses and various diplomas Access to credit	**Category D** *Examples*: Access to public schools Access to electricity and water supplies Basic health services Passport renewals

If corruption means that already scarce public benefits, such as organ transplants or building permits, are allocated according to beneficiaries' willingness to pay bribes, instead of according to a confirmed need, qualifications, or some form of competitive process, the consequences for society are both higher prices for the benefits and a failure to reach those in need who cannot or will not pay a bribe. As shown in category A, the consequence is therefore a combination of higher costs and allocation effects. In other cases, like those listed in category B, the demand for bribes may limit the access to public benefits that are meant to be abundant, such as vaccinations and routine hospital services. The costs to society are fewer benefits allocated than is optimal or intended, or higher expenses for beneficiaries. Hence, the consequence is primarily a cost-effect, which may lead to limited access for those who cannot pay the extra expense.

As indicated by the columns in Table 2.1, we should distinguish between benefits allocated upon some assessment of a client's qualifications (such as driving licenses offered upon a passed exam – see the left-hand side of Table 2.1) and benefits that are supposed to be offered regardless of what qualifications the client holds (such as public schooling for children – see the right-hand side of Table 2.1). There is usually a good reason why a state institution is supposed to assess qualifications before it provides a certain benefit, and the consequences of offering benefits in exchange for a bribe, instead of after seeing evidence of the required qualifications, can inflict considerable damage on society. If driving licenses are allocated to drivers who have paid a bribe, instead of being given to drivers who have passed a test, for example, unsafe drivers are let loose on the roads.[11] For those individuals who are never likely to qualify for a certain benefit, the bribe they are willing to offer might be very high, and thus outweigh a public servant's moral reluctance to participate in corruption.

Under circumstances in which there is no scarcity and benefits are supposed to be allocated to every client who wants them (category D) but, because of corruption, benefits are allocated at a higher price (that is, payment of a bribe), the direct damage caused is the accumulated higher expense. Examples could include extra payments demanded for access to publicly available infrastructure (such as electricity or water). The illegal profit obtained can be significant for those who demand the bribes. At the same time, the expense for each citizen can be small. Thus individual citizens may not feel victimized, and, for society as a whole, the consequences may appear diminished. The exact scope of the damage is difficult to specify.

Within each of the four categories in Table 2.1, the magnitude of the consequences depends on the specific context. The consequences can be dramatic, such as death or the denial of opportunities for individuals and groups to significantly improve the quality of their lives. Especially in cases when qualifications are supposed to be assessed before benefits are allocated, corruption can *facilitate other forms of crime*, such as importing illegal products or committing an act of terrorism, and in these cases the main damage to society caused by the corrupt act is normally the crime it facilitates.[12] To the extent that the categories can be ranked, the most dramatic consequences are generally found in category A (where

---

[11]   See Bertrand et al. (2006); this study is described in this chapter's section 4.

[12]   According to Shelley (2014), corruption has been part of both the planning and the motivation for all the most severe terror attacks since 11 September 2001. Corruption facilitated the accumulation of needed capital, the acquisition of needed permits, and the transportation of weapons, while political corruption made it easier to recruit members of terrorist organizations.

both allocations and prices are distorted), while the least dramatic consequences are found in category D (where the bribe resembles a pure tax added to the formal price). In addition, bribes are typically more distortive of decision-making the less predictable they are, the larger the bribes demanded, and the more they affect service provision (including what happens to those who do not get the services because of corruption).[13] Corruption rarely causes an isolated price effect.[14]

The framework presented here focuses on the direct qualitative consequences of corruption, but corrupt acts usually also generate *indirect* effects. For example, talented youths may compete for positions in which they can solicit bribes, instead of using their talents in occupations that are more likely to produce benefits for society as a whole. Funds are hidden outside the reach of domestic law enforcers, instead of being reinvested for productive activities. Citizens' trust in their government deteriorates if public benefits go primarily to those who pay a bribe, and not to those qualified for the benefits. Weak law enforcement and government-condoned unfairness harm societies in subtle ways.

2.1.2.2 The consequences differ across sectors

Decisions that are distorted by corrupt acts have different direct consequences depending on what form of authority is distorted and what sectors of society the decisions affect. Providing a typology of consequences, Jennifer Bussel (2015) explains the importance of distinguishing between corruption in (i) the legislative and regulations, (ii) public procurement and government contracting, (iii) government employment decisions, and (iv) public sector service provision. These circumstances categorically lead to different corrupt deals and consequences, and when referring to corruption, we should be specific about the circumstance. Moreover, the consequence of what appears to be the same distortion will be very different, depending on the setting. A distorted decision about a multibillion public procurement contract in the defense sector will have a

---

[13]   The examples in Table 2.2 are not 'waterproof;' they are listed with keywords, and for each of them there might be circumstances around the allocation of benefits that would warrant a different place in the table. The renewal of a passport, for example, is normally a benefit available to everyone, but that benefit becomes more expensive if awarded only in exchange for a bribe. Under certain circumstances, however, a passport applicant may need specific qualifications, and if so, the award of a passport in exchange for a bribe can have damages beyond a pure price effect.
[14]   See OECD (2015:72–73), where I first made these points about the consequences of bribes.

very different impact than a distorted decision about a contract for the supply of textbooks in public schools. The consequences of improper customs clearance for a group of Norwegian retirees who are illegally bringing back cheese from a Swiss vacation will have profoundly different dimensions than improper customs clearance offered to a group of terrorists who are importing weapons illegally. The same forms of decisions are distorted but the consequences can hardly be compared.

While it is impossible to acquire a comprehensive and nuanced overview of the consequences of corruption in an economy or society, we can improve our understanding by investigating and comparing impacts in different situations and sectors. Together with a group of researchers, I prepared a report in 2014 for the OECD to be used in the G20 Anti-Corruption Working Group.[15] For each of four different sectors – infrastructure, extractive industries (natural resources), health, and education – we mapped research results on how the kinds of distortions presented in Table 2.1 play out in practice. Features such as scarcity, distorted allocation of benefits (with or without assessment of qualification), and facilitation of other forms of crime were considered.

Table 2.2 summarizes the mechanisms identified. Similar corruption mechanisms will typically have very different consequences in different sectors. The effect of inflated prices for medicines will have different consequences than inflated prices in construction, for example. When comparing sectors, there are similar consequences associated with very different situations and problems. For example, distortions regarding access to benefits have obvious cross-cutting consequences when those distortions happen in the education sector. In the extractive industries, similar distortions will typically affect the selection of producers and their operational conditions, with apparently much narrower consequences. However, since the production curve, production technology, and the tax regime determine the amount of oil pumped up from an oilfield, the integrity in regulatory institutions significantly affects the amount of state revenues from the sector – and thus, the problem is not so narrow after all.[16] What we also see is how corrupt distortions in political budget allocation tend to cause overspending in some sectors, such as infrastructure, while causing cuts in others, such as health and

---

[15]   The study was a review of research results on the consequences of corruption. See OECD (2015). We conducted the study under the leadership of the OECD Secretariat in collaboration with staff of the World Bank. See the OECD website for details regarding the G20 working group on corruption: http://www.oecd.org/g20/topics/anti-corruption/.

[16]   The argument is spelled out by Al Kasim, Søreide, and Williams (2013).

education. Cuts in revenues from oil production and export may well harm the education level as much as the corrupt distortions that take place in the sector itself.

Each sector appears to have its own unique distortions as a result of corruption. The bureaucratic corruption that takes place within the education sector damages the moral leadership far more than would a cut in state revenues (even if that cut is a result of corruption). Corruption in education tend to facilitate the embezzlement of funds (that is, funds do not reach the schools) and encourage teacher absenteeism (also referred to as the phenomenon of 'ghost teachers').[17] Other serious consequences are the obvious long-term impacts on competence in society, as well as the distortion of recruitment processes for jobs and positions because attestations of educational qualifications cannot be trusted to reflect individuals' true competence.

When it comes to the health sector, corruption makes health services more expensive or inaccessible for those in need.[18] Corruption also facilitates other offenses, including the sale of fake medicines (sometimes supplied by organized crime), and major insurance fraud. High-level corruption in large-scale public procurement in this sector affects the selection and quality of services and products. In the infrastructure sector, corruption distorts utility regulation, leads to expensive subsidies, and state-owned entities are privatized with their market power intact. Services such as the provision of electricity, water, ports, and roads become more expensive than they would have been without distortions. Investment projects become less targeted to society's needs. In addition, the construction of new infrastructure is highly exposed to corruption. With large and complicated projects, the difficulty to plan for each and every expense intensifies, and the room for flexible and corrupt solutions is larger than in many types of government financed projects. In this sector it is also not uncommon to see costs that are cut illegally by lowering the level of quality, and maintenance that is ignored due to some corrupt agreement.

When we turn to the production and sale of nonrenewable extractives we find again that corruption has unique consequences that are sector-specific. Political corruption affecting this sector causes not only a loss of state revenues, it also encourages a tendency to neglect the importance of other sectors.[19] Corruption in resource-rich economies is also associated

---

[17] Poisson (2014) provides a brief and useful review of issues.
[18] Described in more detail by Vian (2008).
[19] Explained by Kolstad and Wiig (2012).

with inferior framework conditions for business, in some countries leading to lower foreign direct investment in the economy. Table 2.2 presents an overview of these results.

Table 2.2   Consequences of corruption across sectors

	Extractives	**Infrastructure**	**Health**	**Education**
Misallocation of state revenues	Budget skewed away from services for the poor. Resource dependency common.	Overinvestment and mis-investment in infrastructure facilities.	Budget cuts. Health and pharmaceutical subsidies. 'Corruption-friendly investments' (construction, building, consultancy services).	Lower value for money (education is one of the bigger amounts in national budgets).
Wasted resources	Illicit financial flows may reflect stolen state revenues. Inefficient sector governance hampers production and revenue potential.	Too expensive subsidies. Overinflated costs in construction cause losses for taxpayers.	Ghost workers and absenteeism.	Leakage of funds allocated for education. Ghost workers and absenteeism.
Inflated prices	Framework conditions for industrial development in other sectors of the economy largely neglected, resulting in uncompetitive prices for individuals and firms.	Bribes demanded for access to water and electricity. More expensive power supply.	Inflated prices of medicines and services.	Extra (informal) payments for textbooks, certificates/ grades. and teachers' salaries.
Reduced quality	Few consequences if services are inferior. Lower quality of basic service delivery, including health and education.	Low-quality roads and other construction. Poorer utility service provisions (for example, power cuts).	Substandard and fake medicine. Lower quality of health services offered.	Inferior teaching. Lower-quality school facilities. False diplomas (grades not reflecting qualifications).
Scarcity	'Scarcity' of competitors if tenders for oil licenses are manipulated.	Network services not necessarily provided to all districts despite contractual commitments.	Lack of medicines (unavailable, substandard, fake, ineffective).	Teaching not taking place. Insufficient supply of teaching services and school supplies.

Table 2.2 (continued)

	Extractives	Infrastructure	Health	Education
Unfair allocation of benefits	Political corruption causes income inequalities.	Poor segments more exposed if there is government failure behind the provision of electricity, water, and sanitation.	Health care allocated to those who pay bribes; allocated less upon needs.	Good grades for those who pay bribes. Private schools not available for poor segments.
Other negative consequences	Conflict/civil war, terror attacks, bunkering (stolen oil), illegal mining, environmental damage, lack of safety in production (causes health damage and deaths).	Tax/ accounting-related fraud. Theft of electricity supply. Embezzlement in construction. Low-quality construction causes deaths.	Fake medicines sold by help of corruption and linked to organized crime. Lack of treatment causes deaths.	Embezzlement of public funds on the way from central level to individual schools.

Note: The report is available on the OECD website at: http://www.oecd.org/publications/consequences-of-corruption-at-the-sector-level-and-implications-for-economic-growth-and-development-9789264230781-en.htm (August 2015). Examples of other volumes containing presentations of how corruption takes shape in different sectors include Campos and Pradhan (2007) and Søreide and Williams (2014), while the U4 Anti-Corruption Resource Centre provides numerous sector reports. For G20 Australia, see their website at: http://www.g20australia.org/official_resources/g20_high_level_principles_corruption_and_growth.

Source: The table was prepared by the author for the report *Consequences of Corruption at the Sector Level and Implications for Economic Growth and Development* (OECD: Paris, 2015). Authors involved in the study included Antonio Estache, Jacques Hallak, Philippe Le Billon, Muriel Poisson, Vincent Somville, and Taryn Vian, in addition to myself. The table is reproduced with permission from the OECD.

Upon the overwhelming amount of research confirming that corruption harms development, the leaders of the G20 countries came to an agreement during their 2014 meetings in Australia where they acknowledged the damaging consequences of corruption. This agreement includes seven statements, the first being:

'Corruption damages citizens' confidence in governance institutions and their supporting integrity systems, and weakens the rule of law,'

and the second:

'Corruption impacts the costs of goods and services provided by government, decreasing their quality and directly increasing the cost for business, reducing access to services by the poor, ultimately increasing social inequality.'

The next five statements, which can be found on the G20 Australia official website,[20] address corruption's impact on foreign direct investment, healthy competition, the political allocation of resources, national security, money laundering, financial integrity, transnational organized crime, tax evasion, the effect of development assistance, as well as our collective ability to reach global development goals.

2.1.2.3   The consequences depend on one's perspective

The consequences of corruption for development must be considered also in light of *whose development* we are talking about. Individuals experience corruption very differently, depending on a host of factors, among them ethnicity, social status, and personal income or wealth. A wealthy business leader may well be concerned about corruption in society and what it does to her industry and investments. For the poor farmer who loses her land because of the problem, the situation is very different and the consequences far more dire. Furthermore, these women will have very unequal opportunities to voice their concerns.

The cost of people killed because of corruption, or of journalists imprisoned because of the corruption they try to reveal, is hard to quantify in economic terms but nevertheless carries a very high price for both individual victims and entire societies in terms of political freedom and human rights. At the government level, policymakers and politicians often concentrate on the overall economic consequences of corruption for the country, not least its tendency to impede *macroeconomic* development, though increasing income differences and a general sense of unfairness also harm society. The vulnerability of the victims of corruption is – or should be – highly relevant in any debate about development, but all too often this perspective is overshadowed by macroeconomic concerns about growth and national income levels.

The trickle-down effects of economic growth cannot be taken for granted, especially not in countries where corruption distorts markets and government policies so that they benefit the few, not the population as a whole. It is not 'the people' who gain from corruption. The results of Thomas Piketty's (2014) groundbreaking research on inequality are starting to 'trickle up' to political leaders – and the experts associated with policy hubs, such as the OECD, the World Bank, the International Monetary Fund (IMF), and the World Economic Forum – who are

---

[20] The OECD Secretariat managed this in 2014. See the G20 Australia official website (retrieved July 2015): http://www.g20australia.org/official_resources/g20_high_level_principles_corruption_and_growth.

starting to accept that narrowly accumulated wealth, partly a result of corruption or similar forms of grabbing, endangers not only economic growth but also political and social stability and government legitimacy.

The various kinds of damage that corruption can cause, and the range of perspectives brought to bear on it, are well illustrated in the accompanying textbox describing elephant poaching in Africa.

BOX 2.1   CORRUPTION'S ROLE IN ELEPHANT POACHING

Africa had millions of elephants a few decades ago, but these animals are now at risk of extinction. Part of the reason for this alarming decline in the elephant population is the development of land for infrastructure, and cities' and society's need to secure food, including large-scale supplies of meat for underfinanced government troops and rebel fighters. The most important factor, however, is the illegal poaching conducted to supply Asian markets with ivory. In 2013 alone, 41.5 tons of ivory were seized. With an interdiction rate assumed (optimistically) to be 10 percent, an estimated 400 tons were traded – which would mean, in effect, that more than 50 000 elephants were killed for their tusks.

Elephant poaching is an organized illegal industry. Following an international agreement in 1989, poaching was criminalized; however, instead of reducing the problem, criminalization simply spurred higher prices and turned ivory into a very lucrative contraband item.[21] According to Varun Vira and Thomas Ewing (2014), who have investigated the economics of poaching across the African continent, corruption facilitates all parts of this industry's 'value chain,' from poaching and trafficking to retail. This illegal business secures profit not only for the poachers, criminal networks, and traders involved, but also for terrorist groups such as Al-Shabab, the military in several countries, civil servants in wildlife parks who turn a blind eye to the crime, custom officials who allow the export of ivory, and even politicians who are paid or rewarded with powerful political support if they ignore large-scale violations of national park conservation rules. In addition, many of the players who are formally expected to enforce the law benefit informally from ignoring poaching.

Despite international pressure, criminalization, and a near global ban on the ivory trade, elephants are poorly protected. Many law enforcement initiatives have been targeted at detecting and sanctioning poachers, who are typically poor villagers at the bottom of the ivory trade hierarchy. These poachers are protected from law enforcement initiatives by allies higher in the government system. Efforts to enforce anti-poaching laws have therefore proved risky, and in several countries, those who report poaching are often met with threats and informal sanctions, and some have been murdered. Unless the high-level corruption behind this illegal business is understood and efficiently addressed, the African elephant will soon be extinct.

---

[21]   In end-user markets, ivory was sold in 2014 at more than US$300 per kilogram, while in 1976 the price was less than $6 per kilogram (Vira and Ewing 2014:5).

The problem of elephant poaching illustrates the different costs of corruption, including the direct economic consequences associated with a lack of security and reduced tourism, the non-monetary costs associated with having far fewer elephants in the world, and the huge illegal resources made available to support terrorist groups on the African continent. This story of how organized crime has developed with the support of corrupt politicians – across countries governed in close collaboration with multilateral development partners, including on issues of anticorruption – is a window into the real world of corruption. We need to generate data on the problem, but the real consequences of corruption can never be reflected in a figure on economic growth or captured by a country's position on a corruption index. The story of elephant poaching is a story of how challenging it can be for public institutions and civil society organizations to promote law enforcement – no matter what international support they may have – when it goes against the personal interests of incumbent politicians.

2.2 ARENAS PARTICULARLY EXPOSED TO CORRUPTION

The extent of corruption and its consequences depend on the reasons why corrupt acts occur and the frequency with which these reasons are present. Even in the most corrupt societies, the opportunity to benefit from corruption is limited to certain situations. The damage of corruption will thus be easier to understand by considering when these situations occur.

If we define corrupt acts as *trade in decisions that should not be for sale*, corruption requires at least one individual with delegated authority who is prepared to sell a decision. However, the corrupt bargain takes place only if the decision-maker calculates that the value of the resulting decision, once the size of the offered bribe has been subtracted, exceeds his or her risks and costs, including the moral concerns associated with a corrupt decision. Whether or not someone will pay a sufficiently high amount for the decision depends on its value for a potential buyer. Under very asymmetric allocation of bargaining powers, however, the buyer may be 'willingly forced to buy' – in the sense of being exposed to extortion for a benefit that he or she in principle can refuse but strongly prefers to obtain.

Based on these intuitive observations, we can establish three criteria for corruption to happen:

(1) decision-makers have control over monetary or nonmonetary *values*;
(2) decision-makers have discretionary *authority*; and

(3)   there are players/counterparts with the *moral capacity* to (illegally)
offer and pay for a certain decision.

When combined, these factors create an environment in which corruption
can occur, and the *more* that these factors are present (that is, the more
control and the more authority that decision-makers possess, and the
more the moral capacity of the players allows corruption), the higher the
risk of corruption. The scope of the (direct) damage caused by this
corruption can be defined as *the impact of distorted decisions multiplied
by their frequency*. The greater the values at stake, the higher the
willingness there is to pay for the decisions (that is, greater values
encourage larger bribes), and the more likely it is that corruption will in
fact occur.

Although corruption occurs in many different situations, the three
criteria for corruption are found more often in some situations than in
others. The following subsections highlight four of these high-risk
situations: unchecked state administrative authority; government regulation of the private sector; financial/transaction secrecy; and unchecked
political (mis)spending.[22]

2.2.1   Unchecked State Authority

State administrations make numerous decisions that members of society
might want to influence. The risk of corruption in state administration
depends not only on the types and severity of controls in place to deter
corruption and to promote transparency in decision-making, but also on
what characterizes the decisions at stake and *how civil servants' decision-
making authority is delegated and organized*. As in other markets, a
buyer's willingness to pay depends on the value at stake for the buyer,
including both monetary and nonmonetary values (for example, the
patient who needs heart surgery is likely to be more willing to pay,
legally or illegally, for that surgery than a patient who needs a knee
operation). The price will also depend on the cost, which in this setting
refers to the risk for the decision-maker of getting caught and the
consequences she or he will face if caught. If the briber's goal is to
obtain a civil servant's help in undertaking something *illegal*, such as
smuggling narcotics or dumping poisoned material in a river, the
consequences for the civil servant if caught are higher, and therefore, the
bribe paid for having the crime overlooked is typically higher (as

[22]   This section is largely based on arguments previously presented with a
richer literature review in Søreide (2014a).

illustrated by the example of elephant poaching: see Box 2.1 in this chapter). However, the risk of facing a sanction depends on the extent of the decision-maker's discretionary authority. A civil servant who exercises a monopoly on decision-making, left unchecked can decide, for example, who will get treatment and in what order, will be able to demand bribes from clients along the whole demand curve. Such a civil servant can allocate benefits according to which bribe is offered, and thus each bribe reflects each client's willingness (and ability) to pay. A corrupt decision-maker in this situation can usually enhance his or her illegal revenues by forcing clients to wait, because time will often be more valuable to the clients than to the civil servant. Thus, higher bribes can be extracted by first making clients wait and then, in exchange for bribes, giving them what they want. Examples of circumstances for such *queuing* scenarios are customs, public health services and schools with restricted entry, public housing arrangements and license-dependent access to markets.

The opportunity for demanding bribes will depend on how civil servants and clients 'find each other.' In the case of queuing, the civil servant can choose between clients in the queue, and determine whom to serve when. In cases in which a client, by contrast, can choose which civil servant to consult – choosing, for example which tax officer to consult or tax office to visit – the situation is completely different, because now, if faced with a demand for a bribe, the client can simply turn to another, and perhaps more honest, civil servant. The more *visible* each decision-making unit's service delivery performance is, the more difficult it is for offices or civil servants to facilitate corruption and get away with inefficient solutions. If the civil servants *collude* in the corruption, however, the client is met with a demand for a bribe whomever he or she addresses, and the bribe can (again) be set at the clients' willingness to pay. This is obviously also the result when the corruption is management-steered.

For these different reasons, state authority can be *reorganized for anticorruption.* For instance, elements of 'competition' can be introduced into state administration by allocating authority over a certain thematic or geographic area to several officials, instead of just one, or by giving them overlapping responsibilities, or by letting not one but several expert committees offer advice on important decisions. Monitoring should be arranged so that those with incentives to react on misuse of authority are also informed about performance. Although more anticorruption monitoring risks compromising the efficiency gains associated with discretionary authority given to honest civil servants, this risk can be mitigated by state administrative entities that understand the dangers and are organized accordingly.[23]

2.2.2 Manipulated Regulation for Market Power

State administrative institutions' independence from the executive is supposed to deter populist political agendas from overruling laws regulating institutional performance. This independence, however, may also give these institutions the space within which to make biased, bribe-induced decisions. This risk is particularly high in the field of industry regulation.

Governments largely determine the framework conditions for doing business in a country, and they thereby influence private-sector entities' profit-making opportunities. Decisions at the political level are implemented and enforced at the administrative level by an industry regulation unit. When decisions are biased to the benefit of private-sector entities, at the expense of society at large, it can be difficult to determine whether decisions are corrupted at the political level or the administrative level. Besides, the many aims that lie behind industry regulation – including helping to set prices, ensuring quality, expanding or monitoring labor markets, developing domestic industry, protecting the environment, and so forth – make it relatively easy for a government to defend almost any decision, including the corrupt ones. The difficulty of determining if regulatory decisions have been bought, together with the huge profits at stake and the low risk of politicians being held responsible by voters in democratic elections or of officials being sanctioned by government control units, makes industry regulation a high-risk area for corruption.[24]

The government decisions that may attract attempts to bribe officials are those that are likely to affect a firm's market power, its cost savings, and its opportunities to win contracts. Such decisions are common in sectors where government intervention is especially needed or easy to

---

[23] Further aspects regarding monitoring and responses on misuse of authority are discussed in Chapter 3. For explanation of how the organization of state administration matters for the risk of corruption, see Rose-Ackerman (1978) and Søreide and Rose-Ackerman (2016). On elements of competition in state administration, see Tirole (1986) among others.

[24] Many authors describe the problem of corruption in the regulation of utilities – among them Dal Bo (2006), Martimort and Straub (2009), Estache (2011), Auriol and Straub (2011), Auriol and Blanc (2009), and Kenny and Søreide (2008).

defend, such as in infrastructure, health, defense, and extractive industries. Such sectors, therefore, are more exposed to corruption than other
sectors, and in many countries they are considered arenas for corruption.[25] Associating risks with a particular sector, however, may be unfair
to countries where regulations for that sector function well, and by
labeling some sectors 'more corrupt,' one may discourage adequate
monitoring of sectors that are traditionally regarded as 'less corrupt.' It is,
therefore, necessary to maintain a conceptual understanding of the
mechanisms and circumstances that expose a sector to corruption.

Regulatory decisions exposed to corrupt influence are those that affect
private-sector players' competitive pressure, costs, or contracts. Decisions
that relieve *competitive pressure* are those that lead to higher (formal or
informal) entry barriers for foreign producers, produce greater tolerance
for single-source supplier agreements, and impede enforcement of competition law (accepting acquisitions or indirectly facilitating cartel
collaboration, for example). In many countries, competition authority
decisions made at the administrative level can be overruled at the
political level, and political decisions are exposed to corrupt bargains or
other forms of undue influence.[26] When it comes to *cost savings*,
decisions that significantly influence the prospects for profits among
private-sector players concern industry tax cuts, opportunities for tax
avoidance and evasion, access to low-priced credit, room for vertical
cooperation upstream (securing low-priced production inputs), and biased
enforcement of the laws that affect cost-savings in production (including
matters regarding taxation, safety, environmental standards, or labor
laws). The perhaps most obvious risk is related to decisions that will
improve the opportunity for private players to win *contracts* with the
government. Government investment plans and state budgets, tender
criteria (to match certain products or services), offset arrangements,[27]
diplomatic pressure on foreign governments, and tied development aid or

---

[25]   Transparency International's Corruption Barometer is the most comprehensive cross-country survey of which sectors and industries are perceived to be
the most corrupt, see http://www.transparency.org/gcb2013.

[26]   This is why the connection between corruption and competition was a main
theme at the OECD Global Forum on Competition 2014. See http://www.oecd.
org /competition/globalforum/ fighting-corruption-and-promoting - competition . htm.
Arguments here are further elaborated in Søreide (2014b).

[27]   Offsets are a counter-trade mechanism agreed between purchasing governments and supplying companies that require the latter to put in place a number of
additional investments, often unconnected to the main contract, as a condition of
undertaking it (as defined by Transparency International UK's Defense and
Security Programme, see http://www.ti-defence.org/17-category-what-we-do/

credits (that is, funds that must be spent on goods or services from a donor country) are all areas in which decisions can be skewed to the benefit of a particular supplier. The extent to which such biased decision-making can go on unchecked determines the scope of corrupt damage.

Strategies introduced to reduce the risk of business-related corruption have often concentrated on public procurement procedures. Given the many at risk, however, a focus on certain decisions and procedures is likely to be too narrow, and aspects of industry regulation give stake-holders the misleading impression that significant steps are being taken to reduce the risk of unfair private-sector influence on government spending. Procurement reform has rarely altered the perceived extent of corruption. Unless governments also seek to develop or maintain a (de facto) pro-competition business regulation culture, and take various industry performance assessments into account when they shape this area of governance, the various arenas identified here will remain exposed to corruption.

2.2.3 Secrecy in the World of Business

A well-functioning international infrastructure for the flow of capital facilitates investment, trade, productivity, and innovation. This infra-structure, combined with institutions that secure a safe and stable society with protected property rights and predictable law enforcement, makes it possible for players to (honestly) make a profit while markets are supplied with in-demand products and services. The main obligation of all those who benefit from this infrastructure is to recognize the rules of the game and make the tax payments required for maintaining the system. However, because each country has its own political environment and the right to determine its own laws and tax rates, the system does not work as smoothly as it could if all countries shared the same rules, rates, and controls. From an anticorruption perspective, the major challenges presented by this infrastructure are associated with countries and finan-cial institutions that offer very low tax rates, individual tax agreements, or secrecy when it comes to the identity of owners, their transactions, and the sources of funds.[28]

Secret ownership makes it possible for players to profit from a well-functioning, market-based capital system while avoiding the risk of

---

104-offsets.html. These deals are common in the defense sector, but occur in the extractive industries and infrastructure sectors as well.

[28] Schjelderup (2015) provides a useful introduction to these challenges and the urgent need for better solutions.

being held responsible when they break the rules. The most far-reaching consequence is probably tax evasion, which causes dramatic cuts in a government's revenue base and undermines markets due to unfair competition. The impact of secrecy is not limited to tax evasion, however. The same structures used to hide ownership are also used to conceal corrupt transactions and conflicts of interest. Without facts about the owner of a company, bizarre situations can arise in which, for example, a minister with sector oversight responsibility determines the framework conditions of his or her own companies, and thus makes it possible for those companies to make huge profits, apparently without breaking any laws. Other crimes facilitated by financial secrecy include money laundering, insurance fraud, mafia activities, and terrorism, each of which, of course, has its own potentially severe consequences. The international process of harmonizing rules and controls has been slow, often held back by those who profit from loopholes and low political accountability at home for problems whose consequences occur primarily abroad. A clearer understanding of the role of corporations, financial institutions, legal advisers, and governments, and of the ties between them, is essential for developing efficient law enforcement solutions and for securing a fair allocation of benefits.[29]

A different form of secrecy that enhances the risk of corruption among private-sector players is the uncertainty business representatives may have about when a bribe 'should' be paid to a decision-maker and how large the bribe should be. A government or administration that has a *reputation* for corruption fuels an expectation among private-sector players that they must pay a bribe in order to obtain a certain benefit, have their application considered, or in other ways secure 'fair treatment.' Such a reputation facilitates corruption and leads clients to offer bribes even if no demand for bribes has been expressed by the ultimate decision-maker. Unreliable signals of requested bribes spread more readily if there is a market for middlemen (for example, intermediaries between foreign firms and a state administration), who might have everything to gain from driving up the level of bribery.[30] In the short

---

[29] For details on this agenda, see the website of the Financial Action Task Force (FATF) – http://www.fatf-gafi.org/ – including the reports presenting results on how countries follow up on international agreement regarding financial transparency and suspicious transactions. For details, estimates and cases, see also the websites of Tax Justice Network (http://www.taxjustice.net) and Global Financial Integrity (http://www.gfintegrity.org/).

[30] See Hasker and Okten (2008) and Bjorvatn, Torsvik, and Tungodden (2005).

term, at least, and especially in countries ranked poorly on cross-country perceptions-based corruption indices, signals of expected corruption *drive* corruption, even if the signals are wrong. Countering the impact of a reputation for corruption is very difficult, but its consequences could probably be reduced with a more balanced presentation of the problems and with more emphasis on the likelihood of meeting an honest decision-maker.

2.2.4   Unbridled Access to State Revenues

Most countries' constitutions stipulate a separation between government authority, on the one side, and control of high-level decision-making processes regarding the expenditure of state revenues, on the other. De jure stipulations and de facto practices, however, are often only distantly related. Governments that control state revenues without any effective monitoring are often associated with corruption risks. A number of factors may explain why a country's constitutional provisions are ignored or neglected, including recent or ongoing civil conflict or a colonized past. Another reason – and one that is a powerful driver of corruption – is the difficulty that many governments encounter when they receive large state revenues from abroad, typically in the form of development support or from export of natural resources.

Many countries with abundant natural resources experience weak or even negative economic development when they start exporting their resources. Among the several factors that help explain why this should be the case, one of the most influential is that the export of natural resources creates higher risks of rent-seeking and corruption.[31] The risks can be understood in light of how citizens adapt to expected revenues. Consider a scenario where a country is starting up petroleum production. In this early phase, many citizens try to secure a position where they can benefit from the expected revenue flow. Competition for such positions intensifies. The authority to allocate positions becomes more valuable, and this triggers a rivalry to acquire such power, including at the top level of governance. For the incumbent regime, the expectation or reality of

---

[31]   Such mechanisms are explained by Ross (2013), Karl (1997), Robinson, Torvik, and Verdier (2006), Torvik (2009) – among others. Le Billon (2014) underscores the importance of nuancing between corruption, illegal exploitation, and tax evasion, because these factors occur at different stages of the process toward production and have different beneficiaries. Gamu, Le Billon, and Spiegel (2015) find governance dysfunctions to be the main category of explanatory factors behind a link between revenues from extractive industries and poverty.

increased revenues makes it yet more important to retain political power. The threat of another group taking power becomes too serious for the government and its allies among the country's elite to allow the risk of democratic mechanisms to prevent them from continued control. With an increase in revenues coming from abroad, a consequent decrease in the relative importance of tax revenues from society, and a fading willingness to protect democratic values, the government's accountability vis-à-vis the population falls. Citizens become dissatisfied and frustrated, and civil unrest grows, prompting the regime to expand its use of security mechanisms such as covert intelligence gathering and brutal policing. Enhanced security for the incumbent regime typically requires or fosters a closer relationship between government leaders and military leaders, and politicians bribe generals to retain their loyalty. Supporters of the incumbent regime are rewarded with official positions, personal enrichment, and, in some cases, immunity from prosecution. As a small segment of society becomes ever richer, the poorest segments of the population become even poorer, their circumstances growing far worse than they were before their country's natural resources began to be exported.[32]

This depressing scenario does not play out in all resource-rich economies, but where it does, theories about the mechanisms at work help us understand how the changes in a country's industrial composition and revenue base can entirely alter the risks of high-level corruption.[33] Financial support in the form of aid and development lending can also lead to similar corruption risks. These forms of support are typically accompanied by external controls on spending, public statements from donors about the kinds of results they expect to see in terms of development, and demands from the international community for integrity in state administrative institutions. In practice, however, development partners have found it difficult to place integrity-related conditionalities on transfers to governments, because, in many cases, governments have obtained cheap loans simply by promising to introduce reforms, new laws, or a development agenda; how the governments actually perform in

---

[32] Vicente (2010, 2011) explains why these mechanisms may start even if no revenues from resource production ever materialize; the sheer expectation of revenues is sufficient for the domino effect to begin.

[33] For a useful, more nuanced yet brief literature review, see Gilberthorpe and Papyrakis (2015).

practice has little or no impact on the funding they receive.[34] Far from reducing corruption, this form of negligence may have nurtured the problem.

2.2.5 Worst Case Scenarios

Some societies struggle with more deep-seated corruption problems than others – often referred to as 'entrenched corruption.' While there is corruption in all societies where the checks and balances in governance do not work well, there are some societies where the extent is not 'merely' one among several forms of crime – it is pervasive and chronic. The level of governance dysfunction is equally severe, and the problem is rather associated with constitutional failure, if not a complete breakdown in governance caused by the incumbent regime's loss of legitimacy. These are definitely arenas for corruption, yet the problem is cross-cutting, and not associated with specific mechanisms.

In these contexts, the corruption terminology has its shortcomings. When corruption and other severe development problems all spring from the same fundamental problem (that is, profound governance dys-function), then what appear to be the consequences of corrupt acts (in the narrow, criminal law sense) are, in fact, the consequences of the underlying root problem. In other words, observed cases of corruption are the *expressions* of something more ingrained, and it is difficult to disentangle the impacts of corrupt acts from the damage associated with constitutional problems and an overly weak or overbearing state. How can we understand corruption and its consequences in cases of severe governance problems, where corruption is obviously a problem but not the whole story? Three explanations seem particularly useful: the situation when grabbing simply pays more than honesty, the case of a disconnected government, and brutal kleptocracy.

2.2.5.1 Thievery pays
The instinctive economic approach to understanding entrenched corruption is to investigate *what individuals seek to achieve* by the choices they make, choices that are either development-friendly or not. More specific-ally, economists are likely to search for the factors that explain why so many individuals continuously benefit more from grabbing at the expense of society than from honest production and service delivery. One of the

---

[34] See Kabur and Webb (2000) for results and discussion. We return to these challenges in Chapter 6.

economists who has had much to say about how governance dysfunctions shape incentives is Gordon Tullock. In simple words he explains why an institutional environment might create incentives for grabbing. In the absence of property rights, he says, 'it is almost always true that the most highly profitable 'investment' is to take something from your neighbor' (Tullock 2005:13). The problem is twofold. First, while society would benefit from the results of productive activity, investing time and funds in productive labor will not make much sense if there are no returns from the investment. For each individual, it makes better sense to exploit one's opportunities for theft. A general disinclination to invest in productivity undermines any attempt of triggering economic development. Second, the costs associated with protection from theft are much higher than the expense of carrying out the thievery. While the theft can be carried out quickly, the victim will normally be unable to tell when and in what way the theft will happen, and therefore, protection requires constant aware-ness and multi-dimensional anti-theft strategies. This need for protection adds to the costs associated with the grabbing.

Cheating, theft, fraud, and extortion all have the effects of preventing productive investments, motivating the strong and talented to steal instead of produce, and causing costs that would not be necessary if law and order prevailed. Furthermore, entrenched corruption implies a waste of citizens' investment in a state structure. If a government fails to deliver the services and law enforcement that justifies its existence, these services are replaced in other informal, creative ways, or through private sector solutions, and while citizens will have higher expenses than necessary, they will continue to manage – even if development is hampered by the corruption. The biggest problem in these situations is how 'corruption corrupts' – societies struggling against the most entrenched forms of corruption have difficulties getting out of the situation because there are so many factors that make it more rewarding, or more convenient, to be part of a corruption culture than trying to work against it. Law enforcement has broken down. Honesty is not rewarded.[35]

2.2.5.2 Disconnected governance
A more anthropological approach to entrenched corruption would involve investigating deep-seated governance problems in light of *informal authority and societal norms*. Powerful players' eagerness to implement

---

[35] Andvig and Moene (1989) explain how 'corruption corrupts' in the sense of triggering multiplier effects once corruption begins to increase. The problem of a bad law enforcement equilibrium is further addressed in Chapter 6.

laws and construct formal institutions may have led them to ignore the importance of building the state's legitimacy in society, a task that requires dialogue with representatives of the different areas and segments of the society and an attempt to align the state with informal norms where possible. It requires a recognition of citizens' right to choose their leaders, while agreed upon norms and formal rules are departed upon only incrementally and for publicly justified reasons. Failure from the side of the incumbent regime to recognize the mechanisms through which norms are created and adopted may have undermined the process of connecting formal laws to moral values, and even spurred individuals' propensity to commit 'crime' – as most citizens judge their own acts differently than the representatives of the incumbent regime. Obstacles to good governance may thus be understood as the result of a moral order with which the state is insufficiently aligned.

The state is not necessarily recognized as an authority embedded in society, and for this reason informal structures of authority may well dominate whatever bureaucratic structures the government tries to build. For the individual, corruption is not only a trade-off between benefits and costs; it is also the result of which moral codes to obey and where to place one's loyalty. From this perspective, an act of corruption can be a moral duty for a person who would never commit a 'crime,' in his or her *informal* sense of the word. The long-term benefits for an individual of making choices in line with informal norms may well outweigh the benefits for a citizen of recognizing a formal law. The individual civil servant who adheres to this informal attitude toward the state administration may well get used to exploiting his or her public authority for his or her personal benefit and for the benefit of his or her family and allies. The more such attitudes and patterns are developed and established, the more difficult it is for a development-friendly government to carry out anticorruption reforms.

2.2.5.3 Brutal kleptocracy

In many societies, however, the problem is not that the state is too weak or undisciplined but that it is too strong, and that those in power use that power to benefit a narrow group of allies instead of society as a whole. Increasing voter discontent will not necessarily lead to development in countries with a weak democratic tradition, low unity in the opposition, and an incumbent with a strong grip on revenues and military forces. Under these circumstances, what might have started as a democracy is efficiently diluted with brutal oppression against criticism (the more criticism, the more brutal), generous benefits for supporters in private as well as public institutions, reduced access to correct information, and increasing centralization of state administration. The more concentrated the political control, the more the state can be seen as a single unit, a predatory institution designed and developed to secure benefits for the group of individuals who control it. Such a state not only lacks legitimacy; most citizens consider it a threat to both their economic and physical well-being. For the members of the privileged group involved in government decision-making, this alienation of the state from society may create a 'we/they' attitude toward ordinary citizens. The members of the elite find it easier to neglect their formal duties, and see themselves as morally justified in using excessive force to repress dissent while grabbing what they can from the state coffers and breaking the law in various other ways.[36]

These activities should not be understood 'simply' as a matter of corruption, although there is definitely something rotten going on. In fact, law enforcers may not be able to hold those involved in corruption liable for their acts, because the elite may be in a position to modify the law and set the rules so that their grabbing from the state is made nominally legal.[37] The governance problem is far too big to be addressed with a transaction-based approach (that is, a criminal law process for individual acts). Any attempt to solve the problem must also involve a thorough examination of the government's excessive use of authority and the factors that allow the government to operate without the effective checks on governance associated with modern constitutions and well-functioning societies.

What these three explanations of governance dysfunctions tell us is that cross-country correlations showing a negative relationship between the perceived extent of corruption and various development-friendly social features and economic trends, including GDP growth, should not be interpreted simply as a consequence of corrupt acts. The correlations will easily confirm the existence of 'something rotten' and associated problems, but the relationship must be studied more carefully – and with

---

[36] Acemoglu, Johnson, and Robinson (2005) explain why a ruler in such circumstances needs to control when laws are enforced and when they are ignored. Through a divide-and-rule strategy, the ruler can prevent the development of a strong opposition. While condoning extensive corruption among allies, the ruler applies the law on an ad hoc basis to sanction disloyal officials or demonstrate authority. By displaying how those who violate the law are (sometimes) held responsible, the incumbent courts popular support despite his (or occasionally her) own theft of state revenues.

[37] Kaufmann and Vicente (2011) refer to 'legal corruption' when those in control of governance can adjust the laws to match their corruption.

due awareness of a society's unique history and complex situation – in order to determine the factors driving the relationship. Only then can plausible conclusions regarding the impact of corruption be drawn.

Furthermore, if we define corruption to mean 'something rotten in state administration and governance,' it becomes almost impossible to conceptually determine the damage corruption causes. The concept of something rotten is too unclear to permit analytical and empirical assessments of its consequences *unless* (1) one understands the matter as a conceptual debate about the state's legitimacy in society, or (2) one defines 'corruption' more narrowly, which reduces the term to the classification of certain acts. While state legitimacy is essential for a criminal justice system to function well (a matter discussed later in this book), the latter option – devising a more precise terminology – is the most relevant and fruitful for those interested in improving the enforcement of criminal law on a day-to-day basis and determining appropriate and effective sentencing practices by the courts.

With these different perspectives in mind, and with a keen awareness of the conceptual difficulty of determining the impact of corruption, we now turn to the empirical side of the problem. How can we assess corruption and its consequences?

2.3 METHODOLOGICAL APPROACHES AND CHALLENGES

The data we do have on corruption confirm what all logical reasoning suggests: corruption causes damage to society. How much damage it causes, however, can be difficult to gauge. As we have just seen, in highly corrupt countries, the estimates on corruption are difficult to separate from constitutional frailties, state weakness, and other deep-seated governance problems. In the countries perceived to be less exposed to the problem, some forms of corruption are very subtle and fly under the radar of the corruption indicators. In general, those involved in corruption do not want to be studied, which of course complicates most data-collecting exercises. We have rough estimates of corruption, but however sophisticated the statistical methodologies applied in analyzing the available data, we are limited in the conclusions we can draw. For policy purposes as well as for scholarly research, more nuanced information is necessary. But while we await better data, we should ensure that we know the main categories of existing information about corruption and are aware of their major strengths and weaknesses.

Fact-based information that can safely be used for the development of better estimates of corruption levels is thin on the ground. Some datasets with revealed and prosecuted corruption cases are available, such as the OECD overview of bribe payer cases (OECD, 2014), and these are valuable. However, because we do not know how many instances of corruption pass undetected and unprosecuted, we have no way of knowing if the datasets that are available are representative of the problem as a whole; consequently, such datasets cannot be used to draw generalized conclusions. Similarly, *evidence of suspicious financial trans-fers* can sometimes lead to the detection of corrupt acts, but even if oversight and access to financial information were to improve substantially, the cases observed could not be used as reliable indicators of the frequency of corruption. The *number of court cases* depends on multiple and diverse factors (such as the readiness of whistle-blowers to report what they see, the capacity of investigators to unravel complex crimes, and the political independence of prosecutors) and thus tells us little about the problem's magnitude: an increased number of corruption cases may simply reflect enhanced efficiency in the criminal justice system. The frequency of *cases reported by the press* is not a particularly useful indicator because such figures depend on editorial judgments about what people want to read, as well as levels of press freedom. When it comes to *complaints by those victimized* by corruption (for example, those who suffer from the corrupt application of procurement rules), the number of complaints will depend on what the complainers hope to achieve by complaining – and in highly corrupt societies, they usually expect to accomplish little or nothing. In addition, in many corruption cases, the victims are not easily identified (for example, in cases in which state revenues are wasted or stolen, so that the costs are borne by the state and society as a whole, not by specific individuals), and thus no one sees a reason to speak out.

In response to these difficulties, researchers have come up with solutions that go in three different directions: *macro-level perceptions-based corruption indices; micro-level controlled experiments*; and *self-reporting surveys of experiences* with the problem.[38] This section examines each of these in turn. All have their benefits in terms of

---

[38] In addition, there are sources of data that indicate that corruption may occur, including certain information about taxation, price development, budget transfers, and expenses. Especially relevant are public-sector expenditure-tracking surveys (PETS), which are financial oversight initiatives conducted with the purpose of 'following the money' – for example, from a central decision-making level and all the way down to various user-units such as health or

expanding our body of empirical knowledge on corruption. All also have
their weaknesses, however, and these weaknesses should inspire some
caution about how and when to use the information to justify policy
choices, sanctions, or reform strategies.

2.3.1 Corruption Indices

Many data analyses of corruption apply perceptions-based cross-country
corruption indicators.[39] This category of data is the best-known source of
information about the extent of corruption. The index prepared yearly by
Transparency International, the Corruption Perceptions Index (CPI) –
illustrated in Table 2.1 in this chapter, is probably the most widely cited.
This index, which ranks a large number of countries according to the
perceived extent of their exposure to corruption, is a *composite index*, a
combination of surveys and assessments of corruption collected by a
variety of reputable institutions. The surveys used to compile the CPI do
not cover all countries listed in the CPI, but each country is covered by at
least three different sources. Each country, therefore, is not assessed in
exactly the same way, but there is a certain consistency in the reference
to the corruption phenomenon, which is understood as the abuse of
entrusted power for private gain.[40]

The enormous attention paid to this index worldwide has contributed to
awareness of the need for efficient barriers against corruption, and for
international collaboration as well as investment in research to better
combat corruption. When released each year, the CPI often spurs intense
debate, especially in countries that had hoped to perform better than their
neighbors. Opposition politicians use their country's position on the
index for what it is worth (and more), citing the index ranking as
evidence of the incumbent's greed, shortcomings in the fight against
corruption, and readiness to see income disparities widen. Apparently, the
index triggers a competitive spirit in terms of a country's anticorruption
performance – a sentiment that could help drive healthy development.

---

education facilities. Though relevant for understanding corruption risks, these are
all indirect sources of information and will not be addressed here.

[39]   This subsection draws heavily on some paragraphs in Søreide (2013,
Chapter 3), first presented in a paper for an international anticorruption conference in Brasilia, 2005 (see Søreide, 2005).

[40]   The index with all countries listed and the methodology guide is available
on the Transparency International website, see http://www.transparency.org/
cpi2013. This reference to corruption is Transparency International's definition of
the problem.

A problem with the index, however, is associated with the way in which it is interpreted, which involves simplifying a very complex phenomenon. The index has often been (mis)interpreted by researchers, journalists, and policy analysts as a reliable estimate of the actual magnitude of corruption in the countries included. But the CPI's methodology precludes it from being highly reliable in that sense. Gathering together individuals' perceptions of something that takes place in secrecy will not generate accurate information about the extent of the act no matter how many (more or less uninformed) individuals are asked for their opinion. As Bjørn Høyland, Kalle Moene, and Fredrik Willumsen (2012:1) put it – with reference to perceptions-based governance indicators in general: 'The appeal of the reported rankings lies in their simplicity. They provide an instant idea of the success of countries relative to others. Their users need no more statistical knowledge than readers of sports news.'

The frequency with which references to the corruption index are made makes it all the more important to be aware of its shortcomings. First of all, the index seeks to capture the perceptions of ordinary citizens, expert observers, and foreigners. Subjective survey responses about the magnitude of a problem are inherently vague. Assessments such as 'substantial,' 'serious,' or 'frequent' depend on the respondent's personal reference point, which might be an ideal situation, a comparison with a neighboring society, or a recollection of the situation some years earlier. Expert assessments may be colored by personal experiences or the lack thereof, cases discussed in the press, the observations made by other experts,[41] and the last year's index results. The number of sources is no guarantee of an unbiased result, because similar weaknesses may afflict many sources.[42]

The underlying surveys refer to broad and diverse concepts of corruption, making it difficult to tell exactly what acts 'the perceived extent of' refers to. Corruption takes many forms, and different countries criminalize some of these but not others. For many users of the CPI, this is not a problem, because they want to see all forms of governance-related grabbing controlled. Corruption is regulated by criminal law, however, and those who do not want to categorize a society and its members as corrupt under false pretenses must tread warily in the presence of vague definitions and inconsistent approaches to criminalization. The problem

---

[41] For discussion of cascade information problems in empirics on corruption, see Andvig (2005).
[42] In statistical terms, the margin of error may well correlate between different data sources.

is not easily solved for the index makers. A corruption index that attempts to use the same definition across all countries will capture a combination of both legal and illegal acts. If keeping strictly to each country's legal definition, however, one could not compare the results across countries. A reported index score must therefore be understood as reflecting a very approximate and broadly defined phenomenon: namely, the extent of the feeling that something about the given country's government is rotten.

Even if we assume that users of the index understand this limitation, the way in which the index results are calculated and presented poses other concerns. Despite the use of several surveys to calculate a country's index score, the figure given is imprecise. Index details, which are available on the Transparency International website, reveal large margins of error, which means that a country's real level of *perceived* corruption is likely to be within a range of scores, and is not necessarily correctly reflected in the given ranking (the higher a country's ranking, the lower the level of perceived corruption in that country). Consider, for example, the United States, which was given a score of 74 on the 2014 index. Its 90 percent confidence interval ranges from a score of 60 (where it would be placed with Spain, which is ranked thirty-seventh) to 89 (where it would be alongside Australia, ranked eleventh). With a probability of 90 percent, the United States' true level of *perceived* corruption lies within this wide area on the list of countries.[43] Thus, not only should we be concerned about the distance between perceptions and actual levels of corruption; we should also be worried that there might be a wide gap between *estimated* perceptions of corruption and actual perceptions. In short, the index is not even exact when it comes to informing us about *what people think* of corruption (even if corruption is broadly understood as 'something rotten').

A different concern associated with this source of data is how the index may affect governments' various anticorruption priorities. The attention paid to the index by a wide variety of users, combined with its lack of nuance, might have tempted some governments to focus more on elevating their ranking on the index than on improving their real performance. Høyland, Moene, and Willumsen (2012) have even coined a term, '*rank-seeking behavior*,' to describe this phenomenon, which is most likely to affect countries trying to attract business or obtain

---

[43] For details, see the index's methodology, which is available on the Transparency International website: www.transparency.org. Saisana and Saltelli (2012) describe how the index has been improved in recent years.

unrestricted development loans. Observers who contribute to the underlying surveys that feed into the index may be blinded by a government's introduction of new anticorruption laws, procedures, and institutions, regardless of their actual impact in society. In the absence of strenuous efforts to compare a country's progress within the index with its progress on the ground, the index may even boost incentives for a government to develop façade institutions behind which corruption can continue undetected.[44]

To its credit, Transparency International informs users about the methodology it employs to construct the index and cautions them to avoid far-reaching interpretations. Nonetheless, the problems just described are largely ignored in the literature on corruption. Numerous statistical exercises have applied the CPI data in pursuit of a better understanding of corruption and its causes. Regardless of how the CPI's results are distorted by data inaccuracies, they have been, and still frequently are, presented with great confidence. Several attempts have been made to investigate correlations between the index and other data that may better reflect actual levels of corruption.[45] These studies suggest that the index seems to capture quite well the extent to which a country suffers from serious governance problems. As such, a low ranking on the CPI serves as a warning signal which should be heeded by investors, development partners, and others who operate in a country that is low or falling on the index. A more attentive attitude toward the government of a poorly ranked country may also motivate research and anticorruption action, even if the index result itself says little about what to act on and how to do so. Furthermore, although the index cannot be used as a reliable estimate of corruption risks in a given setting, it is likely to paint a more accurate picture of the general risk of extortive corruption, which is more observable (and perceivable), than of collusive corruption, which is more hidden and more difficult to classify according to legal terms.[46]

2.3.2 Micro-Level Controlled Experiments

A completely different approach to investigating the mechanisms of corruption and its consequences is found in the literature on controlled experiments. These studies are tightly focused, involving, for example,

---

[44] An argument about how institutional façades facilitate grabbing is presented by Moene and Søreide (2015).

[45] See discussion and empirical comparisons of data sources in Lin and Yu (2014) and Foster, Horowitz, and Méndez (2012), among others.

[46] See Auriol (2014).

the investigation of a public service or a certain market in a particular sector in a specific country. The investigators identify a particular group of individuals and closely observe them, monitoring their activities, transactions, income, and any other facets of their lives that may indicate if they are accepting bribes.[47] One such study examined the award of drivers' licenses in New Delhi and discovered convincing evidence on the distortive consequences of corruption. Drivers' licenses, which of course should be awarded only to candidates who have demonstrated their driving skills and knowledge of traffic rules in an exam, were instead awarded upon the payment of a bribe. With corruption, the exam became irrelevant and the bribery put unsafe drivers on the road. Those who obtained their licenses in exchange for a bribe had lower driving qualifications, and those who refused to pay bribes were often denied a license, regardless of their skills. Many of those who offered bribes did not even have to take a driving test to get a license.[48]

The most comprehensive field experiment on corruption to date was conducted by Ben Olken in Indonesia. Olken, the World Bank, and the Indonesian government wanted to discover the extent to which corruption affects the quality of roads, as well as how much local-level corruption citizens in a given community perceive. Around six hundred villages received government funding for local infrastructure projects (for example, the construction or repair of roads and bridges). A large proportion of them were randomly selected for a careful government audit, and as part of the audit, engineers assessed the quality of the resulting construction work (that is, they dug holes in completed roads to evaluate their quality). What Olken found was that prices of the construction projects could easily be inflated and quality reduced without producing any reaction from the citizens who would benefit from the projects. Grassroots controls were thus found to be inefficient for detecting corruption in projects where the final result is difficult for outsiders to observe. Careful audits proved to be far more effective in detecting and preventing fraud and corruption, and despite the costs of performing the audits, they resulted in a clear net gain for the villages involved.[49]

What these examples tell us is that quite exact information about corruption is obtainable if the problem is limited geographically and to certain situations. Such field experiments for better understanding of

---

[47] See Olken and Pande (2012) for details and review of the literature.

[48] Study conducted by Bertrand, Djankov, Henna, and Mullainathan (2006).

[49] For more examples of controlled experiments on corruption and discussion, see Abbink (2006), Peisakhin (2011), and Lambsdorff (2012).

corruption can be done in most high-risk settings, especially if governments are supportive and help facilitate the study. The exact approach for collecting valid data depends on the context and the targeted form of corruption. Each of the different forms of corruption listed in section 1.2.3 of Chapter 1 requires its own data-generating approach and definition of extent. Under certain circumstances, the corrupt transactions can be observed – and if so, the extent of the problem can be measured by the number and size of bribes, the number of corrupted decisions, the amount of illegal revenue, and so forth. These projects are difficult to carry out, however, because they usually require considerable creativity, resources, and access to information. Besides, valid results require some form of *randomization*, such as drawing participants randomly from a larger population. In cases of impact evaluation, randomly selected observations must be categorized into a 'treatment group' (that is, a group induced to act on a certain stimuli, such as more monitoring, education, or exposure to some moral values) and a control group (a group that receives no such stimuli). The results for the two groups must be compared to identify the counterfactual – that is, what would have happened if the initiative (in other words, the stimuli or anticorruption effort) was not introduced. A carefully customized research design and the use of randomization reduce the risk of biases, and are therefore critical for obtaining reliable results.[50]

In addition to the use of precise definitions and randomization, micro-level data-collection exercises are usually built on a solid understanding of the mechanisms at play in the specific setting, which in turn is developed through, for example, preparatory studies of cases, interviews, observations, literature reviews, and theoretical analyses. This means that such projects demand a lot of time and resources, and it is reasonable to ask if this research is worth the expense. While the answer depends on the specific study, it should be kept in mind that this category of empirical studies is the only category that provides exact knowledge about the problem. Despite the fact that these experiments are conducted in a carefully circumscribed environment, they contribute significantly to our knowledge about corruption, especially if their results are combined with theoretical insights. Such combinations can help us understand human traits and how players tend to respond to certain stimuli. The

---

[50]　Jøhnson and Søreide (2013) explain why randomization is necessary for obtaining reliable impact assessments of anticorruption policy work – and provide examples to illustrate the point.

downside is that the high-quality data generated by micro-level experiments are necessarily highly context specific and thus one cannot use their results to develop reliable generalizations or provide the comprehensive set of information policymakers need for risk mapping and policy design. Therefore, while controlled experiments are invaluable in developing our knowledge-base on corruption, their limits (and costs) make them insufficient for conclusions of the general damage caused by corruption, and their results are rarely sufficiently generalizable to justify a change of direction in criminal law policy work.

2.3.3 Questionnaire-Based Surveys

Due to the difficulty of counting a representative number of corruption cases and determining their consequences, assessments of the problem will often rely on *second-best data*, such as asking various players if they themselves have been involved in or observed incidents of corruption. Over the last decade or so, these kinds of surveys have been conducted systematically and have used consistent methodological approaches. Thanks to such efforts worldwide, we are now able to point with confidence to variations across countries, sectors, and industries; researchers are also getting closer to describing how different risks depend on certain contextual factors. Although the survey results do not accurately reflect the frequency with which corruption occurs, our level of confidence in the results increases as the number of consistent results from different data sources grows. Unlike the composite corruption indices, the results of surveys are usually presented with a wealth of supporting detail, allowing researchers to quickly identify the strengths and weaknesses of each survey. The surveys are not, however, free from data weaknesses, and thus efforts to correlate the data with other factors or problems in society produce distorted statistics – which should not, of course, be used to shape or legitimate nuanced policy designs.

Nonetheless, a variety of forms of such second-best sources are helping researchers develop a body of knowledge on corruption that, with each passing year, brings us closer to 'first-best' information. Some of the most useful survey-based data sources are *business surveys*, many of which encompass multiple countries. The most systematic and comprehensive study is the World Bank's Enterprise Survey. Numerous useful but less comprehensive such surveys are conducted every year, including by international consultancies such as PriceWaterhouseCoopers, Deloitte, and Ernst & Young. A further category is the *citizens- and household-surveys* conducted among a representative selection of a population and used to understand how corruption affects, for example, service delivery. Useful data of this sort are collected through the United Nations' many Crime Victimization surveys.

The largest surveys of how citizens around the globe experience corruption in different sectors of the state administration and beyond is undertaken by Transparency International's Global Corruption Barometer. For their latest 2013 survey, they asked over 114,000 individuals in 107 countries for their experiences with corruption. The result is a useful overview of which forms of corruption challenge people's daily lives the most, and which institutions are seen as the most corrupt across countries.[51]

2.4 CONCLUSION: CORRUPTION'S DAMAGING CONSEQUENCES

There are no entirely reliable estimates of the total costs of corruption in a country or industry. As this chapter has described, a conceptual understanding of the various direct and indirect corruption consequences is far from obvious, and they are no easier to quantify. Besides, while one can study the direct distortions caused by corruption in specific settings, the scope of the consequences will always depend on one's perspective. The poor will have a different understanding of the consequences than the wealthy, and many of the consequences are impossible to quantify, such as the loss of life, ratcheting up oppression and violence, and endangering the environment and animal life. In many countries, severe but indirect consequences of corruption are difficult to disentangle from the impacts of other challenges in those societies. In societies with entrenched corruption, the problem must be assessed not only as a sequence of discrete corrupt acts, but also as a reflection of constitutional breakdown.

Since the late 1990s, however, we have witnessed a tremendous development in empirical approaches to understanding corruption and a considerable expansion of the knowledge base about the problem. We know a lot more than before about how corruption harms societies and how the problem unfolds in different countries. We have sufficient and compelling evidence to confirm that corruption has harmful consequences. This is now considered a fact, whereas at the end of the last century it was still disputed by academic writers. The evidence we now

---

[51] http://www.transparency.org/gcb2013.

have comes from surveys, micro-level experiments, and macro-level indicators, while criminal law cases detail how corruption acts are carried out. In addition, we have numerous reports from investigative journalists and civil society activists and organizations that describe various aspects of corruption, reveal specific cases, or evaluate the overall quality of an integrity system. Given this body of evidence, we can say with certainty that corruption leads to the unfair allocation of benefits, distorted assessments of qualifications for benefits, higher costs for governments, a reduced quality of goods and services, and higher expenses for citizens and the private sector. The different sources of information, especially when used in combination, also provide useful information about the extent of corruption in a given society. There is no doubt that corruption hinders development and facilitates others forms of crime.

The recent accumulation of empirical knowledge has prompted action against the problem and has had a multiplier effect. Non-governmental organizations, multilateral organizations, and other players have launched a variety of anticorruption activities, and these have often involved data collecting and fact-finding initiatives.

When it comes to deducing policy implications from our new empirical insights, we must not forget the weaknesses of the data we have. The more uncertain our empirical results on the consequences of corruption, the more humble we must be when putting forward policy recommendations and setting anticorruption priorities. We must not pretend that the information about corruption is more reliable than it actually is. At the same time, that uncertainty should not excuse inaction; our knowledge about integrity mechanisms has improved as well, and there are plenty of initiatives that can safely be introduced for those who want to clean up their state administration.

From an efficiency perspective, however, it is important to make priorities so that initiatives are targeted at the most serious consequences of corruption, instead of being adapted to what will most readily find support in the political environment. The more solid the information about consequences and the impact of anticorruption initiatives, the easier it will be to secure traction for important initiatives. To move forward with this knowledge-generating agenda, we need to combine the insights we have gleaned from conceptual analyses with systematic reviews of empirical insights and findings. Preliminary results, like those listed in each of the cells in Table 2.2, can be subject to more robust research, and each such study would advance our quest for knowledge about corruption.

When it comes to the implications for criminal justice systems, the knowledge of corruption's consequences is essential for political motivation to act on the problem and hence, for criminal law regulation. As we will see in Chapter 3, however, there is a substantial failure to act on this form of crime – even in the most developed countries.

3. Practical obstacles to efficient criminal law enforcement

As the preceding chapters have emphasized, many factors help explain corruption, including factors that lie beyond what criminal law can regulate. Nonetheless, as shown in Figure 3.1, there is a clear relationship between the perceived extent of corruption and the ability of the law enforcement system to sanction it. The graph, prepared with data from the World Justice Project, shows absence of corruption on the vertical axis and the propensity to sanction governance misconduct on the horizontal axis. Even though this graph cannot tell us anything about causal relationships,[1] it strongly suggests that countries with a fairly well-functioning law enforcement system are able to control corruption, and that the more corruption there is in a society, the weaker the law enforcement system's ability is to sanction government misconduct.

This means that we have every reason to ask the question crucial to our hopes of making law enforcement systems more efficient at preventing, detecting, and sanctioning corruption: What are the main obstacles to successful law enforcement? This question lies at the heart of this chapter, which focuses on practical obstacles within the world of criminal law.

The ambition of the chapter is to describe what the law enforcement obstacles look like *when they do occur*. It does not try to gauge their magnitude, nor does it seek to suggest that the problems are present in all societies at all times, or even in particular societies much of the time. The examples given in this chapter are chosen merely to illustrate law enforcement challenges, not to create the (false) impression that Country X is always bested by Problem A and that Country Y wrestles continually with Problem B. Most of the examples feature OECD countries, and many examples are drawn from the reports issued by the OECD Working Group on Bribery (WGB), which are informative and detailed, and address primarily cases of foreign bribery (that is, cases in which firms

---

[1] The variables at the vertical and horizontal axes are both indicators of institutional performance, which means that they can stem from the same underlying causes, as discussed in Chapter 2.

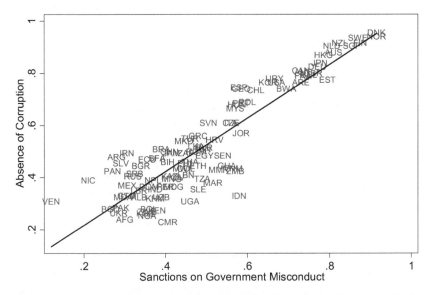

Source of data: World Justice Project (WJP) 2014 Rule of Law Index. The horizontal axis presents the WJP factor 'Government officials are sanctioned for misconduct' (sub-factor 1.4 in the 2014 WJP Report). The vertical axis presents 'Absence of corruption' (WJP factor 2 in the 2014 WJP Report). The correlation's slope is 1.03.

The WJP Rule of Law Index is constructed on the basis of survey information from 100,000 citizens and experts in 99 countries. The respondents answer questions referring to examples and cases, and these responses feed into an index consisting of nine main factors. For details about the WJP Rule of Law Index, see their webpage at: http://worldjusticeproject.org/rule-of-law-index.

Figure 3.1   Correlation between corruption control and the likelihood that government misconduct is sanctioned when disclosed

and individuals are prosecuted at home for the bribery they have committed abroad). This material from the OECD provides unique insights into developed countries' law enforcement shortcomings.[2] While some of the hindrances occur primarily in cases of foreign bribery, most

---

[2]   The OECD reports reviewed for this study are all OECD Phase 3 reports. The background to, purposes of, contents of, and procedures followed in producing these evaluations are described on the OECD website. All the reports are publicly available: see http://www.oecd.org/daf/anti-bribery/countryreports ontheimplementationoftheoecdanti-briberyconvention.htm (retrieved February 2015).

examples reflect dysfunctions that might affect enforcement also in cases of domestic corruption. I draw on other official evaluation processes as well, including reports by the Group of States against Corruption (GRECO), a useful source of systematic evaluations of integrity mechanisms more broadly, and various reports addressing performance under the United Nations Convention against Corruption (UNCAC).[3] (The reports issued by these bodies are referred to in this chapter as 'OECD WGB reports,' and 'GRECO reports' while the relevant UN reports differ in type and will be cited accordingly.) Countering stereotypes or naïve assumptions about some societies being nearly immune to corruption would have been a good reason to portray law enforcement obstacles in the most developed countries. However, the reports are selected primarily because they are the results of rigorous, peer reviewed studies and are widely available.

The chapter begins by discussing barriers to law enforcement encountered at the political level, but continues by examining obstacles that can arise even when there is sincere and significant political support for anticorruption efforts. These latter obstructions include poorly formulated laws and poorly defined crimes, obstacles encountered in investigation and prosecution, and problems associated with verdicts and sanctions. The last section of the chapter looks at what happens when the very institutions supposed to enforce the laws are subject to corrupt influence.

3.1 OBSTACLES AT THE POLITICAL LEVEL

Political support affects law enforcement performance throughout the law enforcement value chain, from the political allocation of resources to the definition of crimes and the appetite for international collaboration. As is explained below, politicians can also help shape the environment for unbiased court judgments. Instead of being part of the solution, however, politicians are sometimes part of the problem. What are the features of politically-steered obstacles to efficient law enforcement?

---

[3] The UN reports were prepared for the Fifth session of the Conference of the States Parties to the United Nations Convention against Corruption and are all available on the website of UNODC: https://www.unodc.org/unodc/en/ treaties/CAC/CAC-COSP-session5.html. The GRECO reports reviewed for this book are those prepared for the fourth round of evaluations: https://www.coe.int/ t/dghl/monitoring/greco/evaluations/round4/ReportsRound4_en.asp.

3.1.1 Weak Political Commitment

The development in the legal sphere of anticorruption over the last decades (as described in Chapter 1) is remarkable, and would never have happened without sincere commitment from influential political leaders. Governments around the world have signed and implemented ground-breaking conventions. Thanks in part to the campaigning efforts of civil society organizations, the names of transparency and integrity initiatives such as 'the EITI,' 'CoST,' 'StAR,' 'the UN Compact,' and 'Sarbanes Oxley & Dodd Frank' have become part of a common anticorruption vocabulary. Law enforcement collaboration between governments has increased the likelihood of detection of those involved in the crime. Severe sanctions are imposed on individuals and firms, and the skeletons in corporate closets are being brought into the bright, public light when past corrupt deals are exposed in court cases. The development community, backed by political leaders, has been nurturing initiatives for better governance in client economies while pushing for anticorruption action in richer economies. With the support of the OECD headquarters, the governments of the world's twenty largest economies, the G20, committed in 2015 to the seven high-level principles on corruption and growth, described in Chapter 2, declaring that corruption is damaging to governance and development.

This anticorruption landscape can be viewed in several ways. It can be seen as a success story, because it shows clear signs of step-by-step progress toward a less corrupt world. At the same time, it can inspire disappointment among those who know the scale of the challenges. Despite this international cooperation in formulating common standards, it is still a struggle to get governments to enforce the laws and convince them to accept the fact that corruption is intolerable. Corruption has distorted governments as long as countries have existed, yet the powerful G20 governments had to be cajoled and persuaded to formally agree to acknowledge this inescapable reality.

The adoption of declarations, conventions, agendas, and strategies is encouraging, but corruption is dealt with only to the extent that publicly enunciated ambitions actually lead to actions that deliver results on the ground. And on the ground, there is a furious demand for more convincing political action against the problem. People demonstrate against dishonest leaders; individuals risk their lives revealing cases involving corrupt government decision-makers; the entire Arab Spring was seen by many people as an uprising against corrupt elites.[4] Voters demand not only honesty from their governments, but also the information they need to assess political performance – information that is hard and sometimes even risky to uncover. At the same time, there are plenty of indicators that corruption goes on. A substantial proportion of firms in international markets claim to be the victims of corruption, even acknowledging and reporting their own bribery expenses. Household surveys from many countries reveal the perception that public office is gravely misused, constantly exposing citizens and firms to extortive corruption. According to Transparency International's Corruption Barometer, citizens in most countries suspect corruption in central government institutions. It is often seen as a problem that governments allow to continue; their citizens believe that their law enforcement systems would have been strengthened if there was sufficient political commitment to do so.

Considering political commitment, it is essential to keep in mind the difference between the *de jure* façades and the *de facto* shortcomings in law enforcement. Consider, for example, the Petrobras corruption scandal in Brazil, investigations into which started in 2014. Brazil is a country with updated legislation on corruption and competent law enforcement institutions. Like the counterparts in other countries, politicians in Brazil have spoken passionately about the problem of corruption for years and have demonstrated their commitment by signing and implementing the most important international anticorruption conventions. Nevertheless, the legal institutions and declared political commitment to fight the challenge could not prevent a comprehensive corruption scheme involving the highest levels of governance and successful businessmen from taking place. The grand scheme, which has shaken not just oil and gas markets (and whose aftershocks have rumbled far beyond Brazil's borders), but apparently also includes cartel collaboration between the country's largest construction companies and billions of dollars transferred between Petrobras, politicians, and construction firms, was revealed by a coincidence. Investigators in the Brazilian state of Parana decided to check the current status of a black market money dealer, Alberto Youssef – and discovered that he happened to have one of the most famous Petrobras directors, Refinery Chief Alberto Costa, on his list of money laundering clients.

---

[4] Anderson (2011) describes explanatory factors behind the Arab Spring uprisings.

Hence, the reason the Petrobras case came to light was not because some politicians with bad consciences realized that these transactions were illegal and were unwilling to bear the moral burden anymore. It was not revealed because one of the many firms involved in the cartel scandal reported the case to the police or the competition authority. The board members of Petrobras (who later claimed that they were given fewer details about business decisions than they should have been given in light of their formal responsibilities) did not voice suspicions to the authorities. If the investigators in Parana had not done their routine check, the illegal cartel would probably still be in business.[5] The just case is one out of numerous examples from around the world confirming that public commitment to anticorruption might be at odds with what politicians do in private.

3.1.2   Opportunities for Undue Personal Benefits

Politicians are in a position to secure substantial personal benefits as long as they ignore the anticorruption agenda or actively prevent enforcement of anticorruption measures. Their reluctance to enforce anticorruption laws take different forms. The following three features are common:

(1)   the corruption is carried out with the help of 'corruption-like circumstances' where the formalities are such that it is difficult to hold those involved accountable;
(2)   a symbiosis between the state administration and politicians develops, in which politicians obtain benefits by facilitating corruption in the state administration; and
(3)   those involved in corruption have taken steps to secure their personal impunity.

The first point refers to politicians' space for exploiting the lack of a clear distinction between the legal and the illegal. This space depends on the legislation regulating what politicians can do and not do, and is addressed in the following section on law formulation and crime definitions (see sub-section 3.2.1.1). Some comments on the two other features follow.

---

[5]   The Petrobras scandal has been well covered by the press. See, for example, BloombergBusiness 'Brazil Fixated as 'Human Bomb' Revelations Rock Elections,' on 21 October 2014, http://www.bloomberg.com/news/articles/2014-10-21/brazil-fixated-as-human-bomb-revelations-rock-elections.

3.1.2.1 Collusion with corrupt state institutions

Collusion between politicians and state administration involved in corrupt deals is a major reason why so often none of them are apprehended. A symbiosis may occur where state administration and politicians corrupt each other; especially a risk in societies where informal connections matter more than formal authorities. For example, a study in which I was involved revealed how the Ministry of Finance budgeted extra funds for travel so that public officials could manipulate and inflate their travel expenses.[6] In return, it appeared, politicians could 'rely on' the loyalty of their staff in the state administration, who would not speak out about political corruption. Corruption in politics and corruption in state administration are often treated as separate problems, and the literature on the connections between the two is not as extensive as one might expect. An early study that did focus on this symbiosis was Robert Wade's 1982 analysis of canal irrigation in South India. After discovering that the water sector, and canal irrigation in particular, was highly inefficient, Wade investigated the power and incentive structures among the main players involved. He found that civil engineers in the public sector had substantial discretionary authority and, on that basis, could generate huge amounts of illicit revenue. Not only did they control the allocation of contracts for firms supplying the sector, but their decisions influenced the perceived performance of politicians, and thus the politicians' prospects of being re-elected. For their part, the politicians controlled recruitment systems and framework conditions for the sector.

Political corruption (and corruption-resembling practices) kept secret with the support of civil servants is a risk in any society. Incumbent politicians that allow or ignore biased decision-making in the state administration may also benefit from the state administration's loyalty when they themselves commit more serious crimes, including the theft of state revenues.

3.1.2.2 Impunity for law breakers

'Impunity' refers to the fact that some individuals (in contrast to their acts) are shielded from the powers of the criminal justice system. Even upon the discovery of clear evidence of their involvement in corrupt acts, and regardless of the contents of the law, certain privileged offenders are not held liable for their corruption. Most countries offer some form of functional immunity from prosecution, which is justified in terms of the value to the state of protecting individuals in certain high-ranking

---

[6]   Søreide et al. (2012).

positions. Their responsibilities would imply too high a risk of being held liable, and, therefore, without the immunity they could not be expected to perform their important work and qualified candidates would be deterred from accepting these positions. In addition, diplomats and their families are given immunity to prevent retaliation against them in case of conflict between states. There are legitimate reasons for formal immunity, but of course such privileges can be misused for personal benefit.

In addition to the formal rules of immunity, privileged decision-makers sometimes obtain de facto impunity. Legislation can be manipulated for this purpose – one example being state-owned entities placed outside the reach of criminal law so that the entity can be controlled politically as a corrupt scheme while those involved are shielded from investigation and prosecution.[7] Another risk of impunity is associated with undefined responsibility: in other words, instances of alleged corruption can be claimed to have happened outside the sphere of the beneficiary's responsibility. Problems with inadequate legal definitions, discussed in section 2 of this chapter, can thus be rooted in the attraction decision-makers' feel for the personal benefits of corruption.

In settings where investigations of corrupt politicians are actually carried out, the case sometimes ends because of a dearth or disappearance of reliable facts (the standard of evidence may suddenly become very high, or documents may disappear from investigators' offices), or a failure to find any witnesses who dare to speak out (in the face of the very real risk that the accused may use their power to take reprisals against witnesses).[8] A further way of securing effective impunity is to prolong the prosecution process by repeatedly appealing convictions – an option that is available primarily to offenders rich enough to afford high defense costs.[9]

---

[7] Concerns have been raised by the United Nations, see, for example, UNODC document CAC/COSP/2013/7. For examples of how state entities are protected or privatized with their market power intact, see Manzetti (1999) and Black, Kraakman, and Tarassova. The problem of 'national champions' is not uncommon in Europe, as is well described by Estache (2011) – see, in particular, Thatcher (2011). The problem is mentioned in several OECD antibribery evaluation reports. For example, the OECD Phase 3 Report on the Slovak Republic recommends that the government take steps so that state-owned and state-controlled companies can also be subject to sanctions (the compilation of recommendations, p. 120).

[8] For more details and policy recommendations, see Freedom House (2014) and Transparency International's website: www.transparency.org.

[9] The statute of limitations may even have been shortened simply to facilitate such impunity. Such allegations were raised regarding former Italian

3.1.3   Commercial Benefits at the Expense of Anticorruption

Close ties between politicians and firms can help explain political disincentives for criminal law enforcement. Especially in foreign bribery cases, some governments refuse to let corruption stand in the way of their firms' entry into prospective markets, or they ignore the problem out of a concern for the country's reputation if suspected bribery is investigated. The problem is hinted at in several of the OECD WBG reports. Regarding Finland for example, the OECD WGB raises concerns about increasing investments in Russia and the country's growing trade links with China. According to the report, Finnish business expansion to countries with a 'high risk of bribe solicitation,' combined with the complete lack of convictions for foreign bribery in Finland's criminal justice system, highlights the concern that realpolitik stands in the way of efficient law enforcement. Transparency International, which offers its own review of foreign bribery enforcement problems, recommended that Italy put in place corruption prevention and monitoring mechanisms for companies, especially for the 'often state-backed' companies in the energy and defense sectors.[10] This recommendation might have been inspired by allegations that 'the state-backed [Italian] military equipment company Finmeccania' was involved in bribery of foreign officials in Panama, Colombia, Malaysia, India, and Saudi Arabia with the object of gaining 'contracts in the military, defense and security sectors.'

Several WGB reports hint at realpolitik obstructing law enforcement when cases are not prosecuted. When looking at Sweden, the WGB notes that very few cases on foreign bribery have been brought since the antibribery convention entered into force, and concludes that 'something is not working,' especially because there have been 'several allegations reported by the media involving Swedish companies.' The report discusses the apparent enforcement failure in light of Swedish industry's likely exposure to corruption risks, given the size of their firms and the

---

prime minister Silvio Berlusconi, who, although found guilty of corruption, could not be imprisoned because the statute of limitations was too short for securing his rights to appeal, and thus, he could not be punished. See *New York Times* on 8 July 2015 (Berlusconi is Convicted in Graft Case): http://www. nytimes.com/aponline/2015/07/08/world/europe/ap-eu-italy-berlusconi-trial.html? _r=0: 'In Italy, defendants serve time only after two different courts have completed two levels of appeals trials, a process that normally takes years.' The rules regarding statutes of limitations in Italian criminal law were modified under Berlusconi's regime.

[10]   Transparency International (2012:25–26).

international areas in which they operate.[11] Similar concerns are raised by the WGB in regard to Japan over the same period.[12]

In some cases, the hint of political unwillingness to enforce the laws is associated with a specific rule which can easily be seen as a loophole for facilitating corruption. For example, tax deductibility for bribes paid abroad was a frequent practice in the OECD area just a few decades ago, but is now generally outlawed. When it comes to Greek shipping companies (a powerful force in the Greek economy), the rule does not apply because they are taxed differently, under a law 'which does not expressly prohibit the tax deduction of bribes.'[13] Being the result of political commitment or not, more examples of how governments have kept openings for corruption follow below.

3.1.4   Insufficient Prosecutorial Independence

For societies with weak anticorruption commitment at the government level, it is a major problem if the country's prosecutorial independence is low. If the careers of judges and investigators or the resources available for their work depend on how those individuals adapt and react to signals from government representatives, they are not sufficiently independent to pursue corruption cases. In practice, the lack of independence permits government representatives to interfere in the investigation and prosecution of cases. This might have been what happened in South Africa in a case opened in 2012, which centered on a South African telecom company that allegedly bribed foreign (and domestic) public officials for the award of a license abroad.[14] In fact, the WGB report points at several cases where major state-owned companies in South Africa allegedly offered bribes in exchange for business benefits. The report points to a clear failure to investigate the corruption, and to investigations being brought to a close due to the 'high-level connections [with] political influence' of the people being investigated.[15]

The WGB has raised general concerns about low prosecutorial independence in the evaluation of several other countries, including the Czech Republic and France. In the latter, the WGB suggested that prosecutors'

---

[11]   OECD WGB Phase 3 Report Sweden, p. 5.
[12]   OECD WGB Phase 3 Report Japan, p. 5.
[13]   OECD WGB Phase 3 Report Greece, pp. 34–35.
[14]   OECD WGO South Africa, pp. 10–11.
[15]   OECD WGO Phase 3 Report South Africa, pp. 35–36. A particular concern regarding state-owned firms was raised by the OECD WBG for other signatory countries as well, including Iceland and Portugal.

independence might be jeopardized by the fact that the minister of justice is authorized to intervene in individual cases, including in criminal law proceedings with instructions to the prosecutors (a concern echoed in a GRECO report).[16] No major French companies, the report observed, had been investigated for foreign bribery since the law was implemented. The structural protection of the prosecutor's independence is very important for criminal justice efficiency, and the prosecutor's position for prosecution of corruption cases will be further addressed in Chapter 5.

We now turn to performance problems in law enforcement institutions, but as we do so it is important to keep in mind how direct or indirect political influence can affect law enforcement opportunities all along the criminal justice value chain. Determining if politicians' personal agendas and corruption-like political circumstances are undermining law enforcement or if law enforcement's shortcomings have a different cause is difficult, however, which is why it is necessary to consider the possible weaknesses of all the main institutions involved. We begin with the law itself, and investigate why fuzzy formulations and innovative definitions sometimes prevent efficient law enforcement.

3.2 INADEQUATE LAW FORMULATION AND CRIME DEFINITIONS

Corrupt acts are frequently assumed to have an illegal status, but in reality that is often not the case. Across legal systems, there is a kernel of agreement about what constitutes a corrupt act in the sense that both the offer and the acceptance of bribes are now illegal in most countries. In practice, however, efficient law enforcement encounters considerable obstacles presented by undefined or vaguely defined legal terms, uncertainties in the interpretation of the law, unclear coordination with other laws, and indeterminate standards of evidence. The anticorruption conventions of the United Nations (UNCAC) and the OECD (the OECD Anti-Bribery Convention) are impressively clear in their principles,[17] but in terms of legal definitions – especially as implemented at the national level – a good deal of imprecision is to be found. As this section explains, a flurry of legal debates are taking place in countries around the world about questions such as what defines corruption (undue influence or undue benefit, for example), who is 'a civil servant,' to what extent

---

[16] GRECO Report Fourth Round on France.

[17] If judged as the largest denominator obtainable in dialogue between many country representatives.

must a corrupt deal be subject to mutual agreement between the parties, and to what extent should individual liability reduce corporate criminal liability?[18]

3.2.1 Weakly Enforceable Legal Solutions and Definitions

Difficulties in enforcing anticorruption regulations are often reflected in an overly narrow interpretation of international agreements. Furthermore, some countries – inadvertently or otherwise – organize their anticorruption legislation in a confusing fashion, which makes enforcement difficult. Despite such obstacles, however, investigators often work hard to find ways to enforce the principles behind their implemented anticorruption conventions, sometimes finding creative solutions for problems caused by imprecisely worded laws.

3.2.1.1 Corruption-like circumstances

'Corruption-like circumstances' refer to various gray areas which provide openings for both civil servants and politicians to secure extra revenues for their personal consumption. Democratically elected politicians are entrusted by voters, and are normally given wide authorities. While the risk of undue influence on decisions to the benefit of politicians, their friends or firms, creates popular debates about the strength of barriers against political corruption, they rarely lead to law enforcement action.

The provider of 'bribery-resembling' revenues, often a private-sector player, normally expects something in return, such as a more profitable industry regulation, protection from competition, diplomatic collaboration in marketing abroad, government subsidies, cheap access to finance, protection from investigation, or contracts disguised as development aid. These 'legal bribes' can be disguised, for example, as an appointment to a well-compensated position on a firm's board, career opportunities for family members, luxury vacations, or a transfer of funds to a civil society organization under the control of the given politician or high-ranking civil servant. The resulting wealth can be hidden from the public. Registries of parliamentarians' wealth are often incomplete, excluding, for example, shareholder activities, remunerations, overseas

---

[18] For reviews of concerns regarding the impact of inefficient legal definitions and solutions on law enforcement, see the volume on the OECD convention by Pieth, Low, and Bonucci (2014). UNODC (2009) offers a technical guide on the UN convention.

bank accounts, and spouses' wealth.[19] Campaign contributions from the
private sector are used to buy political decisions (or the political direction
of a political party), and the funds are sometimes spent – discretely – by
party leaders.[20] Former politicians and civil servants who were privy to
secret information as part of their official duties may move into private-
sector positions, where that information may help a firm secure unfair
advantages over its competitors. These problems are common across the
world. Many European countries with long democratic traditions and
highly regarded judiciaries have very porous barriers to political corruption,[21] and their criminal justice systems cannot be relied on to address
problems that hide within legal gray areas.

3.2.1.2   Narrow interpretation of international agreements

While the international anticorruption conventions are generally wide in
their scope, law enforcement ambitions are often more modest at the
national level, especially in foreign bribery cases. Regarding France, for
example, the OECD WGB found that the jurisdiction's narrow interpretation of the offense of foreign bribery leads to an 'extremely low number
of final convictions' and concludes that France should interpret the
criteria of the convention 'in a sufficiently flexible and broad manner' so
that agreed-upon forms of problems are criminalized.[22] In the case of
Canada, the OECD WGB recommended an amendment of national
legislation so that it clearly covers not only bribery for profit, but also
bribery in the conduct of all international business.[23] The report on
Bulgaria highlighted the need 'to ensure that judges, prosecutors and
investigators' learn that 'bribes of a non-material nature' are covered by
the penal code. In Austria, the foreign bribery rules apply only if the
offense is carried out by an Austrian national or company or partnership
that is incorporated in Austria, a limitation not set by the convention.[24]

---

[19]   Incomplete registry of parliamentarians' wealth has been criticized in
several GRECO reports, including my own country (Norway). The Vice-
President of the Parliament (Svein Roald Hansen) agreed to consider the matter,
but also defended the practice by claiming that parliamentarians are elected and
should be trusted, not controlled in each and every matter: News at NRK
(www.nrk.no) on 14 July 2014 – by Veronica Westhrin and Anne Mone Nordahl.
[20]   Fisman and Miguel (2010) present their research on connections between
politicians and firms, and refer to campaign finance as a legal form of corruption.
[21]   See Transparency International (2012) for a summary of the results of
National Integrity Studies across Europe, https://www.transparency.org/enis.
[22]   See OECD WGB Phase 3 Report France.
[23]   OECD WGB Phase 3 Canada, p. 23.
[24]   OECD WGB Phase 3 Austria and Bulgaria (regarding Bulgaria: p. 19).

Similarly, in Italy, regardless of how far the corruption has Italian beneficiaries, the offense must have been carried out by an Italian national or by an Italian national company's executive or employee, which excludes the many cases in which bribery is handled by middle-men. In Bosnia and Herzegovina, the foreign bribery rules apply only if the offender was in Bosnia at the time of the offense. Such restrictions in the laws' coverage impede efficient law enforcement.[25]

Some terms in the laws have been particularly difficult to define, one of them being the term 'public official' when used to describe a recipient of bribes. When it comes to the scope of coverage of this term, the United Nations expresses concerns regarding how some jurisdictions 'did not cover the main categories of persons enumerated in the Convention or used inconsistent terms.'[26] The problem of narrow definition is especially pronounced in foreign bribery cases. The WGB found that Finland's criminal law definition of a foreign public official is too narrow, because it fails to include a person holding a legislative office in a foreign country. While Finland's government insists that foreign bribery can still be prosecuted under a combination of other laws, the report concludes that the current status is too unclear for 'Finnish businesses to know and be aware of the impermissibility of such bribery.'[27]

Regarding foreign bribery cases, many jurisdictions insist that the offense must also be illegal in the country where the bribe was offered, a substantial obstacle to prosecution because the legal status has to be established in two different jurisdictions.[28] The OECD WGB found this dual criminality requirement to be a problem in France,[29] and expressed concern that its standard of evidence was too narrow for practical enforcement of the law, especially as investigators are required to prove that a foreign public official participated 'directly' in awarding the advantage or contract for the briber. When tested in the law enforcement system, the French standard of proof was found to be very high, as it specifically required the official's signature on a contract awarding the corrupt advantage. Such a criteria of 'direct intervention' does not follow from the OECD convention, and excludes cases of foreign bribery in which, for instance, an official is bribed to use his position to make another public official grant the briber a contract or advantage. According

---

[25] Regarding Italy and Bosnia and Herzegovina, see the CMS guide (see section 2.1.2 for further reference).

[26] UNODC: CAC/COSP/2013/6.

[27] OECD Phase 3 Report Finland.

[28] CMS Guide to Anti-Bribery and Corruption Laws (that is, CMS, 2014).

[29] Art. 113-6 of the Code Penal (CP).

to the report, efficient investigation and prosecution require criminalization that is broader and more flexible on this point, according to the
OECD WGB.[30]

3.2.1.3 Confusing organization of the relevant legislation

According to the CMS Guide – a cross-country overview of criminal law
regulation on corruption produced by CMS, a private-sector supplier of
legal services on corruption – UNCAC and the OECD Convention have
'led to an increasing convergence ... in the sorts of conduct that are
criminalized [in national legislation], but not necessarily [in] how they
are criminalized.'[31] Corruption offenses are not always regulated by
criminal law. Private-sector bribery, for example, is sometimes treated
differently, as is the case in India, Bosnia and Herzegovina, and until
recently, France. In most countries, bribery conducted outside the country
is regulated in a similar fashion as domestic bribery, but there are many
exceptions, and these exceptions take different forms because countries
implement the conventions very differently. In Ireland, for example,
foreign bribery offenses are criminalized in two different statutes, one
that criminalizes the bribing of a foreign public official, and the other
that criminalizes the bribing of officials when the bribery occurs in
Europe.[32] According to the OECD WGB, this arrangement creates
'certain inconsistencies,' and Ireland's legislation needs to be 'consoli-
dated and harmonized' to comply with the OECD Convention. The
problem is yet more complicated in Greece, where the WGB found it
difficult to determine how far the legislation is in line with the convention, because the government had introduced a 'multiplicity of foreign
bribery offences,' with different laws for the implementation of different
conventions (for example, one law for the OECD Anti-Bribery Convention, one for the Council of Europe Convention, one for UNCAC, and
two different laws for EU treaties). At the same time, the offenses in the
different laws did 'not cover all non-Greek public officials as required by
the Anti-Bribery Convention,'[33] and they applied different provisions for
the liability of legal persons, a fact that resulted in 'problems for
implementation.'[34] In Japan the government placed the foreign bribery

---

[30] OECD WGB Phase 3 Report France, pp. 13–14.
[31] CMS (2014:4).
[32] OECD WGB Phase 3 Report Ireland. The two different statutes are the
Prevention of Corruption Act 2001 (POCA) and the Criminal Justice (Theft and
Fraud) Offences Act 2001 (CJOA).
[33] OECD WGB Phase 3 Report Greece, p. 10.
[34] OECD WGB Phase 3 Report Greece, pp. 12–13.

offense in the Unfair Competition Prevention Law (UCPL), not in the penal code, and the WGB questioned if this might explain the country's very low number of investigations and prosecutions of foreign bribery cases. However, the solution is in line with the Japanese legislative tradition – which includes only 'core criminal offences' in the penal code – and the OECD WGB therefore recommends that Japan should 'focus its efforts on making the most of the legislative technique that has been chosen, and improve implementation of the foreign bribery offence in the UCPL.'[35]

The problems of poorly formulated laws and fuzzy definitions of crime have prompted some prosecutors to use creative approaches to ensure enforcement of criminal justice principles. In Germany, for example, cases of alleged foreign bribery have been prosecuted and charged under legislation other than the legislation intended to regulate foreign bribery cases. That specific legislation demands proof of 'elements of the offence going beyond the requirements in Article 1 of the Convention,' which the OECD WGB considers 'a practical impediment to the prosecution of the offence of foreign bribery.' The creative solution, which was defended with reference to economic concerns and human rights,[36] resulted in convictions for commercial bribery, breach of trust, or an administrative offense of 'lack of supervision' instead of foreign bribery, which requires a lower level of evidence. This also happened in the Siemens (Enel) case, where individuals were convicted for 'breach of trust' under the criminal code instead of foreign bribery, because the court could not determine if 'the recipients of the bribes were foreign public officials.'[37] In that case, the same recipients of the bribe were regarded as foreign public officials under the Italian criminal code (the bribery occurred in Italy), however, and the WGB questioned why a 'different finding of fact' was reached.[38] Creative enforcement is also associated with the United States, where it has been used to significantly extend the reach of the country's foreign bribery jurisdiction. While the relevant US legislation itself is not too different from that in many other OECD countries, the WGB highlights the fact that the United States nevertheless manages to make sure that 'legal persons are liable for crimes committed by employees acting within the scope of their employment.' This is strongly commended and

---

[35] OECD WGB Phase 3 Report Japan, pp. 15–16.
[36] Human Rights: Art. 6 of the ECHR demands a 'hearing within a reasonable time.'
[37] OECD WGB Phase 3 Report Germany, p. 13.
[38] OECD WGB Phase 3 Report Germany, p. 14.

believed to be one of the reasons why the United States has such 'an impressive record of law enforcement actions.'[39]

Inadequate legislation is an obstacle to efficient enforcement in many jurisdictions, but what seems to matter more, however, is a country's criminal justice culture and, in particular, the emphasis given to enforcing the principles behind the law. In countries with a solid track record of enforcing corruption laws, this emphasis seems to be sufficiently strong to prevent the kind of legal battles waged in other countries around the interpretation of details.

3.2.2   Unclear Liability: Legal and Natural Persons

An area where legal confusion clearly prevents efficient law enforcement is corporate criminal liability.[40] As will be further discussed in later chapters, efficient law enforcement requires the ability to hold corporations liable so that owners and leaders cannot profit from the crime while the employees involved are sacrificed as scapegoats.

While this idea may appear simple from a non-legal perspective, it is far from simple when it comes to practical enforcement. Most countries have taken steps toward ensuring liability of legal persons for the crimes listed in the UN convention, but according to the UN observers, there is considerable variation in the resulting scope of the criminal liability.[41] Failure to hold legal persons liable for corruption is expressed in different ways, most commonly, it seems, as clear-cut enforcement failure. Regarding South Africa, for example, the OECD WGB found that the country has a 'broad and flexible ... regime of corporate liability,'[42] but the law is 'hardly enforced in practice.' Likewise, in Bulgaria, the government had made it possible to hold legal persons liable for cases of foreign bribery, yet there are no convincing efforts to enforce the law.

Some countries have made it extremely cumbersome to enforce this form of liability. In Hungary, for example, companies have no liability for crimes, but they can have 'certain criminal sanctions ... imposed on them' in some situations: *if* a 'relevant natural person' commits the crime

---

[39]   OECD WGB Phase 3 Report the US, p. 30.
[40]   Pieth and Ivory (2011) provide a useful overview of the issues.
[41]   Review of implementation of the United Nations Convention against Corruption, CAC/COSP/2013/6, p. 18, available at: http://www.unodc.org/documents/treaties/UNCAC/COSP/session5/V1386475e.pdf.
[42]   Legal persons can be held criminally liable under section 332(1) of the Criminal Procedure Act of 1977 based on 'a culpable act of a representative of the legal person.'

intentionally, *if* the crime was intended to or did in fact give an advantage to the company, *and if* the person who committed the crime was a person acting 'as part of the activity of the company' or 'a member or employee of the company' that could have been stopped by others in the company. Complicated rules also apply in Slovakia, where criminal liability for companies can be applied only where 'persons in charge of management' have committed the crime themselves, or where 'an employee/agent committed the offence' after inadequate supervision by the person in management; conditions that are difficult to prove in practice. Switzerland applies liability for a legal person if it has not made 'all requisite and reasonable organizational precautions' to avoid 'bribery of public officials' – again, a criteria at high risk of being subject to lengthy disputes in court.

The failure to hold corporations liable is often excused with reference to legal loopholes for legal persons. In Estonia, for instance, the WGB detected the risk that legal persons could 'delay court proceedings and avoid liability,' thereby avoiding prosecution. In the case of the Netherlands, the WGB recommended that steps be taken to ensure that 'mailbox companies are considered legal entities under the Dutch Criminal Code,' so that cases involving such firms can be 'investigated, prosecuted and sanctioned as foreign bribery cases.' A further practical problem in many cases relates to the relationship between the liability of legal persons and liability of the natural persons. Several countries – including Greece, Iceland, and Hungary, for example – require a conviction of natural persons as a precondition for pursuing the legal person involved, and Belgium is criticized by the OECD WGB for operating with a 'mutually exclusive liability between the natural and legal person.' In France, legal persons are 'criminally liable for offences committed on their behalf,'[43] a requirement that, in practice, makes it necessary to prove that the company has a policy of encouraging or endorsing bribery – something that is difficult to prove.

Countries also differ significantly in the extent to which they see employees as acting on behalf of companies, so that the company can be held liable for an act committed by its employees. In the United States, the principle of 'respondent superior' places a wide-ranging responsibility on the employer.[44] A company cannot avoid liability by ignoring the risk that its employees may conduct offenses, regardless of how far the

---

[43] Art. 121-2 of the French Penal Code.
[44] See more comprehensive explanation by Lucinda Low in Pieth, Low, and Bonucci (2014).

company as a whole benefits from the crime. In other countries, there is a strict demand for evidence that proves that the employee acted on behalf of the company, which makes it easier for companies to avoid liability by demonstrating that they have robust internal procedures in place to prevent and detect violations. This principle applies, for example, in the United Kingdom; the OECD has raised concerns about the risk of avoiding liability for legal persons by 'using a lower level person to commit the bribery.' Ireland, Australia, and New Zealand have similar traditions. However, the United Kingdom seems to have addressed the matter by imposing liability on legal persons for bribery committed by a person who is 'associated' with the organization if the bribery creates advantages for the organization. An 'associated person' can be either a legal person or a natural person. To strengthen the basis for holding legal persons liable, the United Kingdom has also enacted another rule that 'imposes liability on commercial organizations for failure to prevent bribery.'

3.2.3   Corruption Not Captured by Criminal Law

A further problem associated with inadequate definitions and laws is the fact that many players involved in facilitating corruption are not within the grasp of criminal law enforcement. The most serious forms of corruption will often involve more individuals than the briber and a decision-maker; some of these may be directly involved, while others may only be aware of the crime and obtain indirect benefits from condoning it. These people, especially those indirectly involved, are often effectively immune from prosecution, because their involvement is not pursued under criminal law.

In the case of profit-motivated crime, such as fraud and theft, criminal law typically considers the accomplice to be as guilty as the primary offender. This principle appears to have a weaker standing, however, when it comes to financial institutions handling suspect transactions,[45] to export credit agencies that have a strong incentive to lend money regardless of corruption risks (especially if given kickbacks to do so),[46] to external auditors and tax advisers who are rewarded by a continued demand for their services if they turn a blind eye to corruption,[47] to

---

[45]   For official evaluation reports, see www.fatf-gafi.org.

[46]   See, for example, the allegations regarding Export-Import Bank, *The Wall Street Journal* on 23 June 2014 ('Officials at Ex-Im Bank Face Investigations').

[47]   See for example Mitchell and Sikka (2011) for sharp allegations and details regarding accountancy firms and lawyers.

lawyers who advise clients on corrupt transactions,[48] to civil servants who are informed about biased procurement decisions, and to those in the development community who close their eyes to suspected corruption because calling attention to it could jeopardize diplomatic relations.[49]

The accomplice may not be *as guilty* and criminally liable as the main offenders, but in cases when the crime could not have taken place without the tacit or explicit support of others, there is good reason (for the sake of both justice and deterrence) to expand the categories of players who merit the attention of criminal law investigators. In most jurisdictions, it should be possible (for example, by applying the law on negligence or recklessness to corruption cases) to heighten the level of legal responsibility of those who are in a position to observe corruption being conducted.[50]

3.3 OBSTACLES TO EFFICIENT INVESTIGATION AND PROSECUTION

Regardless of the vagueness or precision of anticorruption laws and guidelines, in many countries the main obstacles to enforcement lie in the area of investigation and prosecution. In some instances, suspected crime is simply not addressed; in other cases, the resources needed to conduct costly investigations are absent; and in yet other instances, evidence is not collected because different domestic law enforcement institutions do not collaborate well or because cross-country collaboration fails.

---

[48] In July 2015, the Director of Norwegian Økokrim – the central unit for investigation and prosecution of economic crime – expressed concern about an increasing tendency to use lawyers for the performance of financial crime and corruption. Professional advisers like lawyers and accountants help conceal the funds' origin, create legitimacy, and provide advice regarding placement of the funds. The trend is expected to continue. See NRK on 3 July 2015: see http://www.nrk.no/norge/okokrim_-okende-tendens-til-a-bruke-advokater-i-okonomisk-kriminalitet-1.12440396.

[49] A problem we return to in Chapter 5 is how public institutions are exempt from corporate liability. In the Czech Republic, Czech companies can be held criminally liable, but '[p]ublic sector organizations are excluded from such liability.'

[50] Negligence and recklessness refer to forms of culpability. The question of guilt under these circumstances is difficult to determine, yet regarding those distantly involved in facilitating corruption cases, the rules appear almost unused. Clarification of their relevance would contribute to more efficient criminal law enforcement. For debate about this form of culpability, see Moore (2010).

3.3.1 Failure to Investigate and Prosecute Suspected Corruption

The World Justice Project (WJP) describes challenges in criminal law enforcement around the world, including issues related to impartiality, prosecutorial independence, and due process for the accused. On the basis of surveys designed to capture opinions, experiences, and expert assessments, every year the WJP generates a Rule of Law Index based on expert assessments (the same dataset used to prepare the graph in the introduction to this chapter). According to the 2015 index, some of the world's largest economies perform miserably in their criminal law enforcement. The criminal justice system in Turkey, ranked at 76, is not performing much better than that of Uganda, Colombia, Mexico, and Pakistan. Russia, given a slightly higher score than Turkey, is found to perform worse than Nigeria, Zimbabwe, and Burkina Faso, whereas Brazil, also a large economy, is ranked behind the Philippines, Tanzania, and Kazakhstan, though ahead of Turkey and Russia.[51] Despite their various reforms and publicly stated ambitions to take firm action against corruption, the criminal justice systems of poorly ranked countries are far from independent and unbiased, their law enforcement processes typically move very slowly, corruption within the law enforcement systems themselves may be a problem, and the accused cannot expect a fair trial. Despite what is written in their criminal law on corruption, the law is not efficiently enforced.

The OECD WGB evaluations, which primarily focus on high-income countries associated with better-performing institutions, also point to prosecution-related enforcement failure. Many of the countries' law enforcement systems simply fail to respond to allegations of corruption. Around twenty of the OECD signatory countries – including Israel, Mexico, Brazil, Spain, and Russia – have not made a single foreign bribery conviction in the fifteen or so years since the convention entered into force. In France, there have only been three cases in which individuals had been convicted for foreign bribery, and only 'minimal penalties' were imposed on the perpetrators, including 'suspended prison sentences' and modest fines.[52] In Chile, allegations of foreign bribery are either not thoroughly investigated or are 'prematurely filed.' Both Poland and Belgium were encouraged by the WGB to raise awareness in their

---

[51] See the WJP index website: http://worldjusticeproject.org/rule-of-law-index (retrieved in July 2015).
[52] OECD WGB Phase 3 Report France, p. 10.

criminal justices system about the importance of effectively enforcing the laws on corruption, including the extraterritorial feature of the antibribery rules.[53]

3.3.1.1 Lack of resources for investigation

One of the most commonly cited reasons why enforcement action fails is the lack of resources to undertake the typically comprehensive investigations and expensive prosecutions that corruption cases entail.

Using panel data on corruption convictions in the United States, James Alt and David Lassen (2012) found that the greater the level of prosecutorial resources, the higher the level of convictions (other things being equal). Increasing the number of attorneys devoted to anti-corruption strengthens law enforcement. Nevertheless, a lack of resources is not as valid an excuse for enforcement failure as it might seem. While all governments must establish priorities, criminal law regulates the most damaging acts in society, and the need for protection against them is one of the fundamental reasons for the existence of state institutions. The optimal law enforcement level is normally below 100 percent (because the marginal enforcement cost increases with the share of cases detected), but for all forms of crime it is far above zero! Some countries do struggle to find the resources necessary to develop competent law enforcement institutions, but in most countries the resources exist. Corruption cases are complicated and expensive in advanced economies, but the levels of income and taxation are substantial as well, and successful investigations bring in substantial amounts in fines and recovered assets from the convicted. The lack of resources may well be a handy excuse for an inability to make the needed priorities.

Many countries subject to evaluation by GRECO or the OECD have been found to under-prioritize anticorruption law enforcement. The United Nations finds that most jurisdictions have created specialized departments to combat corruption (in accordance with article 36 of UNCAC).[54] However, these 'faced common challenges relating to limited capacity and resources for implementation,' and there is a clear need to strengthen both the departments' ability 'to conduct investigations without prior external approval' and the 'expertise and capabilities of staff.' Moreover, the OECD addresses the problem of budget neglect regarding enforcement of antibribery laws. For example, the WGB criticized

---

[53] For an overview of law enforcement statistics on foreign bribery, see Transparency International (2014 – and released yearly) and OECD (2014).

[54] UNODC CAC/COSP/2013/7.

Ireland's lack of resources to 'embark on full-scale investigations and prosecutions of foreign bribery cases; further resources are needed if credible allegations of foreign bribery are to be 'investigated and prosecuted in a timely and efficient manner.'[55] In the case of Belgium, the WGB found an urgent need for more 'human and material resources' for both investigation and prosecution of cases in order to reverse a trend of cases being closed due either to a lack of resources or to investigation and prosecution 'exceeding a reasonable time limit.' Concerning Denmark, the WGB highlighted the fact that only one prosecutor and one police officer are assigned to each foreign bribery case. The government was urged to raise this number, 'given the complexity of many of these cases' and to offer specialized training for law enforcement officials.[56]

Lack of resources (real or not) will often result in a slow law enforcement process, and thus it can lead to charges being dropped because of a jurisdiction's statute of limitations. Greece, for example, is said to suffer from serious 'delays in the administration of justice,'[57] while in Italy, many cases have been dismissed because the cases are not completed in time (see, for example, footnote 9 above).

3.3.1.2 Environments not conducive to whistle-blowers

What might be an equally important factor in understanding prosecution failure is the environment for bringing cases to light. The OECD statistics of enforcement actions (OECD, 2014) found that only two percent of all foreign bribery cases were instigated by whistle-blowers who reported the case external of their organization, including cases reported to the press or other external bodies when ignored internally. The good news is that around one-third of the cases were self-reported, and one in five of them became known because of whistle-blowers who reported (internally) to the company management. However, as UN evaluators have warned, substantial variation exists across countries in their implementation of the steps laid out in the UN convention to protect reporting persons, and by no means all countries have regulations regarding the protection of whistle-blowers.[58] For example, the WGB characterized the lack of whistle-blower protection in Iceland's private sector as a 'significant deficiency in Iceland's fight against bribery.' Finland, too, was found to have no whistle-blower protection, and relied instead on witness

---

[55] OECD WGB Phase 3 Report Ireland, p. 32.
[56] OECD WGB Phase 3 Report Denmark, pp. 32–33.
[57] OECD WGB Phase 3 Report Greece, p. 24.
[58] UNODC: CAC/COSP/2013/7. See also Yeoh (2015) for a useful discussion of whistle-blower rules.

protection regulation, labor laws, and corporate codes of conduct, which the WGB adjudged far from sufficient for efficient law enforcement.[59] In South Africa, according to the WGB, legislative measures to strengthen the protection of whistle-blowers have been made, but whistle-blowers still face reprisals, including the use of death threats and even murder. Part of the risk for whistle-blowers is associated with the South African Protection of State Information Bill, which stipulates that whistle-blowers reporting 'classified information' face up to twenty-five years of imprisonment. Even the United Kingdom, which has been much commended for its whistle-blower protection in other settings, is criticized by the OECD WGB for flaws in these rules, pointing to the fact that although the Public Interest Disclosure Act of 1998 established a system for receiving reports and protecting whistleblowers, the act 'does not apply to expatriate workers of UK companies who are based abroad' if they do not have 'strong connections with Great Britain and British employment law.' The report described these workers as being among the groups of employees who are 'most likely to report ... foreign bribery.'[60]

Encouragingly, many governments have or are about to improve their legislative protections for whistle-blowers. Portugal, for example, launched a website in 2010 on which whistle-blowers could anonymously report cases of corruption. The site received over one thousand reports in its first year, several of which led to investigations. According to the WGB, however, Portugal did not have any specific legislation on whistle-blowing. The WGB also commended the United States for its Dodd-Frank Wall Street Reform and Consumer Protection Act of 2010, which protects individual whistle-blowers and prohibits retaliation from employers, secures compensation for the whistle-blowers, and gives whistle-blowers the right to be reinstated on their former level of employment. Moreover, the law provides for compensation for whistle-blowers of between 10 percent and 30 percent of the monetary sanctions imposed and collected – a strong incentive to provide the authorities with information.[61]

---

[59] Other signatory countries found to lack sufficient whistle-blower protection include Japan, Austria, Czech Republic, Estonia and Slovak Republic. See the OECD WGB reports, including Finland (p. 30) and Iceland (p. 25).

[60] OECD WGB Phase 3 United Kingdom, pp. 55–56.

[61] In order to receive such compensation, a whistle-blower has to voluntarily provide the authorities with original information that contributes to enforcement action of which the sanctions surpass USD 1 million. A risk of counter-intuitive consequences in terms of stigma associated with such rewards and how they run

It is still a common problem in many work environments that whistle-blowers might be seen as traitors or snitches. Legal protection of those who report corruption and knowledge of the damage it causes must be expected to promote development, albeit slowly, toward an environment where those who speak out about crime are seen as responsible and laudable. Such a cultural shift would obviously help to make law enforcement more efficient.

3.3.2 Weak Coordination across Domestic Law Enforcement Institutions

Corruption cases are difficult to investigate when they involve different types of offenses and players. Different law enforcement institutions are typically mandated to control different forms of corruption – be it tax evasion, violation of competition law, organized crime, and so forth – and none of them is in a position to see the entirety of a complex case. To find all the pieces of the crime puzzle, and to see how they fit together, the various law enforcement institutions must coordinate their efforts. For instance, an apparent corruption-related problem detected by tax authorities must be reported to crime investigators for the case to be further pursued, and for this to happen, the tax authorities must have the capacity to understand what kind of problem they are observing. Moreover, the civil servants in various institutions must be motivated to pursue cross-institutional collaboration, rather than seeing it as a 'cost' that involves 'wasting' time and effort to chase after goals that lie outside their own mandate. Thus, when they exist, disincentives for collaboration must be removed.

Those disincentives, however, may be connected to the different functions performed by the different institutions. Competition authorities, for example, may offer lenient treatment to those who report cartel collaboration, but they are often unable to offer leniency for acts regulated by criminal law, even though cartel collaboration is facilitated by corruption. If criminal law investigators are brought into investigations being conducted by a competition authority because corruption is suspected, the involvement of those investigators may undermine the competition authority's efforts to encourage self-reporting in return for

---

counter to moral values is debated by Feldman and Lobel (2009). Blount and Markel (2010) discuss how they can cause problems in a work environment and undermine compliance systems. These problems might be avoided if the rewards function as a compensation for the actual and possible future costs associated with whistle-blowing.

leniency.[62] Such cross-institutional disincentives are not uncommon; indeed, they can be found in most parts of a country's unique landscape of law enforcement institutions. Each country should seek to identify these disincentives and remove them through reorganization or better coordination of enforcement activities.

Cross-institutional coordination of enforcement activities is addressed by the OECD WGB. For example, it raised concerns about Iceland, where different investigative authorities were found to have overlapping competencies – its Economic Crime Unit being responsible for 'investigation and prosecution of serious economic and environmental crimes' while the Office of the Special Prosecutor is responsible for investigation of 'suspicions of criminal actions connected with the operations of financial undertakings,' and there being 'no formal coordination mechanisms' between the two bodies. The problem has resulted in 'duplication of work where both bodies were unknowingly investigating the same case.'[63] Iceland was also criticized for a case in which the tax authorities received information about a possible instance of foreign bribery but chose to take 'no further action.'[64] In South Africa, different agencies and courts (for example, Special Commercial Crime Courts, the Directorate for Priority Crime Investigation, and the Anti-Corruption Task Team) were all found responsible for the investigation and prosecution of foreign bribery, while no cases have been successfully pursued, and the WGB highlighted the absence of cooperation between law enforcement bodies. The problem came to light in a case in which investigation was terminated after two years because there was no 'coordination between prosecutors and the police.'[65]

Most coordination problems reported by the WGB relate to collaboration between criminal investigators and tax authorities and financial institutions. Bribers sometimes report the bribes they have paid on their tax returns as tax-deductible expenses. Tax authorities, however, often fail to realize this or, if they do, fail to report it to law enforcement authorities. Bulgaria, for instance, was encouraged by the WGB to review its laws on taxation to make sure there are no 'loopholes for hiding

---

[62]   Also discussed by Søreide (2014b).

[63]   OECD WGB Phase 3 Report Iceland, p. 16.

[64]   In this case a person called the Internal Revenue Directorate 'inquiring on the tax deductibility of a bribe paid to a Nigerian public official.' The authorities chose not to act on the call, as the caller did not provide information on his/her name.

[65]   OECD WGB Phase 3 Report South Africa, pp. 26–28 (the 'Middle East Business Interests Case').

foreign bribery as tax-deductible expenses,' and to 'provide guidelines and training to tax inspectors' in what 'types of expenses constitute bribes to foreign public officials.' Poland was urged to take all 'steps within its legal system' to make sure that all bribery of foreign officials that violates Article 229.5 of the Penal Code 'are not tax deductible.' Austria was instructed to address a different problem, namely, its 'routine practice of confronting tax payers' who are suspected of bribery 'before reporting them to the law enforcement authorities,' thereby giving them an opportunity to destroy or conceal evidence.[66] Japan, in contrast, was commended for allowing different teams of investigators to investigate different parts of the same crime puzzles.[67]

Weak coordination between crime investigative units and financial institutions that are in a position to connect money laundering attempts to corruption cases has undermined many law enforcement actions. The WGB strongly recommended that the Czech Republic, for example, ensured a more effective enforcement of money laundering in connection with foreign bribery cases. Ireland was similarly encouraged to amend its Criminal Justice (Money Laundering and Terrorist Financing) Act 2010 to make sure that foreign bribery is regarded as a 'predicate offence for money laundering,' regardless of where the bribery took place. Japan was criticized for lacking legislation that prohibits money laundering of the proceeds of foreign bribery, a shortcoming that may have limited the number of reported indications or suspicions of foreign bribery. Germany was found to have a criminal law[68] that 'precludes the simultaneous conviction of a person for money laundering and foreign bribery.' A person could not be convicted of money laundering if the person was already convicted for the predicate offense (foreign bribery is regarded as a predicate offense to money laundering under German law), and the German government was encouraged to amend the legislation on money laundering so that the 'bribery of foreign and international MPs' is added to 'the list of predicate offences to money laundering.' Common law countries appear less exposed to the problem of weak cross-institutional coordination. In the United States, for example, the Foreign Corrupt Practices Act provides for both criminal and civil proceedings, which may take place concurrently in one and the same case, a practice that is less common in civil law countries.

---

[66] Compilation of Recommendations made in The Phase 3 Reports, p. 13.
[67] OECD WGB Phase 3 Report Japan, p. 26. The case is described on p. 19.
[68] Germany's penal code section 261(9).

An obvious precondition for law enforcement coordination across institutions is that the responsible authorities are willing to share information and cooperate on whether or not to enter into proceedings. This willingness (or lack thereof) might have more to do with culture and a determination to enforce the laws rather than institutional arrangements. Protection of turf, a preoccupation with advancing one's own career, or an overly protective approach to sensitive personal information despite suspected crime, are factors that may distort the sharing of information required for successful anticorruption law enforcement. And as if the lack of coordination is not a big enough problem domestically, within one and the same jurisdiction, it is even more daunting a challenge when coordination is needed between institutions in different countries.

3.3.3 Insufficient International Legal Assistance

Article 48 of the UN convention calls for '[c]hannels of communication between competent anti-corruption and law enforcement authorities' on 'bilateral, regional and global levels.' This kind of communication is considered of 'particular importance' at the regional level, and different regional law enforcement mechanisms are in place to promote interaction, including the European Police Office, the European Anti-fraud Office, the Schengen Information System, and the Asset Recovery Network of the Financial Action Task Force of South America against Money Laundering.[69] Membership of INTERPOL, which has established a secure global communications system (I-24/7), is a further prerequisite for effective international law enforcement cooperation.[70] This kind of cooperation, the United Nations notes, should 'not replace direct channels of communication with law enforcement authorities of other States,' and Article 49 explicitly encourages joint investigations as well as the establishment of joint investigative bodies in different regions (the advantages of which include the ability to bridge between civil and common law systems).[71] The channels established for cross-country investigatory collaboration are now facilitating progress in many cases. For example, in the case against executives of the international fertilizer

---

[69] For a more comprehensive list of such regional collaboration and updates, see the UNODC website at: https://www.unodc.org/unodc/en/money-laundering/imolin-amlid.html.

[70] INTERPOL's I-24/7 system, see http://www.interpol.int/INTERPOL-expertise/Data-exchange/I-24-7, see in particular INTERPOL Factsheet COM/FS/2015-02/GI-03.

[71] UN Report CAC/COSP/2013/10.

producer Yara, which led to the conviction of four directors in July 2015, Norwegian investigators requested and received legal assistance from law enforcement systems in thirteen different countries – and this support was considered critical to the prosecution of the case.[72] While such comprehensive international collaboration in investigation and prosecution might be time-consuming, the result is a victory for all those who seek to promote the principles embedded in the United Nations convention and strengthen the channels for such collaboration.

At the same time, reluctance or failure to collaborate is frequently reported. For example, a case against electrical products manufacturer Philips was not prosecuted because of tardy cooperation. The alleged bribery took place in Poland, and in order to prosecute the legal person, Polish authorities sent a request to the Netherlands, the country where Philips is headquartered, for assistance in carrying out a raid of Philips' offices in the Netherlands. According to Transparency International (2012), Poland's investigators sent the request in March 2008 but did not receive a response until October 2009, which was too late for the Polish investigators to make use of the Dutch information. The case led to the conviction for bribery 'of three Polish former managers of Philips,' but 'Philips as a legal entity could not be prosecuted.'[73]

Nonetheless, *intra*regional collaboration tends to function more smoothly than *inter*regional collaboration. For example, investigators complain about a 'legal firewall' between China and the West that blocks any attempt to trace funds that end up in China. The relevance of the problem became apparent in June 2015, when investigators in Florence, Italy 'discovered that more than 4.5 billion euros ($4.9 billion) – the proceeds of counterfeiting, prostitution, labor exploitation, and tax evasion – had been smuggled out of Italy to China in less than four years using a money-transfer service. Nearly half that money was funneled through one of China's largest state banks, the Bank of China, which earned more than EUR 758,000 in commissions on the transfers, according to Italian investigative documents obtained by The Associated Press. Italian officials said that when they tried to appeal to Chinese

---

[72] The Norwegian investigators benefited from close collaboration with colleagues in Switzerland, the United States and France. They requested and received mutual legal assistance from Sweden, the Netherlands, the United Kingdom, Austria, and Monaco. Likewise, mutual legal assistance was provided by the British Virgin Islands, Hong Kong, and Belize. Lebanon was the only country approached that did not respond. Personal dialogue with Chief Investigator of the case, Marianne Djupesland, August 2015.

[73] Transparency International (2012: 29–30).

authorities for help, they got nowhere.' According to Chinese authorities, however, 'judicial cooperation has become a top priority for China's Communist Party, which is ramping up efforts to repatriate corrupt officials who have fled overseas.'[74]

3.4 UNPREDICTABLE PENALTIES, SANCTIONS, AND CONSEQUENCES

As we will discuss in Chapter 4, predictable criminal law sanctions are considered a precondition for crime deterrence, as well as for fairness and criminal justice legitimacy. Within a jurisdiction, judges generally strive for consistency across cases, and as long as no undue elements interfere with the cases, corrupt civil servants, as well as corrupt citizens and firms, can expect fairly similar criminal justice treatment within the same jurisdiction. But if we look at corruption cases from an international perspective, the picture is different.

3.4.1 Variation in Repression Levels

As mentioned in Chapter 1, the penalties most commonly applied in corruption cases include a civil or criminal fine, the confiscation of assets, imprisonment (or a suspended prison sentence), compensation, and some form of injunction. Variation across countries in repression levels depends on cultural factors, and especially the society's confidence in sanctions as a crime deterrent. Many countries, however, are reluctant to judge someone as guilty. In Brazil, for example, many defendants have been convicted of corruption in lower court, but on appeal to a higher court, the accused have generally been found not guilty and thus released.[75] When it comes to foreign bribery cases, the OECD convention requires sanctions that are 'effective, proportionate and dissuasive.' As already noted, however, many of the countries that have criminalized foreign bribery in the past fifteen or so years have yet to convict a single natural or legal person of the crime, or they have taken only very minor law enforcement actions.

---

[74] Reported by *New York Times* in June 2015: 'Correction: China-Italy-Money Laundering Story' (by Frances D'Emilio for the Associated Press).

[75] For details, see a review of the Brazilian law enforcement situation by Carson and Mota Prado (2014).

3.4.1.1   The repression level

For those who are convicted *and* sanctioned, the extent and the nature of the sanction depend on the country in which they are prosecuted. Some examples illustrate the cross-country variation. When it comes to fines, France, for example, imposes fines for natural persons of up to EUR 150,000 if the corruption happens in the public sector and fines of up to EUR 75,000 if it happens in the private sector; both sides of the transaction can be sanctioned equally. For legal persons, the maximum fine is EUR 750,000.[76] Germany has a fine ceiling of EUR 1,000,000 for players in the private and public sectors, including for directors, board members, and officials when the corruption is a result of 'insufficient organization, instruction and supervision.'[77] The United Kingdom and India have no precise fine limits; in Russia, the fines can be 'up to 100 times the amount of the bribe.'[78] In practice, the level of fines is sometimes lower when it comes to cases of foreign bribery, and a recurrent criticism voiced by the OECD WGB is that governments need to raise their sanction level for this form of corruption.

Debates have been stirred by the realization that international corporations may profit far more from an instance of corruption than they would have to pay if caught, convicted, and forced to pay the maximum fine. The fact that French aviation and defense companies, which seek to win enormously valuable contracts, face no more than a fine of EUR 750,000 has been called 'derisory'; that amount is so low as to bear no 'relation to actual or expected profits.'[79] Japan has imposed very mild sanctions in cases of foreign bribery, and in Austria the fines for legal persons for foreign bribery offenses were found to be notably *lower* than the fines for natural persons.[80] The United States, by contrast, imposes very large fines, which are considered by the WGB to have a clear deterrent effect. The combination of hefty fines and the large number of companies and individuals prosecuted for foreign bribery is 'felt to be the main reason why many companies have taken steps to improve their anti-bribery measures.'[81] In the world of scholarly research, however, we

---

[76]   CMS (2014:20–21).
[77]   CMS (2014:23).
[78]   CMS (2014:37).
[79]   OECD Phase 3 Report France, p. 27.
[80]   OECD WGB Austria and Japan.
[81]   OECD Phase 3 US.

have very little evidence to confirm a causal link between the level of fines and deterrent effects.[82]

When it comes to the use of imprisonment as a sanction for corruption offenses, the variation across countries is substantial. Countries with legislation that distinguishes between active bribery (the briber) and passive bribery (the recipient of bribes) tend to punish passive bribery more severely, and bribery in the public sector is generally punished more severely than bribery in the private sector. Many countries allow for very long terms of imprisonment for corruption: in Bulgaria, one can be imprisoned for up to thirty years; in Italy, up to twenty years for judicial bribery; in Russia, up to fifteen years; in China, the briber can be sentenced to life imprisonment – and a public official who has received a bribe can be given the death penalty. Most countries have lower maximum levels: Brazil and Albania, for instance, have a maximum of twelve years; France, the United Kingdom, and Norway have a maximum of ten years; and Switzerland has a limit of five years.

3.4.1.2 Debarment

Natural and legal persons who are found guilty of corruption can be formally excluded from offering services, holding office, and bidding for public tenders. Such exclusion and debarment may follow as the direct result of a court decision or it may be the result of a decision made by other players in society after a verdict is delivered; for example, a procurement agency or a bank may decide not to accept clients convicted of corruption. From a legal perspective, it matters if the exclusion is part of a legal verdict. From an economic perspective, what matters is the actual consequence for the offenders. Whether debarment follows a court ruling, public procurement procedures, or some employment decision, it may contribute to a public perception that crime has been met by justice. For that perception to develop, however, predictability is important, but in practice this predictability is scarce, regardless of whether a private or public sector actor imposed the debarment.

Within the OECD area, it is quite common to have debarment listed as a possible criminal law sanction. In most countries a public official who accepts bribes can face disqualification from similar posts in the future.

---

[82] A concern regarding the calculation of fines, which will be returned to later in the book, is the importance of securing transparency around the law enforcement action and, if relevant, the negotiated settlement or the court's verdict. In many cases, few details are made public about the law enforcement action and subsequent verdict, which makes it difficult to predict what kind of crime-preventing effects the case may have.

And in France, for example, corruption in the private sector implies a risk of professional restrictions. In Germany, the criminal may face an occupational ban. In the Netherlands, too, criminal law penalties may include a ban of 'practicing the profession in which the person committed the crime.' In Switzerland, those found guilty risk being removed from a position of director or executive officer.[83] When it comes to legal persons, most countries' legislation allows penalties that involve some kind of restriction of the operation of the company, a termination of the company, and/or a debarment from competing for public contracts and benefits. Some jurisdictions – including Austria, China, and Russia – still do not have such rules.[84]

In practice, however, it does not seem to matter much what a country's *criminal* law stipulates in this regard, because these rules are rarely applied in corruption cases, especially not when it comes to legal persons. In Norway, for example, debarment or other forms of exclusion have never been used in any criminal law verdict on corruption. When the OECD WGB urges countries to strengthen and clarify their debarment practices, with particular reference to their public procurement practices, it generally refers to institutions outside the criminal justice system, and primarily public procurement entities. For example, France has been encouraged to make sure that all 'the additional penalties available in law' are being used on legal persons, 'in particular debarment from public procurement,' so that the 'sanctions are effective, proportionate and dissuasive.' Denmark has been urged to clarify the 'maximum period of debarment' and to take steps to ensure that the 'records of criminal convictions' are upheld for 'at least as long as' the maximum period. The WGB has called on Mexico to include debarment 'as a sanction in all cases of foreign bribery in the context of international business.' These are all references to 'sanctions' enforced by those who buy services and products for state institutions.[85]

A major problem with the practice of debarment outside criminal law is that those who regulate debarment rules are often in a position to make exceptions to the rules. For example, corrupt suppliers are not accepted as bidders in public procurement because they cannot be trusted. The procurement agents, whom the suppliers might want to bribe, are nonetheless trusted to evaluate the situation and to determine if exemptions from the rules should be made. A corrupt procurement agent could

---

[83] These examples are all found in CMS (2014).
[84] See CMS (2014).
[85] See the OECD WGB Phase 3 reports for the mentioned countries.

thus set aside the very debarment sanction that is intended to prevent corruption. A further problem of debarment – if actually enforced in settings where corruption is a problem – is that it heightens the risk of collusion between the remaining players, which in turn may raise the price of the goods and services to be procured.[86] For these reasons, which will be further addressed in Chapter 5, the question of how far an act of corruption should result in a service provider or individual being found unqualified as a supplier or employee should be part of the judgment conducted by those who consider the criminal liability, and not the procurement agents whose main objective is to secure value for money in public contracting.

3.4.2 Difficulties with Asset Recovery and Neglected Victim Compensation

Asset recovery is a minimum criminal law sanction, because it implies that the profit generated through the corruption is confiscated – in the same way that an apprehended jewelry thief is not permitted to keep the jewelry. In corruption cases, the assets to be recovered equal the bribe payment or the estimated value of a nonmonetary benefit. For the briber, it is supposed to match the benefit obtained through bribery.

While returning the assets lost in corruption may seem to be the most reasonable form of victim compensation, the substantial international development of anticorruption legislation since the late 1990s has not been matched by greater attention to this issue. According to the United Nations, there is little consistency between law enforcement capacities and how governments address the need to protect and offer compensation to victims.[87] Few assets are recovered from those involved in corruption, and out of those assets that have been seized, very little goes to the victims as a form of reparation.

A report by StAR (2013) – a joint initiative of the World Bank and the United Nations established to combat money laundering and promote asset recovery – presents the result of a review of 395 settlements in cross-border corruption cases that took place between 1999 and 2012. While these cases resulted in a total of US $6.9 billion in sanctions, only 3 percent (US $197 million) was returned or ordered to be returned to the countries whose officials were accused of accepting bribes. According to

---

[86] For a presentation of the legal regulation and discussion of inconsistent principles, see Hjelmeng and Søreide (2014). Auriol and Søreide (2015) describe the market consequences of enforced debarment rules.

[87] UN CAC/COSP/2013/7.

another report by StAR (2014), awareness of the importance of victim compensation in cross-border corruption cases is increasing, as is the value of assets recovered and returned.

However, despite the signs of progress and the achievements in the form of strengthened international collaboration for this cause, there are some substantial hurdles that seem to hinder substantial progress. Most but not all countries offer a legal basis for confiscating such assets, John Hatchard (2014) explains. And the most straightforward way of recovering assets – conviction-based forfeiture – can be used only upon a criminal conviction. Given the many difficulties associated with these criminal law processes, as discussed earlier in this chapter, the attempt of prosecuting and securing such conviction often fails or they take years to reach a conclusion. Therefore, the asset recovery successes that have taken place are often 'non-conviction-based asset forfeiture.' One of the 'advantages' of this approach, according to Hatchard (2014:319) – in addition to the chances of securing assets without the dependence on a court verdict – is that 'proof that the property constitutes the proceeds of corruption is established on a balance of probabilities;' it is not evaluated by a court. As StAR (2014) explains, the procedures associated with settlements and other out of court approaches are the 'most efficient' strategies as they allow the proceeds to be located, frozen and recovered faster and thus more securely than conviction-based approaches.

One of the problems with this approach is what Hatchard (2014:320) describes as 'constitutional issues' – namely, the right to a fair trial and the right not to be arbitrarily deprived of property. Radha Ivory (2014) adds nuance to this point, and explains 'the human rights of the bad guys.' The calls for more and quicker asset recovery as part of law enforcement actions against corruption are legitimate and must be met with clearer rules and efficient enforcement. In the jungle of treaties, rights and jurisdictions, there are trade-offs between benefits and costs, and a narrow focus on one goal will easily lead to consequences for other goals, and especially in the area of human rights.

The way forward seems to be a combination of criminal sanctions and civil remedies as well as closer collaboration between law enforcement institutions, yet in the process of facilitating this work at the international level, there are also hurdles in the form of cultural differences between the countries involved, lack of trust in those who may receive the transfers, a desire in the most developed countries to monitor how the recipient government spends the assets that are returned to the country, and these challenges come on top of the difficulty of localizing the funds and calculating which victims should be compensated and for how much.

3.5 CORRUPTION IN LAW ENFORCEMENT AND OVERSIGHT INSTITUTIONS

Police corruption is documented in countries across the world. It does not seem to be restricted to any particular ranks within the police. And when courts prosecute against it, they are vulnerable to undue influence both from other (corrupt) government institutions and directly from the accused. The risk of undue influence on law enforcement is a particular concern in corruption cases, as those who are accused of corruption (usually upon strong evidence) may well be inclined to offer bribes to law enforcement officials in the hope of securing more lenient treatment or seeing the charges against them dropped.

3.5.1 Corruption Risks along the Law Enforcement Value Chain

Risks of corruption exist throughout the law enforcement value chain, and despite the deterrent risk of sanctions, the risks may increase with the risk of incarceration or substantial loss of status or wealth as the amount at stake for those involved increases.[88] At the level of investigation, there is the risk of *'recursive corruption,'* which means that an official who has been detected as being involved in corruption may try to bribe the official who caught him or her, and thus avoid sanctions.[89] The problem is associated with corrupt networks in police force governance, including manipulated management decisions regarding personnel and resource allocations (for example, fewer resources are allocated to those individuals or departments that are willing to respond to signals from higher up in the system about which cases to shield from investigation). Through such mechanisms, some offenders are protected from law enforcement actions even before they are investigated.

Entrenched corruption in police forces involves colleagues protecting one another from consequences when they commit some breach of duty, including corruption; officers can thus demand bribes safe in the knowledge that they are unlikely to be reported by their colleagues.[90] The

---

[88] Corruption risks along the law enforcement value chain are described in greater detail by Messick and Schutte (2015).

[89] This is a problem much addressed in the economic literature as well, see for example Polinsky and Shavell (2001), Marjit and Shi (1998) and Mookherjee and Png (1995).

[90] Such situations are described in numerous publications, see for example Andvig and Barasa (2013) regarding Kenya, Aspinall and Van Klinken (2011) regarding Indonesia, Bonner (2012) regarding Mexico.

extent of this problem varies. In some situations, colleagues are friends who would not report each other's actions; in other settings, corrupt officials systematically extort bribes from clients and share the proceeds.

Prosecutorial corruption involves a suspect either avoiding charges by influencing the evidence and selection of witnesses or being given milder treatment by prosecutors. Such challenges are difficult to detect and address due to the prosecutors' discretion to dismiss a case and negotiate charges. Heicke Gramkow provides an overview of these risks, and explains how prosecutors under corrupt influence may delay cases, alter police records, lose documents, and alter charges.[91] They may falsify evidence, support unreasonable bail requirements, rig the jury selection, not disclose exculpatory evidence, intimidate witnesses, or handpick the trial attorney. In some cases, the prosecutor can even influence the choice of judge or court. It should be noted that law enforcement actors who refuse to accept bribes are sometimes threatened with violence – threats that can be all too credible when made by members of organized crime networks. Outsiders may find it difficult to determine if an apparently highly biased law enforcement system is simply greedy or is the victim of organized crime.

Indirectly, the final court decision is subject to the various corruption risks throughout the law enforcement value chain. But of course, where judicial corruption is a problem, there is also the risk that the judge is *directly* involved. In many countries, a single judge alone decides the sentence in a given case, which increases the risk of corruption compared with settings in which several individuals are involved in deciding the sentence. A judge may also influence the extent of trial delays – often of significant benefit to the accused – and the conduct of preliminary proceedings (including decisions about whether there is sufficient evidence to justify a trial, whether to set bail and at what level, and so forth). In addition, with or without the judge's awareness, other personnel working in a court may influence decisions such as those regarding the provision of legal advice to victims, the protection of witnesses, and the remuneration of witnesses and more – all of which may help to secure more lenient treatment for the accused. Court assistants may also be offered bribes by those who fear they will not otherwise receive fair

---

[91]   See Messick and Schuette (2015).

treatment in court (especially if the other side in the court case has already paid a bribe to the court personnel).[92]

The law enforcement process does not end with the verdict. The risks of corruption extend to the process of collecting a fine, bringing offenders to prison, and the conditions experienced by an offender in prison. With access to the Internet and a cell phone – and bribes paid to prison management and prison guards to look the other way – an inmate may even continue operating a network of illegal business deals from inside jail, including offering and taking bribes.[93]

3.5.2 No Country is Immune to Corruption in the Judiciary

Judiciaries and police forces in all countries are exposed to the risks of corruption, although the judiciaries in poorer countries are particularly vulnerable. As addressed in Chapter 2, most societies experience a decrease in the most extortive forms of corruption as their income levels increase, and high-income economies tend to have stronger formal and informal integrity mechanisms. However, for several reasons (which will be addressed in Chapter 5), law enforcement institutions are difficult to organize with the purpose of minimizing corruption risks. The individuals representing the institutions – ranging from a lowly police officer to a chief prosecutor or high court judge – are entrusted with a high degree of discretionary power, which is intended to help them retain their independence when making decisions that affect powerful actors, both in the public sector (and at the political level) and in society at large. Those accused in the gravest cases of corruption are often wealthy and influential, and many of them will do whatever they can to avoid investigation and prosecution. Consequently, law enforcement corruption risks are present in countries at any income level.

Because this corruption problem occurs *within* the institutions supposed to deal with corruption in society, it is constructive to have the risks evaluated by experts from other countries. Hence it has been useful that regional institutionalized collaboration, like GRECO in Europe, focuses its evaluations on 'corruption prevention in respect of members

---

[92] For more details of corruption risks in courts, see Transparency International (2015), Gloppen (2014) and Victoria Jennet's section in Messick and Schuette (2015).

[93] Hill (2015) provides a useful introduction to this problem.

of parliament, judges and prosecutors.'[94] These evaluations search for system dysfunctions, not for corruption cases, yet they identify the high-risk areas for corruption. Problems frequently addressed are the risk of political influence in specific investigations and court cases, the appointment of judges and high-ranking civil servants, and guidelines on what is acceptable regarding gifts and paid positions outside the judiciary.

Exact information about the extent of corruption among prosecutors and in courts is obviously difficult to obtain. Risks vary substantially across institutions within the same society. Some macro-level rankings, however, do offer a rough estimate of cross-country variation in perceived risks. The World Justice Project has included some questions on the risk of corruption in criminal justice systems in its broad-ranging cross-country survey. What the results tell us is that some of the top performers on Transparency International's Corruption Perceptions Index are found lower down the rankings for the level of corruption within a country's criminal justice system, and many high-income countries are outperformed on this ranking by countries with lower income levels. Botswana, for example, is ranked higher than Canada and France, and Mongolia and Ecuador are ranked higher than Ukraine and Mexico. The latter two are ranked among the most challenged countries, together with Uzbekistan, Venezuela, Nigeria, and Pakistan, among some others. Indonesia is ranked slightly ahead of these countries, but below, for example, Thailand, the Philippines, and Vietnam, which are ranked similarly to Romania, Argentina, Ethiopia, Croatia, Iran, and India. Estonia and Malaysia are ranked with the better performing Germany and Canada and some others, while top performers are New Zealand and the Nordic countries, with the highest score given to Denmark.

When one compares the results on corruption in criminal justice systems with rankings for the quality of the criminal justice system overall, one finds some surprises. Countries that perform badly on corruption within their criminal justice system compared with the quality of their system overall include Peru, Moldova, Uganda, Bulgaria, Ukraine, Malawi, Kenya, Kyrgyzstan, Tanzania, Albania, Cambodia, Zimbabwe, and Malawi – which means, their criminal justice system is more corrupt than what one might expect when considering only the overall performance. Countries that have a substantially higher criminal

---

[94]   For details and results of the different GRECO evaluation rounds (1-4), see the GRECO website: http://www.coe.int/t/dghl/monitoring/greco/evaluations/index_en.asp. See also The European Commission for the Efficiency of Justice website: http://www.coe.int/T/dghl/cooperation/cepej/default_en.asp and GRECO.

justice integrity (that is, lower corruption) score than what their general performance score would suggest include Japan, New Zealand, Greece, Georgia, Belgium, Chile, Germany, Botswana, the United States, Sweden, Uruguay, Turkey, France, Estonia, Malaysia, the Philippines, and Sri Lanka.

3.6 CONCLUSION: LAW ENFORCEMENT OBSTACLES IN PRACTICE

This chapter has described common types of law enforcement failure along the criminal justice value chain. While such failure is manifested within the law enforcement institutions – most notably, in issues regarding the adequacy of laws and definitions of crime, the conduct of investigations and prosecution, the use and predictability of sanctions, and the presence of corruption within the institutions themselves – the underlying problems are often to be found at the political level. For various reasons, political commitment to the anticorruption agenda may be weak, in contrast to what one should expect from elected and entrusted leaders. Some politicians seek to protect commercial benefits for their country, regardless of what corruption problems exist abroad, ignoring the damage caused in international markets and the reasons why each country must enforce their foreign bribery laws. Others may benefit personally from allowing corruption to go on, for example if they own companies that profit from biased decisions, or if corruption is part of a power game, where a tolerant attitude secures support and loyalty from allies and leaders in the state administration.

However, while the government and politicians are easy to blame, the law enforcement institutions have a responsibility to enforce the rules within the framework conditions they are given, and to demand better conditions from their political masters when necessary. Corruption cases must be thoroughly investigated and prosecuted even if such processes are demanding, and collaboration with other law enforcement bodies must be undertaken even if it might be burdensome. The law enforcement institutions in some countries show great creativity in enforcing the law, whatever the obstacles at the political level. Creating a legal platform for action (something that diplomatic pressures and international conventions have helped to build) is important, but that platform is no more than a tool: *how* the tool is used determines what results are achieved. And how it is used depends on much more than the availability of financial resources for enforcement. As this chapter has revealed, it also depends on culture, ambitions, integrity, and commitment – from the lowest-ranking police officers all the way up to the minister of justice, and from the initial investigation into a possible case of corruption all the way to the enforcement of sanctions after a verdict has been delivered. Within these law enforcement systems, the risks of corruption within the ranks of law enforcers must be addressed, even if it might mean taking enforcement action against colleagues. Any ambition or strategy to promote more efficient law enforcement can be undermined unless the law enforcement institutions are honest and free from undue external interference.

While official international evaluations of law enforcement performance often focus on the details of laws, law enforcement statistics, and the organization of law enforcement institutions, efficient criminal law enforcement against corruption depends on how strategies are developed for influencing the incentives of those involved – and potentially involved – in corruption. This challenging terrain, with its many different concerns and trade-offs, is the subject of the next two chapters.

PART II

Fundamental challenges and the way forward

4. Economic reasoning on corruption

For economists, criminal law is not necessarily the most natural starting point for the design of an anticorruption strategy. With their focus on the power of incentives, rather than on the punitive force of sanctions, economists believe that many effective anticorruption steps can be taken aside from adhering to criminal law – steps that include reorganizing authority and decision-making, enhancing access to information, and letting remuneration depend on the desired performance.[1] Furthermore, many economists are cautious about what they consider a moral classification of acts. During the early stages of systematic research into corruption, which broadly (albeit coincidentally) spanned the period of the Cold War, when we had a very incomplete understanding of corruption's causes and only weak empirical information about its consequences, many economists found it premature to define corrupt acts as crime. Some authors, in fact, defended bribery as a pragmatic response to market failures or to situations in which players had to contend with weak property rights and otherwise challenging institutional framework conditions. The past two decades' increasing store of empirical knowledge about social phenomena, corruption included, have made it impossible for economists to ignore the damaging consequences of corruption, although economists are still quick to point out that different forms of corruption have different consequences (as discussed in Chapter 2). Today, economists still see criminal law as an excessively powerful tool for addressing certain corruption-related problems, but there is also broad agreement that corruption's harmful effects on governance and the performance of markets justify the criminal law approach.

As this recognition has grown so has the realization that general economic arguments about crime control in general also apply to the control of corruption in particular. This increasing awareness brings us to the main question in this chapter: What can the economics of crime tell us about how we should efficiently deal with corruption?

---

[1] For a comprehensive introduction to the economics of corruption and literature review, see Rose-Ackerman and Palifka (2016, especially Chapters 2–6).

As the ambition of this book is to bridge the gap between legal and economic thinking, I begin the chapter with a brief introduction to the basic premises for a criminal law system to undertake an enforcement action. Understood by economists or not, these premises define the framework within which economic solutions can play a practical role. The legal premises for an enforcement action are often anchored in a country's constitution and procedural law, and even if they are not written in stone, they have to be clear and accepted by both legal scholars and economists. Satisfying these premises, or conditions, can be extremely difficult in the case of enforcement actions against corruption. Likewise, legal scholars need to understand the basic economic perspectives on crime and deterrence, laid out in the second section, so as to navigate what is for many of them the unfamiliar terrain of economic reasoning. In the third section, I examine the ways in which the two disciplines' perspectives on deterrence strategies conflict.

While the first half of the chapter thus looks at crime generally, the second half zooms in on corruption specifically. In the fourth section, I explore how economic theories of crime have been adapted to help uncover and explain the unique features of this form of crime. In light of the fact that corruption often involves organizations, the fifth section discusses common economic arguments on law enforcement vis-à-vis corporations. The sixth and final section summarizes the proposals made by economists for generating a more efficient criminal law approach to corruption; subsequent chapters look at the practical applicability and potential value of these proposals.

4.1   PREMISES FOR LAW ENFORCEMENT STRATEGIES AND SANCTIONING

No matter what ideas legal scholars and economists come up with about how and when to use criminal law, those ideas will make sense only if they take into account three things: (1) the legal conditions that must be satisfied before a law enforcement action can be taken; (2) the assumption that humans are (quite) rational decision-makers; and (3) the match between theoretical assumptions behind law enforcement strategies and the knowledge we have about empirical realities, including how individuals make choices.

4.1.1 Legal Conditions for Sanctioning Criminal Law Offenders

Criminal law stipulates how society can and should react when members commit what that society defines as crime. By offering an outlet for anger and retribution, the criminal justice system reduces the risk of vigilantism and increases the chances of peaceful conflict resolution. Rule-based reactions to crime help protect citizens from one another and from their leaders; such reactions also stimulate general recognition of moral values.[2]

In societies with legitimate criminal law systems ('legitimate' here describing systems that are seen by most citizens as fair, nonarbitrary, and rational), a number of basic conditions must be satisfied before criminal sanctions can be applied. The most obvious of these conditions is that *a criminal act must have been committed.*[3] In everyday parlance, we use 'crime' as if the word refers to a clear category of acts. In corruption cases, however, it can be difficult to draw the line between legal acts and crime. An array of examples illustrates this difficulty. First, at what point does lobbyism coupled with transactions to a political party bank account controlled by party leaders cross the line of legality and become corruption? Is it a crime when a high-ranking bureaucrat who regulates a utility provider does so to the benefit of his sister-in-law, who is a major shareholder in the company? How far can a company be held criminally liable for the bribes offered by its sub-sub-suppliers, even though the transaction in the end benefits the company? Is it corruption when a firm renegotiates for more favorable contractual terms after its bid has been accepted by the government if it becomes clear that the government indicated, but did not explicitly state, that such renegotiation was to be expected? How serious in this context is a firm's purchase of information about a competitor's bid? Many governments have criminal-ized the planning of terrorist acts; should the planning of acts of corruption likewise be criminalized, and if so, how early in the planning would the crime definition apply?

Each of these examples presents situations in which corruption could have harmful consequences. Whether or not those acts could be regulated by applying criminal law is generally unclear, however. It can be difficult

---

[2] This part draws heavily on Søreide (2013:184–187), prepared in dialogue with Jørn Jacobsen. For an introduction to the rationale behind criminal law sanctions, see Ashworth (2005).

[3] Some societies deem that criminal liability occurs only when an act has caused damage. Other societies hold that the mere risk of significant damage can be sufficient for an act to be considered a crime.

to draw the line between what is corruption and what is not, and unless that line is clear criminal law enforcement action cannot be taken. Fuzzy definitions of crimes allow for interpretation and discretion in law enforcement, but complicate the task of deciding if a crime has in fact taken place. Strict definitions of crime, in contrast, limit the criminal law's relevance in controlling criminal acts, because such definitions necessarily exclude many acts. Harmonized laws combined with an increasing amount of court cases involving corruption internationally does help national jurisdictions to interpret their own corruption laws and to clarify their own definitions by examining relevant verdicts from other countries. Nonetheless, many countries still need legal amendments or guidelines to draw the line between what is legal and what is criminal, especially in the area of corporate crime.[4]

A second condition for punishment is that *the individual(s) or entity responsible for the crime must be identified.* The fact that murder has taken place is insufficient for the crime to be prosecuted; prosecution requires that there is someone to charge for the crime. This condition may appear obvious, but satisfying it may be difficult. The criminal act may have been committed by a company or by agents acting on more or less explicit orders from a decision-maker who is more powerful than those known to have been involved in the case. The management of a company or a state entity may fiercely reject any allegations of corruption brought forward by investigators, and they may well seek to lay blame on a scapegoat.

The third criminal law condition is that the accused must be *guilty.* This adds to the difficulty of holding an offender criminally liable, because those accused must have understood ex ante the criminal nature of the act, or at least have understood that the act was wrongful and could cause serious consequences, and still have decided to commit the act. The accused will typically deny that this was the case, and proving the contrary can be very difficult. For instance, the accused might claim that a seemingly corrupt transaction via a financial secrecy provider was just an ordinary payment for consultancy services.

---

[4] Chapter 1 suggests adopting a bargaining perspective on corrupt acts in order to grasp conceptually what should be understood as corruption. A legal definition needs more precision, however, and the bargain principle is of help only as a starting point in the search for a criminal law classification of a corrupt act. Chapter 3 described examples of how criminal law amendments might be necessary to avoid the risk of serious forms of corruption being shielded from the attention of criminal law investigators simply because the specific acts are not adequately stipulated in the criminal law definition of corrupt acts.

As if these difficulties – defining the acts of crime, identifying the offender, and placing blame – are not challenging enough, each condition requires *evidence* for it to prompt a criminal law sanction. Different criminal justice systems operate with different demands for evidence. In countries where the criminal justice system is embedded in the society, the risk of sanctioning an innocent individual is typically thought to be more serious than the failure to sanction the actual offender. In other countries, however, the criminal law system appears to prioritize harsh penalties while there is less concern about charging the right individual for an offense – expressed, for example, in the system's propensity to impose sanctions upon confessions produced by the use of torture.

In order to reduce the call from victims for revenge in criminal law cases, the society's formal response to and sanctioning of an act of crime must involve concrete consequences for the offender. For this reason, many criminal acts are seen to justify the use of imprisonment, which is not used for other forms of wrongdoing. Such punishment is a serious infringement of a citizen's liberty, however, and therefore the legitimate use of criminal justice sanctions requires broad consensus in society about when and how they should be applied. To protect citizens' autonomy and their most obvious human rights, including protection against punishment for no good reason, clear restrictions must be placed on a government's use of force, repression, and punishment. This is why most countries have a *criminal procedure act* that stipulates rules regarding investigations, the accused's right to a lawyer, the use of pressure during interrogation, protection against self-incrimination, arrest orders, the length of detainment, the use of evidence, exchange of information, access to information for outsiders, the contents of an indictment, the conduct of court proceedings, and more. The higher the repression level, the more important it is to avoid procedural mistakes, such as imposing sanctions on innocent citizens or using the criminal law to sanction acts that are in fact legal.

Once the different conditions have all been met, and the case has been prosecuted, legal constraints govern the severity of the punishment as well: *the sanction should be set at 'a reasonable level'* given the crime committed and, in many cases, the situation of the criminal, too. The sanction should be *proportional* to the level of sanctions for other forms of crime, and there must be some *consistency* with former judgments on similar acts. What is found reasonable, proportional, and consistent, however, depends on the judge imposing the sanction, as well as the prevailing legal tradition and culture. For the individual court, there may be few guiding principles regarding these judgments, and the justification

for the procedural law requirements is often vague. Within one jurisdiction, the same form of corruption can lead to different sanctions in
legal districts; across jurisdictions, the variation in the use of sanctions is
often huge.[5]

It is within the framework of these legal conditions that governments
can improve their criminal law regulation and use of sanctions (for
example, by considering recommendations from social science research).
While they are rarely debated in the economic literature, these conditions
both complement and restrain the applicability of economic solutions.
Typically, economists write about criminal law as if tacitly recognizing
these conditions. The legitimacy associated with these values – and their
possible indirect influence on moral values – appears to be largely
ignored. This is one of the reasons why legal scholars sometimes have
difficulties accepting economic strategies for crime control: They are
presented without reference to the basic legal premises of law enforcement, and therefore, easily considered irrelevant – even if the mechanisms per se make sense. However, the two disciplines also share some
assumptions, and at the bottom of both economic and legal analyses is
the belief that we act rationally and thus, can be subject to criminal law
regulation.

4.1.2   The Rationality Assumption

Economists and legal scholars have quite high expectations regarding our
inclination to act rationally. What does it mean in practice? According to
the online version of *Merriam-Webster's Dictionary*, being 'rational'
means 'having reason or understanding.' 'Reason' is listed with the
following three definitions: '(1) a statement or fact that explains why
something is the way it is, why someone does, thinks, or says something,
or why someone behaves a certain way; (2) a fact, condition, or situation
that makes it proper or appropriate to do something, feel something, etc.;
and (3) the power of the mind to think and understand in a logical way.'[6]
While economists and legal scholars may endorse these definitions, they
nonetheless tend to have a different understanding of 'rational.'

The point at issue in law is what qualifies as sufficiently rational for
legal liability, a matter of decisive importance for a verdict. From this
perspective, rationality is associated with the question of an offender's

---

[5] Variation in sanctions for corruption cases is discussed further in
Chapter 5.

[6] See Merriam-Webster online: http://www.merriam-webster.com/dictionary/
reason (accessed on 12 July 2015).

mental health – meaning the ability of the offender to understand the consequences of his or her actions. In law, it is usually found meaningless to impose sanctions on those who are too young or too senseless to feel any form of responsibility, because they cannot be *blamed* for their actions. Assessment of the offender's mental health is rarely relevant in cases of corruption, where those involved are often government representatives entrusted with some degree of authority or business people well aware of the trade-offs associated with bribery.

For economic analyses, *rationality* is simply taken for granted. It is, however, defined with more precision and more explicitly in economics than in law. Rationality is defined as an axiomatic concept with a set of conditions that must be met for there to be consistency between preferences and choices. Specifically, an individual makes rational choices if she or he can rank her or his preferences in a set order – which means that the individual knows what outcome is preferred to another. These preferences must be logically consistent (if situation A is preferred to B, and B to C, then C will not be preferred to A), and the ranking must be unaffected by new alternatives (option X will not lead the individual to prefer B to A). In addition, a rational individual is assumed to have full, or 'perfect,' information about what will occur upon any choice made (or at least about the probability that certain consequences will follow), and have the cognitive ability and time to weigh every choice against every other alternative choice. Game theoretical analyses take this assumption even further. They are based on the assumption that individuals can rationally predict *other* individuals' (rational) choices. Thus, these theories are used for describing dynamic developments and equilibria (that is, where a given situation or relationship is stable, simply because under the given assumptions, no individual will deviate from his or her strategic preferences).[7]

Of course, this (economic) rationality assumption is overly optimistic about our cognitive capacity. Few of us behave as if we are as consistent, informed, and efficient as the rationality assumption pictures us all to be. We act on impulses, and our preferences change over time or depend on the specific context (for example, our preferences may change depending on who is watching the choices we make). Besides, many individuals seem to have a substantial gap between their feelings and their good judgment, while rationality implies a substantial overlap (that is, that our feelings match our rational choices; that, for instance, one would never

---

[7]   Premises for economic theory are described by Samuelson (1947), Arrow (1959).

fall in love with a person whose lifestyle one finds difficult to accept). In real life, most of us act on multiple – often conflicting – goals, and the enormous number of choices and amount of information available in today's world makes it difficult even to imagine 'the perfectly informed' individual.

Across disciplines, however, it is considered misleading, rude, and unwise to consider criminal offenders as uninformed *irrational* decision-makers. It is held to be misleading because most individuals act *fairly* rationally, especially regarding decisions that are important to them. Besides, expecting irrationality would make it difficult to bring the criminal justice system to bear, because that system expects moral competence and responsibility – implicitly demanding awareness and accountability. From the legal perspective, a criminal law sanction can be imposed because the offender *is* responsible and, assumingly, rational. For economists, irrationality would imply assumptions of arbitrary choices and that would bring to the fore theoretical predictions with low ability to explain observations in society. Despite some apparent rationality shortages, analytical results that build on rationality assumptions are still useful for understanding choices, especially when it comes to important decisions, repetitive choices, or informed assessments, and many economic theories appear to predict behavior quite well.[8]

4.1.3 Empirical Validation of Theory

Despite the different reasons for expecting citizens to act rationally, a whole new branch of research has emerged over the twentieth century – often referred to as 'behavioral economics,' as though to tell us that humans are not as rational as we try to maintain.[9] What this field of research seeks to identify is the need for more nuanced assumptions about how decisions are made. Given our abiding human characteristics and instincts, we tend to make decisions that predictably deviate from what would otherwise appear rational; thus, we make choices with a 'bounded rationality.' Through creative and systematic research on choices, often using laboratory or field experiments (see Chapter 2), we

---

[8] Harsanyi (1977:16) points out that game theoretical results that build on overly optimistic assumptions about human rationality must be considered in a normative perspective; that is, the results must be understood as indicating *what would have been wise* to do for an individual with a given set of preferences.

[9] Harel (2014) summarizes the insights of behavioral analysis of criminal law.

can learn how to modify our economic analyses of choices – how to interpret those choices differently – including in the area of crime.

One area where such insights have emerged relates to how humans systematically miscalculate risks, and this of course is relevant for understanding the impact of a criminal law strategy. Humans are typically irrationally concerned about big losses, and overestimate the risk of dramatic consequences – a tendency that may explain why so many swimmers worry about shark attacks and so many passengers are anxious about flying. At the same time, humans commonly underestimate high probabilities, and act in ways that deviate from what a rational assessment of the risks would suggest is the wise course – a tendency that may explain smoking.[10] Most humans are risk averse, though to different degrees, and this feature appears to be a deviation from rationality. It makes us accept unnecessary costs simply to avoid uncertainty. However, for an individual who strictly prefers secure outcomes to uncertain outcomes, it *is* rational to accept these costs.

When it comes to uncertain benefits that can be obtained by making a specific choice, humans tend to make inconsistent judgments in different ways. For example, some studies show that we are readier to morally defend a decision if we profit from it ourselves than if the same decision is made for the benefit of someone else. At the same time, other studies confirm that we distinguish the fairness of outcomes from their desirability, which means that we will not necessarily consider all benefits that accrue to ourselves as fair.[11] The risk of harmful consequences is easier to accept for decision-makers if the victims are far away or unknown, which they typically are in cases of corruption, especially in cases of foreign bribery.[12] In addition, we tend to be far more tempted by rewards that emerge soon after an act is taken instead of later (we have a high 'discount factor'), which gives us a near-sighted focus on the benefits of crime rather than a long-sighted recognition of the costs associated with sanctions. When we lose benefits because others misbehave, our impulsive quest for retribution will typically overwhelm our rationality and skew our decision-making.[13]

While economists have traditionally focused on individuals making choices, empirical research has enhanced our understanding of how we

---

[10]　See Kahneman and Tversky (1979, 1986), chapters in Shafir (2012), and Kahneman (2011).

[11]　Tyler (2012) explains how humans often make choices as if driven by social/group motivations.

[12]　See Van Winden and Ash (2009) for details and debate.

[13]　See Shafir (2012, Chapter 10).

make decisions as members of groups. We appear to be socially motivated, and an individual may well accept a decision that creates a disadvantage for herself or himself if it benefits the group as a whole. These choices can be made rationally – that is, the individual acts with consistency between preferences and choices. Group dynamics affect individuals in many different ways, however, and the propensity to adapt to one's group environment and culture (almost irrespective of their particular characteristics) is high.[14]

Such insights from studies of decision-making spotlight the problems with simplistic underlying rationality assumptions in legal and economic reasoning: humans make choices in more complex ways than has often been assumed.[15] Although the rationality assumption continues to be a fundamental premise for analytical reasoning around the impact of criminal law sanctions, economists are paying more attention to bounded rationality and applying more modesty regarding the policy implications of their theoretical analyses.

For any researcher in criminal law, theoretical assumptions behind policy choices must match realities on the ground. For this reason, descriptive empirical analyses of honest and dishonest behavior, as well as careful evaluations of the impacts of strategic choices, are a prerequisite for the development of any academic strategy designed to generate efficient solutions.

4.2 ECONOMIC PERSPECTIVES ON CRIME DETERRENCE

Having laid out the basic premises for a criminal justice approach to crime and corruption, we can now turn to a summary of economic intuition regarding crime. Typically, economists write about criminal law as if tacitly recognizing the legal conditions, and the matter of legitimacy and its possible indirect influence on moral values appears largely ignored, at least until the recent decade. Most economic analyses of criminal law are developed with the narrower objective of optimizing deterrence: A committed crime cannot be undone, but it is possible to

---

[14] Tirole (1996) explains why newcomers in a company are likely to adopt the work ethics of their colleagues. Sarsfield (2012) describes the theories of group dynamics and equilibrium forces (further debated in Chapter 6) with reference to corruption in Mexico. See also Acemoglu and Jackson (2014).

[15] These irrationality patterns were previously reviewed by Søreide (2014: 28–29).

develop strategies for preventing harmful acts in the future. Society's response when crime is revealed is assumed by economists to be a central component of such strategies. Sanctions predictably imposed on those involved, economists reason, may deter rational potential offenders from committing crime. If so, crime rates will decrease, which will make society safer. If sanctions have no such effect, economists argue (at least implicitly), then there are few reasons to impose sanctions (which are typically costly for society) on citizens or organizations.

In studies of optimal crime deterrence, economists traditionally have chosen to focus on four main policy choices: (1) the sanctioning rule, (2) the form of sanction, (3) the magnitude of the sanction (also known as the 'repression level'), and (4) detection strategies. With the ambition of crime deterrence, these policy choices are optimized with respect to trade-offs between the extent of crime, the damage caused, the cost of law enforcement, and the expected impact on potential offenders. This section introduces elementary arguments in this theory.[16]

4.2.1 The Propensity to Commit Crime

The economic starting point of a study of sanctions is typically the potential criminal's assumed utility function; that is, the list of concerns most relevant for his or her choice to commit a crime or remain honest. Crime is preferred if the net benefit associated with such a choice exceeds the expected outcome of honest alternatives. The net benefit is the amount of gains from the crime minus the amount of costs – and both benefits and costs are associated with uncertainties.

The imagined potential criminal's calculation of benefits and costs are not straightforward. For the individual, the benefits of committing an economic crime, such as corruption, include both monetary values and indirect benefits that have less or no monetary value. The marginal value of the *monetary gain* depends on the circumstance. For some offenders, the crime secures subsistence or covers some urgent need, while for others the gains add to an already high consumption of luxury. The *indirect benefits* might include, for example, a higher status – obtained because the crime signals loyalty to corrupt leaders, garners career opportunities (for example by securing successful market access through bribery), or bolsters a reputation in the world of business as a person who can get things done. The benefits of crime may also come from avoiding

---

[16] For more thorough introduction of this theme with literature reviews, see Polinsky and Shavell (2007), Harel (2012), Garoupa (1997), and Posner (1985).

the consequences of remaining honest; for instance, the offender avoids the risk of signaling law-abidingness in an environment where most players benefit from collaborating in crime. Moreover, for some decision-makers, the involvement in crime may even satisfy some *primitive needs* of revenge, envy, control, or risk attraction. All these different factors are included in the economists' basket of thinkable benefits that could be part of the imagined potential offender's cost-benefit assessment, although exactly which of these factors are included in the economic analysis of a specific case depends on the research question.

When it comes to the cost side of the equation, the most important factor that prevents crime is probably the *moral cost* associated with crime. The reason why most citizens do not steal is not simply the low probability of getting away with the crime; they simply just don't steal. They *are not* 'a person who steals.' Of course, the burden of violating formal rules varies across individuals, contexts, and societies, as discussed in Chapter 2.

Another obvious cost factor, and the one that economists have traditionally emphasized, because it can be steered, is the *risk of getting caught* in the crime and sanctioned. Many forms of economic crime, such as corruption, are rarely committed on impulse, and a decision-maker will typically consider the risks of detection – a risk that will depend on the law enforcement situation as well as the given individual's skills in committing the crime while leaving little or no evidence of having done so. The consequences associated with detection will typically exceed the pure expense of a fine or the burden of spending time in prison, because the process of being investigated, accused and, taken to court add to the consequences. The *reputational side* is often equally important. The fall from a position as a high-ranking official or business leader down to the status of a crook who got rich at the expense of others can be precipitous, and the mere contemplation of such a plunge can sometimes induce moral vertigo.

Balancing the perceived costs and expected benefits associated with a crime is a judgment that the potential offender has to make. And it is typically difficult to make that judgment with certainty. Few of the variables involved in the calculation have exact values, several can be only roughly estimated, and a range of probabilities come into play. Like the potential offender weighing costs and benefits, economists making theoretical predictions are beset by high levels of uncertainty.

A common inference from economic theories is that governments can influence the incidence of crime by enhancing the expected costs associated with criminal acts. The assumption is that the benefits of crime can be outweighed by the risk of consequences if caught in the crime. By imposing stricter sanctions, a higher proportion of potential criminals will find their net benefit from crime to be negative, and thus harmful acts will be deterred. This reasoning is not in conflict with the notion of citizens likely to obey the law because they agree with its content, or because they detest the idea of committing harmful acts, or – regardless of their own view about the rules – because they find abiding by the law coherent with a well-functioning society. Instead, criminal law regulations are expected to influence *those who are on the margin* – that is, those who are very close to being tempted by criminal benefits. The closer individuals are to indifference between committing a crime and staying honest, the easier it is to influence their choice. Therefore, the closer they are to indifference, the weaker the criminal law reaction found necessary to prevent crime.[17]

In theory, the reaction would not *have* to be a punishment; it could just as well be a reward for law-abiding behavior. Either option would influence the personal assessment of costs and benefits. For several reasons, however, there are limits to how far a criminal justice system can and should reward honesty. One concern is the practical and financial side of administering such rewards (a relevant concern even if applying non-monetary rewards), because such rewards would be similar to subsidizing non-behavior – as if we would have to determine how much non-crime a citizen has committed. In addition, it would easily undermine the norm-generating effect of taking honesty for granted.[18] Crime should be considered the exception to the norm (regardless of its frequency), and thus law enforcement expenses are spent more cost-efficiently by targeting the exception instead of the common practice.

4.2.2 Sentencing and Repression

So, what should be the leading sentencing principle for law enforcement authorities that aim at preventing corruption? If we assume 'certain enforcement' (that is, we assume that each incident of crime is observed

---

[17] This intuition – the closer individuals are to indifference, the stronger the deterrent effect – has not reached the common legal reasoning around repression levels. The implication of the assumption, that is, the lower sanctions, the more indifferent the potential offenders, must be considered a sub-solution, because of the difficulty of combining the result with the predictability necessary for deterrence. Trade-offs in policy choices are debated in Chapter 5.

[18] See Frey (2009) – and note, in circumstances where crime is indeed the norm, the effect of rewarding deviations – in terms of honesty – may well be the more cost-efficient strategy.

and prosecuted) and perfect information, and take into account the fact that law enforcement is costly, crime would be deterred by an expected sanction that matched the distance between the offender's benefits and costs. The criminal law reaction does not need to reflect the total gain, because committing a crime usually involves costs. In principle, the optimal sanction matches what it takes to change the net benefit associated with the act from a positive to a negative value. According to this logic, a very small difference between the basket of benefits and the basket of costs implies that a very small sanction, such as a small fine or even merely a stern warning, would be sufficient to tilt the balance in favor of law abidingness. When the gain from crime is huge, compared to the costs, the optimal response must intensify accordingly.

We do not have perfect information about the two baskets, however, and, therefore, the practical use of this principle would have to rely on rough assumptions or minimum sanctions (what is necessary to secure the sufficient 'disutility' for a given group of potential offenders). In addition, there is no such thing as certain enforcement, especially not for a crime such as corruption, which is usually difficult to detect. For this reason, the potential offender is assumed to take *the risk* of sanctions into account, assessing the *expected* consequences (that is, the probability of a reaction multiplied by the consequences if the reaction happens). There-fore, for law enforcement to deter crime, the sanction assumed necessary to tilt the balance between the benefits and costs associated with the crime must be multiplied by the probability of detection. This intuition can be expressed as a simple formula: let p represent the probability, S the sanction, and ΔU the difference between benefits and costs associated with the choice of committing crime, and we have the sanction expressed by the following fraction: $S = \Delta U/p$.

A high risk of detection will imply a relatively lower sanction, while a low risk should imply that sanctions are multiplied accordingly. A problem with this simple assumption is that detection rates and sanction levels can influence the propensity to commit crime very differently. For some, the risk of detection matters much more than the sanction level. A high repression level cannot 'compensate' for a low detection rate if a low risk of detection leads the perpetrators to ignore the risk of sanctions.

4.2.2.1   Applying the sanction principle under resource constraints

Assuming for now that the sanction has the assumed impact, namely deterring crime if the repression level reflects the net benefit from crime divided on the probability of getting caught (that is, the formula above). If there are also resource constraints, what implications can be drawn from the relationship between the variables?

The obvious implication is that the more expensive the detection of crime, the higher the repression level should be – while keeping the expected deterrent effect constant. From a government perspective, however, it is important to keep a range of costs at a minimum while productive activity is generally promoted. From that perspective, the repression level is an expense found necessary to control crime, but at the same time, the higher the level, the more it prevents time and money being allocated to more productive uses. Especially when it comes to imprisonment, the burden of the penalty harms citizens who have nothing to do with the crime (such as the family of a prisoner). Accordingly, a heavy sanction must be considered also as a cost to society, and, like other costs, it should be kept as low as possible. And in order to keep the indirect costs associated with penalties at a minimum, the lack of knowledge about the deterrent effect of a sanction may just as well lead to a lower, instead of a higher, repression level, because both outcomes are associated with costs to society.[19]

Apparently, the closer that a sentence can be adjusted to the circumstances of the individual offender, the easier it may be to keep the sanction low – while still within the logic of the sanction principle. Individual variation in sanctions could be combined with the predictability needed for deterrence as long as the *principle* for determining the sanctions is predictable. If so, it might be fair to let a sanction, intended to counterbalance the expected net benefit of crime, differ across individuals. This is an important question: Would it be possible to keep a deterrent effect constant with relatively lower variable sanctions as long as potential perpetrators know that their individual circumstances are the starting point for a principled sanction decision? Among the relevant factors to be considered in such a sanction assessment would be the offender's *attitude toward risk*. For risk-attracted offenders (players on the stock market, for example), or for optimists, deterrence would require a higher sanction than that required to deter risk-averse individuals. Given the complex set of risk factors associated with crime, however, the

---

[19] Criminal justice sanctions will typically depend on the gravity of the crime, a principle associated primarily with retributive concerns, rather than with efficient deterrence. However, in settings where only the harm to society is observed, while the offender's assessment of benefits and costs is unknown, it makes sense to let the sanction reflect the level of harm. Such a rule will induce the decision-maker to take into account the consequences to society when considering a criminal act.

risk attitude is difficult to take into account, even at an abstract level.[20] A further factor (albeit one that is simpler to take into account) relevant for the question of individual sanctions is *crime competence*. Offenders who consider themselves very adept in 'the art of' conducting the specific form of crime, should – according to this concept – be sanctioned harder than those who know that they are clumsy. The clever offenders will have more confidence in their ability to avoid detection, and thus will 'need' a heavier sentence to counterbalance the benefit from crime. In other words, a lower deterrent effect implies a more severe sanction. Along the same lines of reasoning, it would make sense to let the sanction depend on the offender's social status. Famous people with ardent followers, for example, could be treated more severely so as to deter crime more efficiently, while the various indirect costs on society associated with sanctions could be reduced by treating a larger number of ordinary offenders more mildly.

The problem with this reasoning is the indirect consequences of a criminal justice system that operates with a different form of justice depending on the identity of the offender. Sanctioning the famous more heavily, for example, would signal that law abidingness among the more powerful or prominent members of society is seen by the system as more important than law abidingness among 'ordinary' citizens. Besides, a procedure that is supposed to take into account multiple factors that steer offenders' assessments of risks, leads to a very complicated calculation with highly uncertain estimates and assumptions. Instead of serving as a guiding sanction rule, such a calculation would easily expand the space for discretion in sanction decisions, and frustrate any attempt at creating predictability.

At the same time, if the various factors associated with the individual are *not* taken into account, the criminal justice system has to operate with a repression level based on perceived averages of various factors. This implies, however, that the level of deterrence will be suboptimal if the burden of sanctions on society and resource constraints are taken into account in the application of the simple sanction principle. Therefore, given the sanction principle expressed in the equation above, there will be some sub-optimality whether the actual sanctions are adjusted for personal factors or not.

---

[20] For many decision-makers, the risks of losing benefits by not committing crime could be more important than the risk of sanctions; if so, the risk-averse decision-maker would commit crime instead of – as is often assumed – being deterred more easily than risk-neutral decision-makers. (Søreide (2009) makes this point with reference to corruption.)

4.2.2.2 The sanction principle extended

Other factors that should be taken into account when deciding a sentence are 'crime elasticity,' recidivism, 'marginal deterrence,' and indirect consequences of a high repression level – each of which is addressed in turn in the following paragraphs.

Crime elasticity in terms of sanctions refers to the impact of a sanction on the propensity to commit crime.[21] The higher this elasticity (that is, the higher the impact of a sanction on the propensity to commit crime), the lower the sanction can be – while keeping expected crime deterrence constant. Following this reasoning, a serious crime can be met with a low sanction if the risk of being detected and sanctioned matters very much to the offenders. How much this (assumed or observed) elasticity should be taken into account is difficult to determine, because the offender's assessment of costs and benefits may change over time. If sanctions in one period are low because they are expected to have a relatively high impact on crime decisions, the sanction itself may have a lower impact in the next period. Therefore, perpetrators' perceived sensitivity to sanctions is relevant for sentencing and can be taken into account in sentencing if changes in crime elasticity over time are understood.

An obvious challenge to deterrence-based strategy is *recidivism*; repeat offenders demonstratively confirm the failure to deter. Total deterrence ('100 percent deterrence'), it should be noted, is not expected or sought from an economic efficiency perspective, because the marginal cost of pursuing offenders increases with the number of offenders detected and sanctioned, which makes it very costly to find and detect the last few percentage points of wrongdoers. Therefore, while a government can operate with zero tolerance for crime, some crime will continue to occur under the postulated optimal sanction strategy and resource constraints. Besides, offenders' sensitivity to criminal justice strategies will vary, possibly like a normal probability distribution. Offenders who have clearly demonstrated that they are difficult to deter – because they commit crime repeatedly – should face stricter sanctions.[22] To what extent a sanction should depend on an offender's history is not clear, however, especially because the objective of protecting society may be more important than efficient deterrence, and calls for incarceration or debarment from professional services in such cases.

---

[21] The term is explained by Gary Becker (1968) – and his application of the term is further described by Antony Dnes (2000), see in particular, pp. 74–75.

[22] In principle, a sanction strategy that is already found optimal cannot be made more optimal, see Polinsky and Shavel (2007) – and this argument could be seen as an underlying assumption of sub-optimality.

Equally important when it comes to sanctioning offenders who are hard to deter is to adjust the sanction for *marginal deterrence*: In order to prevent an offender from committing several crimes at the same time, the repression level should increase with the number of offenses, that is, added crime is deterred at the margin. The logic is that if we expect some crime to happen, the criminal justice system should aim for sanctions that reduce the damage of the crime that is not deterred. A very brutal sanction, against corruption, for example, may incentivize an offender to kill the witnesses to the corrupt acts, and thus, too harsh a sanction might actually encourage such added crime. And, with the purpose of inducing the offender to refrain from committing the most serious forms of crime, the sanction should be more severe for crimes with more damaging consequences. Hence, marginal deterrence is the economic argument for a harm-based hierarchy of sanctions, while among legal scholars it is often defended with reference to retribution.

Such scaling of sanctions, however, requires space for high repression levels. If the offender has already been sentenced to a hundred years in prison for her corruption, sentencing her to another hundred for money laundering activities makes no sense. Given the aim of general predictability, the concern for marginal deterrence implies upper limits for sentencing; marginal deterrence cannot be taken into account only in those cases where several offenses are combined.

An upper limit on sanctions may be wise for several other reasons, too. One concern is the above-mentioned impact of detection, which may matter relatively more to many offenders than what the simple sanction principle proposes. Another concern is the problems associated with a brutalized criminal justice system. Instead of being faced with widespread condemnation, offenders subject to brutal punishments may excite sympathy or even empathy among the general public. And witnesses may prefer to stay silent, instead of blowing the whistle on crime.

A possible strategy for combining the various arguments on optimal sanctions is to expand the number of sanction options. Economic reasoning around crime strategies tends to address the repression level as a one-dimensional variable (that is, higher or lower repression). Instead, the sentence options could be considered a vector, with multiple sanction options, each with its different purpose and repression levels. Alternatives to monetary fines and imprisonment are community service, victim compensation, exclusion from professional service provision, and various forms of rehabilitation.

4.3 A CLASH BETWEEN CAMPS? LAW'S SKEPTICISM TOWARD ECONOMIC SOLUTIONS

Economic thinking has influenced criminal law significantly in many ways, in many countries, and for many years. Inspired by arguments stemming from Cesare Beccaria's *Of Crimes and Punishments* (1764) and Jeremy Bentham's *An Introduction to the Principles of Morals and Legislation* (1789), economists have enriched the debate about criminal law as a crime prevention strategy and challenged arguments around retribution. With Gary Becker's *Crime and Punishment: An Economic Approach* (1968), the discipline introduced the analytical framework (partly described above) for explaining the trade-offs between enforcement costs and the damage caused by a crime, which led to postulated principles for the optimal allocation of law enforcement resources. The discipline's empirical and theoretical analyses have cast light on how offenders optimize their crime decisions and expanded our understanding of crime combinations and substitute offenses. In combination with sociology, the economic discipline has (to the irritation of many legal scholars) disputed legal doctrines, and its purest utilitarian ideas have provoked legal thinkers to explain and defend the values enshrined in criminal justice systems.

4.3.1 Law's Main Concern about the Economics of Crime

The field of economics shares the legal discipline's strong normative motivation, and members of both disciplines are inclined to ask, 'What is the right, or optimal, response to revealed cases of crime?' For both disciplines, the definition of 'optimal' is a composite one, although the nature of that composition differs substantially. And so, while both disciplines appear fascinated to discover how far crime can be regulated through the criminal justice system, the economist and the legal scholar will develop their strategies on very different sets of premises.

These differences not only prevent many economists and legal scholars from understanding one another's reasoning; their ignorance may also prevent them from seeing what hinders the implementation of their own policy suggestions: The economist explains the steps toward more efficient anticorruption solutions without knowledge about what legal barriers will prevent the efficiency gains from materializing. The legal scholar proposes anticorruption rules without realizing why the economist might be right about the risk of counterintuitive consequences.

Legal scholars rarely, if ever, disagree with the aim of preventing crime, they nonetheless accuse economists of having a simplistic, one-dimensional, deterrence-fixated attitude toward criminal justice processes. The main purpose of such processes, the legal scholars argue, should be to place blame correctly, regardless of what impact the sanctions may have on other members of society. Exactly how blame is placed correctly is not so clear, however. As discussed in Chapter 1, there is substantial variation across countries regarding sentencing principles and practices. Searching for answers in the philosophy of criminal sentencing objectives offers little guidance, as there are so many answers – which in different ways have shaped today's criminal law. Within the legal discipline there is consensus that fairness and moral values matter, but apparently, no clear agreement around what constitutes 'the right repression level.' This perception is confirmed by Michael Tonry, upon a review of the literature, as he maintains that 'it is regrettable that contemporary conceptions of just punishment are at best muddled and morally incoherent and at worst non-existent ...' and he continues, 'we need better ways to talk and think about what may justly be done to and with offenders' (Tonry 2011:24).

What many legal scholars seem to agree on, however, is how economists' narrow focus on deterrence easily leads to perverse effects, with criminal law procedure, human rights, and the offender's rational ability to accept guilt all regarded as of minor importance, as long as someone is punished so that *others* are discouraged from committing crime. Economic reasoning also seems to suggest that the individual who is punished for a crime should be treated harshly, not because he or she necessarily deserves harsh treatment, but for the purpose of achieving larger aims in society. Many legal scholars disapprove of this use (or abuse) of individuals for other ends. From the legal perspective, a fair and transparent criminal justice process is likely to have *indirect deterrent effects* if citizens generally agree with the processes by which law is developed and approve of the performance of criminal justice institutions. The essence of law's criticism of economics is therefore not economists' focus on deterrence per se, but rather the normative implications of the most basic economic analyses, which are interpreted by legal scholars primarily as a defense of a threat-based criminal justice system. This perception is strengthened by the technical way in which economists tend to present their arguments, typically addressing one mechanism at a time; assuming everything else to be either constant, absent, or simplified; and making no reference to the legal conditions for punishing citizens.

4.3.2 Bridging the Camps

Law's criticism of economics is not inaccurate but it is misleading. The law camp should read the economic analyses for what they are. Economic analysis is a tool for investigating the consequences of individual choices and government strategies. Even if most economic models optimize deterrence, the methodology could equally well be applied to optimize strategies for, say, fairness or safety. The methodology's main virtue vis-à-vis many other social science analyses is the precision of the arguments. This precision requires simplification, even though, in practice, many processes, interactions, and decisions happen in parallel. The chosen conjectures for a specific problem are spelled out in the presentation of results, while underlying assumptions are usually left unstated. Options and constraints on decisions are kept to a minimum in these theories. For noneconomists, the results of economic analysis can easily appear to be gross simplifications of the mechanisms at play in a society. Like everybody else, however, economists know that a society's complexity will reduce the general validity of arguments developed under assumptions of an oversimplified reality. What is truly worth critical debate is the selection of factors put into the analysis: Are they really the *most* important ones? We have seen rapid improvements in data sources on a range of areas over the last twenty to thirty years. The more facts that are known about a phenomenon, the sharper can be the critical debate about theoretical assumptions – because, as mentioned above, the theoretical elements included in an analysis should match the available empirical knowledge.

Even if the economic method per se is neutral in terms of value judgments, the discipline can be blamed for indirectly encouraging analysis of certain aspects of decision-making at the expense of others, especially if students learn about theories that systematically omit elements that should not be neglected. Monetary values, for example, are important, even for individuals who consider themselves antimaterialist. Nonetheless, such values may have been overemphasized, especially when it comes to studies of choices by individuals whose basic material needs are already satisfied. Until recently, the matter of fairness was seldom analyzed by economists; thanks to Amartya Sen (2001, 2011), among others, this is now a far more common theme in economic studies, and it has been brought into economic crime research by Thomas Miceli (1991), and Steven Shavell and Mitchell Polinsky (2000), among others. Group dynamics are still not widely studied, but economists such as Jean Tirole (1996) have started to explain why choices will, importantly, often

depend on group belonging and loyalty.[23] Traditionally, the moral cost –
or the individual's emotional burden of violating a law – has often been
treated as an exogenous parameter; encouragingly, many economists have
now started to ask where these moral costs come from.

4.3.3   Humankind as a Moral and Social Animal

The key to bridging law and economics seems to lie in the recognition of
humankind as a moral and social animal. Of course, a constructive
dialogue about how the criminal justice system can and should offer a
corrective to undesired acts by placing blame and imposing sanctions
also requires the participants to accept that neither of the disciplines has
a firmer grasp than the other on the truth. In terms of policy implications,
this is extremely challenging terrain, because the knowledge about how
we behave, what choices we make, and how they can be influenced by
government-steered mechanisms is highly fragmented, and many results
of behavioral studies are hotly disputed.

In order to better understand the importance of the relevant results we
do have in behavioral economics, some of which are listed briefly in this
chapter's first section, I consulted Bertil Tungodden, a professor of
economics at the Norwegian School of Economics (NHH). He is also the
co-director of The Choice Lab, a research center that designs experiments
that are implemented in controlled laboratory or field settings. Among his
research interests are humans' propensity to make ethical choices and the
importance of fairness in a policy perspective.[24] In the interview, Bertil
Tungodden gave an answer to two questions as follows.

Q: How has behavioral economics changed the economics of crime?

A main contribution of behavioral and experimental economics has
been to show convincingly that people are motivated by more than
narrow economic self-interest, in particular, that people in many
situations are morally motivated. An immediate implication of this
insight is that to understand criminal behavior, one has to understand
the moral considerations involved in criminal activity. To illustrate,
think of tax evasion. The classical work on tax evasion by Michael G.
Allingham and Agnar Sandmo [1972] took as a starting point that

---

[23]   See also Bénabou and Tirole (2011), and Acemoglu and Jackson (2014).
[24]   Interview with author, 31 July 2015. See Bertil Tungodden's website at
NHH: http://www.nhh.no/Default.aspx?ID=731. For information about The
Choice Lab, see http://blogg.nhh.no/thechoicelab/.

people made a trade-off between the expected economic gain from avoiding taxes and the expected economic costs if caught and penalized. Inspired by insights from behavioral economics, however, recent work on tax evasion has studied how moral motivation interacts with these economic considerations and how governments may intervene to strengthen the moral motivation of taxpayers. Many interesting research questions arise from this perspective; it is, for example, not obvious that moral motivation always pulls in the direction of less tax evasion (or, more generally, less crime). Many economic experiments have shown that people are conditional contributors, who find it morally right to contribute to a public good if others contribute, but, importantly, also find it morally right not to contribute if others do not contribute. As a consequence, the moral perspective may explain why it is so difficult to get some economies or societies (think, for example, of Greece) out of a bad equilibrium where most people do not pay taxes; in such a setting, people may find it morally justifiable that they themselves do not pay taxes, which makes it hard to build a tax culture. A similar line of reasoning applies to many other important questions in the economics of crime, for example, corruption. Behavioral economics has also brought another research avenue into the economics of crime, by showing that people are also consistently irrational. Phenomena like lack of self-control and loss aversion may also shed light on criminal behavior, so these are exciting times for those who work in the intersection between behavioral economics and the economics of crime.

Q: What is the origin of moral costs?

This is a very deep question that has been discussed extensively in philosophy and is now studied empirically by economists, psychologists, and philosophers. I like to think of us as having a moral capacity in the same way as we have a capacity for language, where this moral capacity is shaped by experiences. Experiences may therefore shape both what we consider the morally right thing to do and the weight we attached to moral considerations, and there are a number of ongoing field experiments that systematically study how childhood experiences, education, political institutions, and other factors shape moral costs. Interestingly, the moral costs may be context dependent; we may have very different moral ideals when acting as a parent than when acting as a business partner. For example, a recent paper in [the journal] *Nature* by Alain Cohn, Ernst Fehr, and Michel André Maréchal [2014] shows experimental evidence of how the prevailing business culture in the banking industry weakens and undermines a norm of honesty. Findings like this open up a new set of questions for economists, because they suggest that we cannot focus only on how to optimally design institutions for a given set of preferences of people (in the private or public sector); we also need to look at how these institutions shape our preferences, including our moral motivation. Another interesting question is how moral costs depend on whether we are observed by others. Some people claim that we only act morally in order to signal to others, but in ongoing work with coauthors I examine evidence suggesting that this is not the full story. Even if no one else observes you, most people choose to behave (at least to some extent) morally. This may serve as a self-signal – we want to show to ourselves that we are decent people – but it may also simply be that we want to do what we think is the right thing in a given situation.

These insights from Bertil Tungodden suggest that economics is a discipline making rapid progress when it comes to exploring the role of moral values and choices. If this development is matched by legal scholars blazing new trails as they search for new knowledge about how to devise efficient strategies for better crime control, the two disciplines may meet up in the same place without the need for bridges. Whether that much of a harmony between the two disciplines is welcome and helpful is another question. Despite various developments toward a common understanding of the mechanisms at play, the economics of crime maintains its utilitarian approach, something that many legal scholars will continue to find difficult to accept. The differences in their approaches reflect the complexity of criminal justice processes in society and the multiplicity of objectives behind criminal justice policies. Whether or not they are closer to singing in harmony with legal scholars, economists will continue enriching (or annoying) legal scholarly debates with their analyses of incentives and efficient strategies, and their empirical scrutiny of established facts. With these perspectives in mind, we now turn to the economics of corruption.

4.4   THE DISTINCT ECONOMIC FEATURES OF CORRUPTION

For several reasons, corruption is different from other forms of crime, and this fact should be reflected in criminal justice responses to the problem. In particular, the specific features of the crime influence the design of optimal systems for monitoring it and define the opportunities for using self-reporting mechanisms to prevent it.

4.4.1 The Crime of Corrupt Decision-Making

As discussed in Chapter 1, it makes sense to study the crime of corruption from a bargain perspective. Corrupt decisions made by public institutions involve state administrative bodies when it comes to both committing the crime and to monitoring and enforcing the laws against the problem. If we are to assess the performance of monitoring and law enforcement, we thus need to understand how closely, formally and informally, the law-breaking institution and the law-enforcing institution are located within a *government hierarchy*.

When the (public) law-enforcing institution and the (public) law-breaking institution are far apart, vertically or horizontally, and function independently, the crime can be investigated and sanctions can be imposed almost as if the crime had been conducted by a player in the private sector. But when the law enforcement institution and the law-breaking institution are very close (geographically, structurally, or informally), they will sometimes act as if they are part of the same decision-making unit. Consider, for example, an oil ministry and a state-owned oil company with industry-regulating responsibility. In Nigeria, Kazakhstan, and Angola, for example, critics have claimed that these institutions act as one unit while still being sufficiently separate enough to hide from public scrutiny the details of comprehensive corruption carried out by regulators and incumbent politicians. Corruption in such cases is facilitated because the checks and balances between the institutions are fictional.[25] Position in a state administrative hierarchy matters no less for law enforcement vis-à-vis individual decision-makers. In many countries, decision-makers above a certain level of authority enjoy a de facto impunity, and thus the outcomes of anticorruption law enforcement actions often depend on *the rank of the offender*, no matter what formal systems of legal egalitarianism exist. While impunity for the powerful is symptomatic for corruption, it is a problem for other forms of crime as well.

Another feature of corruption that differentiates it from most other forms of crime is how it is embedded in the unique powers held by state administrative institutions. Law enforcement itself is therefore vulnerable

---

[25] See debates and results in Victor, Hults and Thurber (2011), Mahdavi (2014), Shaxson (2007), Al-Kasim, Søreide and Williams (2008).

to corruption. The clichéd types of police corruption (for example, traffic officials who demand bribes for not imposing penalties for traffic violations that were never committed) are just one expression of this problem. The problem is also manifested in legal stipulations and bureaucratic rules that are exploited for corrupt gain, and in vague or outdated legal definitions of corruption. This is why the most up-to-date best practice anticorruption legislation is found in countries where the problem is perceived to be relatively minor. Low levels of corruption are not necessarily the result of excellent regulations; they may instead reflect how easily laws are implemented when the society is already receptive to them. In other words, *how corruption may distort criminal justice approaches* throughout the law enforcement value chain is important to understand how corruption in a society is carried out.

Like participants in many other forms of crime, the players involved in corruption act at the mercy of one another. In a corrupt deal, the two sides (if not more) involved must trust each other both to stay silent about the crime and to share the gains according to the illegal agreement they have made. The more symmetric *the bargaining powers* between them, the easier it is to penetrate this trust with law enforcement tools. Corruption differs from other crimes – for example, a bank robbery, where those involved make a deal on how to collaborate to break into a bank and share the proceeds – in that the deal itself *is* the crime. This implies that those involved can better control various crime-determining factors. In particular, if we see corruption as a sale of decisions, the price can be adapted to the cost, and therefore the potential gain for the player with the largest bargaining power becomes endogenous, instead of exogenous. To clarify with an example: Bank robbers can negotiate how to share the proceeds of the crime between them, but those negotiations will not influence the total obtainable gain for those involved, which depends on the amount of gold or cash in the bank vault. When it comes to corruption, the very negotiations *are* what determine the gain from the crime (though within the limits of what each player can control). This is why the allocation of bargaining powers – ranging from very asymmetric and extortive corruption to the more symmetric and collusive deals – is so important to understand the problem's presence and consequences. The bargaining powers in these deals will depend on the discretionary authority of the decision-maker and access to various types of information.

4.4.2 Exchange of Information and Transaction Costs

Economists often emphasize how corruption depends on who knows what. Citizens will normally vote for the leaders they *believe* will act accountably, although they do not know for certain whom they can trust. The true intention of those who come to power is the leaders' *hidden knowledge.* Moreover, regardless of the selected leaders' honesty, once in power, they have to delegate authority in a bureaucratic structure even though they do not have *full information* about their staff's integrity. This lack of oversight by the leadership can be exploited by dishonest staff who are authorized to make decisions on behalf of their state institution. By law, some institutions are kept at arm's length from the political level so as to reduce the risk of populist interference in their work. However, neither politicians nor voters can tell for certain if such independence enhances integrity; there is, in other words, a *lack of information* about true decision-making. Furthermore, the regulatory independence from politics may in fact allow powerful clients more space to influence government decisions, a problem referred to in the literature as 'regulatory capture.'[26] Law enforcement is also vulnerable to this problem, because trusted decision-makers – such as judges in courts – are given wide discretionary authority. For outsiders as well as for those involved, it can be hard to tell how honestly the judges reach their verdicts; we have *incomplete information* about their decision-making processes.[27]

4.4.2.1 Bureaucratic structures

The different cells in Table 2.2 in Chapter 2 contain numerous examples of how corruption is contingent on someone's lack of information, and in each of the cases, corruption may continue if those supposed to exercise oversight of the institutions do not have the information that would otherwise have prompted a reaction against a trusted but dishonest decision-maker. Large parts of the economic literature on corruption apply a principal-agent framework for analyzing the allocation of authority to individuals whose integrity is uncertain, a framework in which the 'principal' (for example, a leader or the voters) faces constraints in

---

[26] See Dal Bo (2006).

[27] By 'transaction costs' economists refer to the costs of taking part in economic activity – broadly understood, the expenses associated with the activity of purchasing or selling goods and services. For more explanation, see Niehans (1987) and Klaes (2000).

monitoring an agent (for example, staff or elected leaders).[28] Principal-agent models assume that the interests of the principal and the agent diverge, meaning that there is 'information asymmetry' to the advantage of the agent while the principal can prescribe the rules regarding factors that are important to the agent, including wages, exact responsibilities, and reporting requirements. In determining these variables, the principal takes into account the trade-offs between the various costs and his or her assumptions about how the agent will adapt to the rules. The problem solved by this field of economic reasoning is how the principal, who bears both the failure costs and the monitoring costs, should seek to induce the agent to perform in line with his or her goals (which are assumed to overlap with the goals of the institution) while keeping inspection costs at a minimum. The principal's challenge is easier to solve to the extent that *the performance targets are more observable* and the *organization's aims are more precisely defined*: the clearer the objectives of the institution, the easier it is to detect departure from them.

Conceptually, the principal-agent framework is useful for understanding corruption risks and solutions. In many settings, however, the principal in reality relies on the reports of a third-party player – a monitor that provides information about several agents' performance. A government agency relies on the observations described by an auditor, a tax official or a customs official, for example, while voters who evaluate the performance of their politicians rely on the 'facts' presented by journalists, civil society, and academic researchers. In such scenarios, it is relevant to ask: What is the principal's optimal control mechanism when there is a high risk of collusion between the monitor and the agent? What is now the most optimal anticorruption strategy? How can this collusion be made more difficult or less tempting, while monitoring costs are minimized?[29]

In many contexts, however, leaders/principals are informed about corruption but nonetheless fail to react against the crime. Why? One reason could be that they are themselves involved in some form of collusion with their dishonest staff/agents. Perhaps they obtain *side-payments* or some nonmonetary compensation for allowing their staff's corruption to continue. Another reason could be that the leaders expect negative net benefit from reacting against the crime. Under circumstances

---

[28] The principal is understood as the one with oversight responsibility and interests that are aligned with an idea of a social optimum/development of society as a whole. For explanation, see Sappington (1991) and Stiglitz (1987).

[29] See Myerson (1986), Rahman (2012), and Ortner and Chassang (2014).

where corruption is entrenched in society, leaders who observe dishonesty in their organizations may find it too difficult or too costly to try to curb the problem, and thus they fail to react against crime. Economists use the term 'coordination problem' to describe a situation in which individual decision-makers – leaders, their subordinates, and their subordinates' subordinates – all seem to consider counteractions too costly, even if each decision-maker might have taken steps if others were inclined to take action as well.[30]

4.4.2.2 Loyalty to the corrupt deal

The matter of asymmetric information is also relevant to understand the deal between the public sector decision-maker (the agent), who demands a bribe, and the external client, who pays the bribe. Depending on the setting, incomplete information creates a lot of 'transaction costs,' including the costs of selecting partners for the corrupt deal, determining the conditions of the deal, finding ways of concealing the deal, laundering the proceedings, and making sure the 'contract' can be enforced. The contract is illegal and obviously cannot be enforced with the help of formal law enforcement institutions. The parties involved will not necessarily deliver their parts of the deal simultaneously, and in many cases there is a risk that the counterpart will deviate from the deal halfway through the plan or, worse, reveal the counterpart's involvement (for example, in exchange for lenient criminal law treatment). Long-term agreements – for example, between private sector corporations and corrupt politicians – are not necessarily stable, because powerful government decision-makers may denounce their connections and end their biased decision-making habits in order to win public approval.

For those involved, the corrupt deals can be more easily enforced – as Johan Graf Lambsdorff (2002) explains – if:

(1)   they are *repeated* (those involved meet several times);
(2)   those involved gain from nurturing a *reputation* for being reliable (as do middlemen or information brokers who have professionalized their corruption-facilitating services);
(3)   those involved can create a *joint unit* that profits from the corrupt deal, typically a co-owned company, so that both parties benefit when their corrupt deal is enforced;

---

[30]   In the literature on corruption, especially in political science, this is also referred to as a problem of 'collective action' – see Persson, Rothstein, and Teorell (2013).

(4)   payments can be made *in steps* (for example, payments are made before and after the counterpart has done his or her part); or

(5)   the deal can be strengthened by *social ties* (for example, members of the same family participate in a corrupt deal).[31]

The difficulties of successfully carrying out corrupt deals helps deter such crime. This is why transparency initiatives will sometimes have a clearer deterrent effect on corruption than the tools applied by the criminal justice system. Enhanced access to information about public contracting, the performance of state institutions, the personal finances for key decision-makers, and potential conflicts of interest are all important anticorruption tools, simply because the availability of such information adds to the transaction costs for those involved in the crime, who have to do more and be more creative to carry out the corruption.

4.4.3   The Impact of Control and Sanctions

The unique mechanisms of corruption determine the likely deterrent impact of monitoring and sanctions. As described in Chapter 2, those who control scarce resources or assess clients' qualifications for receiving certain benefits are in a position to demand bribes. The scarcer the resources, the more decisive the assessment of qualifications, the more important the benefits for the clients, and the higher the client's ability to pay, the higher the obtainable bribes.

The bribe functions as a price that balances demand and supply; thus, the higher the demand, the higher the price. However, the official can *create* shortages if the benefits are not already scarce.[32] For example, even if there is enough space in the port for all ships to offload their cargoes or a sufficient electricity supply to satisfy all who apply for access to it, the official controlling the port or the connectivity to the electricity network may restrict access by working very slowly or creating obstacles for service delivery unless bribes are paid (tactics used even at a political level). Likewise, in order to induce bribery, the official can make it clear that her or his assessment of qualifications will depend

---

[31]   Lambsdorff (2002) and Rose-Ackerman (1999) provide more explanation and examples. The transaction costs associated with corrupt deals are important reasons why it might be difficult for foreign firms to enter a market with high levels of corruption. Even firms that might be inclined to make bribe payments may have difficulties entering a market where business partners have found a way to handle these different aspects of corruption.

[32]   See Rose-Ackerman (1975) for analysis.

on a bribe (for example, by acting as if highly doubtful about the client's qualifications) regardless of whether the client's aim is to obtain a benefit (for example, a license for production or import, or permission to construct a building) or avoid a cost (for example, a fine for pollution or for failing to implement safety measures).

The civil servant's control over the decisions that create the opportunity for corrupt deals influences both the impact of detection strategies and the impact of sanctions. We will consider each in turn.

With corruption, as with other forms of crime, a higher than expected cost associated with committing the crime (a higher risk of detection and/or a higher penalty if caught in the crime) can be expected to have a crime-preventive effect. When it comes to corruption, however, the impact of law enforcement strategies is more difficult to predict because the officials will often be able to adapt their corruption to the form of oversight. An increase in the frequency and intensity of controls ought to reduce the propensities for corruption. But if the corrupt officials control the price of the decisions they sell (for example, because their clients are unqualified for the benefits they are seeking), they can simply let the higher cost be reflected in a higher price, which they can demand to compensate them for the now higher burden (that is, the higher risks) of selling decisions. This means that the frequency of the corrupt decisions can be reduced and/or the proportion of dishonest officials within an institution decreased, but the officials still involved in corruption may earn just as much or even more from it. For society, the decisions that are now for sale at a higher price may well be of a more damaging sort, because the price for selling small deviations from what would otherwise have been decided is now likely to be too low for the official; big deviations can be sold for high prices. Therefore, the risk exists that monitoring may only *appear* to be a successful strategy; in reality, corruption may continue to distort decision-making while those involved reap the same amount of illegal revenue. Even if the consequences of sanctions grow more severe when the size of bribes increases, or the strategies for hiding ill-gotten gains become more cumbersome, the price-effect may well outweigh the higher costs.[33]

The same argument applies when it comes to the likely impact of penalties imposed on those found guilty of corruption: the size of the bribe can be raised to compensate the official for the higher risk

---

[33] The arguments in this section stem from Rose-Ackerman (1978). For further explanation, see Rose-Ackerman and Palifka (2016), and Søreide and Rose-Ackerman (2016).

associated with the sale of government decisions. As long as clients are willing to pay for the decisions in question, the bribe may exceed the expected cost associated with sanctions and thus undermine the deterrent effect of a higher repression level. For this reason, there are limits to what can be achieved in terms of anticorruption by relying solely on recommendations offered by the classic law and economics literature. It is, therefore, important to combine such strategies with other anticorruption approaches. The implementation of controls on procedure should be combined with various forms of control on performance. Institutions can be reorganized, and corruption reduced, by reducing officials' monopoly authority.[34] In organizations where corruption has become entrenched, close ties between corrupt colleagues can be broken, staff can be rotated geographically, authority can be placed in competing units, and officials can be given overlapping jurisdictions (geographically or thematically) so that clients can find an alternative decision-maker if the one they first approach asks for bribes. Third-party players can have enhanced access to information about decision-making. Clients who meet the demand for bribes can be given opportunities to safely file complaints. In addition, a strategy that takes these mechanisms into account should induce the officials that have become deterred from corrupt decision-making (for example, through a strategy of intensified monitoring) to report on their still corrupt colleagues. In fact, there should also be a strategy for encouraging those who are part of the corrupt deal to report their own crime.

4.4.4 Incentives for Self-Reporting

Expecting those who commit a crime to report their own wrongdoings may seem contrary to the rationality assumption discussed in section 1.2. A bank robber is rarely expected to admit her or his crime unless already strongly suspected of the crime and aware that a confession might lead to a milder treatment. Why would those involved in corruption be less reticent?

The answer lies in the nature of the crime: a corrupt deal takes two (or more) players, and the more that these players' attitudes, values, and reference points differ, the easier it is to break whatever trust exists between them. Consider, for example, the business woman meeting a corrupt high-ranking government official to negotiate the details of a

---

[34] Organization and information – Tirole (staff rotation, competition, overlapping jurisdictions).

sole-source procurement bid, which the official will accept in exchange for a bribe to exempt the bid from the rule of competitive bidding. Or consider the farmer who is visited by a corrupt inspector who is supposed to check whether the farm abides by various safety standards. Compared to a group of criminals who collaborate in robbing a bank, the business woman and the official overseeing public procurement, and the farmer and the farm inspector, may have very little in common. The empathy they feel for each other is limited, and unless they need each other for similar deals in the future, each party may have little reason to protect their counterpart.

The more numerous and wider the differences between them – in terms of how they benefit from the deal and their personal characteristics – the more asymmetric the bargaining powers between them, and the more likely they are to betray the deal. In cases of extortive corruption, where the bribe payers hate to pay but feel compelled to do so, they may need little encouragement to admit the facts and betray their counterpart. Offering the bribe payer a small reward for providing the facts of the case instead of imposing a penalty for being part of a corrupt deal will raise the risks for those officials who demand bribes. An individual's growing concern that her or his counterpart will report the crime first, and thereby gain full leniency, leaving the individual to be punished by the criminal justice system, may tip the scales in favor of reporting, even if the individual firmly intended to stick to the deal originally. Martin Dufwenberg and Giancarlo Spagnolo (2015) have studied various aspects of such initiatives.[35] For such a scheme to work, a clear and predictable benefit must be provided to the party who reports the case first. For full leniency to be offered, the case should be admitted before the crime is suspected by investigators. While debates in the literature have circled around the bribers' opportunity to report the demand for bribes, the intended deterrent effect occurs if any of the parties is incentivized to report their corruption. What is particularly important to note is how asymmetric powers between those involved makes it easier to demand a bribe while making it easier for law enforcers to reveal and deal with the problem.[36]

There are trade-offs in the implementation of self-reporting rewards, however. Intuitively, an offender who reports the crime should not be fully excused, as this would limit the deterrent effect of law enforcement

[35] See also Basu and Cordella (2014).
[36] This is why extortive corruption is highly eradicated as countries' income level and institutional capacity improves, while the more collusive forms of corruption – where those involved are less likely to betray their counterpart – are a problem in countries at all income levels (Auriol, 2014).

initiatives. At the same time, the higher the benefits associated with a confession, the more likely the offenders are to self-report. In other words, it is possible to exploit *information asymmetries* between the parties for more efficient law enforcement. The right balance between these concerns is difficult to find, especially in light of the following three reasons:

(1) *Encouraging self-incrimination*: A substantial reward for those who confess may tempt innocent, but suspected, players to admit offenses for which they have no liability so as to avoid what they consider a likely sanction. In the extreme, the real offender may go free.

(2) *Offering sanction rebates:* A substantial sanction rebate (that is, reduced penalty) upon confession when suspected may alter the deterrent effect of a sanction. If it is possible for an individual to make a small payment when detected of wrongdoing, that penalty becomes a price (or a tax) that can be paid for continued corrupt practice. In the extreme, the penalty rebate increases the frequency of the problem instead of deterring the crime.

(3) *Reaching for unsuspected offenders:* Law enforcement expenses would decrease if a penalty rebate or substantial reward were offered to incentivize those who are not already suspected of crime to come forward and confess their crime. Taking such a step, however, intensifies the problems listed under (1) and (2).

So far, economists have found no definitive answer to the problem of how to combine the different goals in crime deterrence while promoting self-reporting. While economic arguments are generally in favor of self-reporting, unanswered questions remain, including at what stage of an investigation leniency should (still) be offered.

Inferences of economic reasoning for the development of criminal justice strategies are summarized at the end of this chapter. What is now important to consider, before we get to that summary, is the economic reasoning around the fact that corruption is often associated with organizations, rather than individual decision-makers.

4.5 THE DISTINCT FEATURE OF CORPORATE LIABILITY

Corruption is a crime that is associated in different ways with the work performed by organizations. Consider for example how officials in state institutions and representatives of political parties may demand bribes because it benefits their cronies. Police or tax officials may share the gains of their corruption with their colleagues. Politicians may spend illegal bribe revenues to campaign for votes for their party; it is not necessarily spent for their personal consumption. Bribes are often paid to secure benefits and profits for an organization. A bribe may be what helps a firm entering a foreign market secure its barriers against competition. A bribe may be the only way for a nongovernmental organization to obtain information needed for its development-motivated work. There is no shortage of examples of bribery conducted for the benefit of organizations.

From a legal perspective, it is difficult to apply the ordinary criminal justice principles[37] when a crime appears to have been committed by organizations, because those principles were developed for the purpose of holding individuals responsible. Economists, who are less wedded to these principles, approach the problem of corrupt organizations by seeking to determine what regulatory steps are required to induce leaders in organizations to control their own and their staffs' inclinations to commit corruption. After all, the leaders are in command and, compared with external monitors, are in a better position to know the organization's various activities. What form of criminal justice strategies and sanctions will induce these leaders to improve their organization's compliance with the law? What trade-offs can be made to help reach this goal? And how can organizations, like individuals, be incentivized to self-report and collaborate with prosecutors? These questions are considered in turn.

4.5.1   Incentivizing Organizations for Compliance

Even if corrupt activity is associated with the economic activities conducted by organizations, including corporations, the decision to commit crime is made by individuals. Under circumstances when (1) an entire organization or a group of colleagues appears to have benefited from a corrupt act, and (2) it is difficult to determine who in an organization conducted the crime, as well as who made or condoned the decision to go ahead with the crime, a law enforcement solution is to sanction the organization or group as a whole; the alternative option is simply to do nothing – to fail to react against the crime because it is impossible to tell who within an organization is criminally liable.

---

[37]   Described above, section 4.1.

For law enforcers who have this goal and have the tool of criminal justice sanctions at their disposal, two options present themselves: sanctioning the organization for what its members have done, or sanctioning individual members for what the organization has done. In practice, whichever of these options is taken seems to depend largely on the form or nature of the organization. For example, if it is known that a crime has been committed by a family member or a villager, but it is not known exactly who is responsible, most jurisdictions do not hold the whole family or entire village criminally liable (even if such sanctions would have induced group pressure for law compliance). However, when it comes to *organized crime*, many jurisdictions do hold individual members liable for the crime committed by the organization (that is, individuals are charged because of their membership or because membership is illegal). When it comes to *organizations that sometimes commit crime* (such as registered corporations and civil society organizations), a third approach is common: the organization is sanctioned (for example, with a heavy fine) but its employees (including the individuals who were in a position to decide to conduct the crime and/or who have profited from the crime) are not held liable unless evidence for their direct involvement is available.

From an economic perspective, distinguishing between these different categories of law enforcement problems vis-à-vis organizations is conceptually challenging. An individual's ability to choose whether to be involved in a crime or not could be one important factor in determining group liability. Family members and villagers can rarely choose their family or neighbors. Most organizations, however, consist of members or employees who can choose to leave. The difference between a mafia group that commits serious crime but also offers many services that citizens appreciate (for example, financial services, insurance, security, and conflict resolution), and a registered organization that commits serious crime and also offers various services or products that citizens appreciate is not clear, however. Mafia organizations are often associated with violent acts, but this is not a precondition for network-based crime. Furthermore, the corruption and other forms of crime conducted or encouraged by formally registered corporations can also involve violence, including murder. Unless a clear and substantial distinction can be found, it is difficult to defend different approaches to law enforcement vis-à-vis the different forms of organization.[38]

---

[38]   The organized crime definition is not necessarily set by the group itself, and the group members are not necessarily mandated to break the law and use

Leaving that difficulty aside for a while, consider for the sake of simplicity a private sector corporation: What form of group liability will best serve to prevent crime? According to the logic of the deterrence strategy described above, guilty individuals typically escape with lower than expected consequences when group sanctions are applied, as compared with the situation in which the guilty are identified and sanctioned while the organization as a whole and remaining staff face no criminal law enforcement reaction. Given the economic cost-benefit approach to optimal law enforcement, the intuitive solution would be an adjustment of the sanction, with group sanctions set at a sufficiently severe level that individual decision-makers (whoever they are) will take into account the consequences of the sanctions (for the organization and, indirectly, for themselves) even if they personally can hide behind corporate structures or liability placed on the organization's management. Such sanctions will promote self-policing in the organization, and a higher level of compliance will follow as a result.

The problem with this approach is that higher risk is imposed on those who are innocent, whether they are lower-level staff members, who may be punished indirectly if a sanction compels an organization to lay off staff, or high-level leaders, who may go to prison for the crimes committed by members of their staff. This higher risk is a burden, particularly for those who are honest and who have no control over the decision to commit a crime. Traditionally, *economic* reasoning around crime deterrence has not been constrained by legal principles about innocence, guilt, and human rights.[39] Rather, economists typically focus on the associated transaction costs. A high repression level that is supposed to target all group members in case an act of crime is detected may lead many group members, who are not able to influence the crime itself, to invest in strategies for avoiding exposure to the undesired consequence of a criminal justice sanction and the associated reputational burden. Those strategies might include having options for alternative

---

violence. What is considered to be an organized crime group might be a network of allies with little influence over one another. It might be an organization with both peaceful and violent branches – possibly a guerrilla organization in opposition to a corrupt government. In these cases, it might appear inconsistent to hold any group member liable for crimes committed by the organization that is defined as an organized crime group, whereas the employees of a corporation – that also commits crime that kills – are *not* held liable for what the corporation has done.

[39] Unless these values are important to maximize deterrence, as we return to in Chapter 6.

employment, obtaining financial insurance to offset the costs of a sanction, and securing legal assistance to defend oneself against a sanction.

In theory, these costs could be exactly what it takes to secure sufficient pressure against those in command of a crime-inclined organization. The expected burden on group members could induce powerful decision-makers to introduce effective oversight mechanisms and efficiently prevent crime from taking place. This assumption will not hold, however, if the benefits of committing the crime exceed the expected aggregated costs of a sanction for the organization's members. In particular, this sanction shortcoming is a particular problem when the benefits accrue primarily to a limited group of members (such as the owners or leaders of an organization) while the cost associated with a criminal justice penalty harms the whole organization. A penalty sufficiently high to alter the cost-benefit assessment of the crime, as postulated by the economic deterrence theory, will likely threaten the very existence of the organization (if, for example, innocent members flee the organization or the size of a monetary penalty exceeds the organization's total revenues). In the extreme, the 'optimal' sanction intended to deter organizations from committing a crime could have more severe consequences for society than the consequences of the crime.[40]

In other words, a penalty against an organization (such as a monetary fine, determined in accordance with the sanction principle) will not automatically induce main decision-makers to do what they can to prevent crime from taking place. Leaders make decisions both on behalf of their organization and on behalf of themselves as individuals. Consequently, a penalty intended to influence corporate strategies will not necessarily prevent leaders from seeking benefits through corruption. Whatever the interests of owners, a leader may boost her or his annual bonus by securing market entry through corruption, while a penalty placed on the company might not be imposed until years later, if at all, and might not harm the decision-maker's personal economy. For outsiders and law enforcers, such cases are difficult to judge, especially when an organization's owners, managers, and staff all benefit from the crime.[41]

---

[40] Especially if applying the economic principle of placing sanctions that are sufficient for altering the crime decision, not reflecting the consequences of the crime.

[41] For more thorough discussions of shortcomings with deterrence-based strategies vis-à-vis organizations, see Oded (2013, Chapter 2).

4.5.2 Duty-Based Liability

The *perfect* form of group liability – one that avoids these difficulties and efficiently prevents crime – is difficult to imagine. Over the past twenty years or so, however, the idea of a duty-based sanctions regime has gained ground among legal scholars, economists, and practitioners of various sorts. At the heart of such a regime is the notion that criminal justice sanctions should depend on what the given organization has done to prevent crime, report any criminal acts, and limit their harmful consequences. When the identity of the individuals involved in committing the crime is unknown, the question of criminal liability is turned into a question of how far the company carried out certain *duties*. Its performance when it comes to stipulated responsibilities – including reporting the crime when detected, implementing strategies to prevent and detect crime, and demonstrating a clear and consistent zero tolerance for crime among the top leadership of the organization – determines the penalty.

The better the organization's performance, the lower the likely corporate criminal sanction is if a case of corruption is detected. This approach will not remove the temptation of benefiting from bribery, however. A substantial 'benchmark penalty' (that is, the gross penalty from various sanction rebates are made upon modifying factors), sufficient even to eradicate an organization if imposed (based on the logic that crime-inclined firms may well be removed from the market), combined with a sharp decline in the penalty for each successful self-regulation mechanism in operation, enables the criminal justice regime to encourage corporate compliance. Upon such a regime, owners will (convincingly) encourage self-regulation, and leaders, who may think they can benefit from corruption while hiding their own involvement behind corporate structures, will face the risk of charges simply because they did not do enough to prevent the crime from happening. Board members, sharing some of this leadership liability, will become more inclined to demand compliance and to monitor oversight systems. Hence, according to this line of reasoning, a well-designed duty-based regime combines sanctions imposed on the organization and the individual, thus avoiding some of the incentive problems described above. It should be noted, though, that the organization's criminal liability under this logic is reduced to *the failure to ensure* a well-functioning internal compliance regime; the organization is not exposed to full criminal liability for the corrupt acts.[42]

In practice, however, there are several difficulties associated with the arrangement. The most obvious problem is the risk of 'window-dressing' – namely, that corporations appear to have a well-functioning compliance system and zero tolerance against corruption, but make bribe payments in secret. Many bribes are paid at the political level, handled 'above' the bureaucracy of the corporation and arranged in a very sophisticated fashion that makes it extremely difficult to trace the transactions. Corruption, fraud, and collusion can go on despite the organization having an active compliance system; the Enron case is a well-known case in point.[43] If, against the odds, corruption is detected, the management simply points to its excellent compliance system, insists that it did what it could to prevent the case from happening, and vows that it will collaborate with the criminal justice system and let investigators have whatever information they want. In order to prevent such window-dressing situations, according to research conducted by Jennifer Arlen and Reinier Kraakman, a duty-based sanctions regime should be combined with 'strict residual responsibility.' This means that a certain sanction is imposed on the corporation if a crime is detected, no matter what compliance system the corporation has in place.[44]

---

[42] Some prosecutors, who are used to such compliance-based assessment of liability (for example, in the United States and increasingly in the United Kingdom), are now seeking to expand their authority so that they can sanction organizations for not having anticorruption systems in place, even if it has not actually been proved that any cases of corruption have taken place. Such sanctions would be authorized under administrative law, and would therefore be of lower amounts and have a different legal status than criminal law sanctions for verified cases of corruption. Such sanctions would be consistent with the monitoring of safety standards more generally. However, regardless of the legal status of such sanctions, they imply a cost on organizations even if no crime has actually taken place, and especially when the expected compliance regime is poorly defined, firms face a burden in terms of being uncertain about what they can be held liable for.

[43] The Enron scandal, revealed in October 2001, is the biggest business bankruptcy ever. Enron, an American energy company, collapsed as the result of a huge audit fraud. It led to the dissolution of Arthur Andersen (a global auditing consultancy), numerous families losing their pension savings, and debates about 'who guards the guardians' and how short-sighted profit hunts degrade morality (see *The Economist*: 'Enron: The Real Scandal' on 17 January 2002; and *Forbes*: 'Enron, Ethics and Today's Corporate Values' – a comment by Ken Silverstein on 14 May 2013).

[44] Most of the arguments presented here draw heavily on Arlen (2012).

Logically, the solution is a result of the difficulty of observing performance; that is, there is asymmetric information between law enforcement authorities and the corporate management. In one way or the other, the criminal justice system should act on what *is* observable, instead of some assumption of compliance or corruption. It would be counterintuitive, however, to *reward* companies that are never suspected of corruption (or other forms of crime).[45] What the law enforcement system can do is to impose a sanction on any firm that evidently fails to self-regulate. Those that are not involved will 'be rewarded' by facing no reaction, regardless of whether the reason for noninvolvement is the organization's well-functioning compliance system or its leaders' moral barriers against committing a crime.

The idea of adding strict residual liability is useful in the search for a more efficient law enforcement response to corruption, but, of course, strict residual liability will not solve all difficulties. A further challenge with the duty-based sanctions regime is to decide the correct sanction resulting from strict residual liability and to determine how much sanction rebate should be offered in exchange for maintaining a robust self-regulation regime and collaborating with investigators. If the regime is to influence future crime decisions with the help of criminal justice strategies, the criminal justice system must operate with predictable sanction principles. Upon demonstrating a set of stipulated self-regulation measures, such as self-policing (conducting surveillance within the organization), self-reporting (informing the criminal justice system when crime in the organization is suspected or detected), and sincere commitment (encouraging and protecting whistle-blowers), a rebate can be calculated in line with explicit guidelines. Exactly what the eventual sanctions should be will depend on the specific case and jurisdiction. Nonetheless, from an economic perspective, this logic behind the sentencing principle – that is, a heavy benchmark sentence with a sharp rebate for performance measure and strict liability if cases are detected – makes good sense.

In practice, however, there are difficulties implementing such a regime because it challenges core principles associated with traditional criminal justice systems. Criminal justice systems are developed to enable the investigation and prosecution of cases of crime, not to regulate and assess the quality of a corporation's whistle-blower program. Which government institution would be fit to judge the quality of a compliance system – without interfering with the work of investigators? And what should the

---

[45] For all we know, these firms might be better at hiding the acts.

arena for the required dialogue between the organization and those who assess its compliance program be, bearing in mind that a criminal justice system should maintain a clear distance between the prosecutor and the offender? Especially during the early phases of a criminal justice investigation of corporate crime, when the firm (in line with its compliance system) is expected to place evidence on the table, some form of dialogue will occur around compliance and self-reporting; in other words, the offender is expected to 'collaborate' with prosecutors, and this collaboration will have consequences for the eventual sanction.

4.5.3   Negotiated Settlements

An assessment of compliance systems and corporate performance, when it comes to preventing and detecting crime, cannot be conducted without *any* dialogue between representatives of the criminal justice system and representatives of the organization that allegedly has been involved in corruption. The corporation must provide details about itself, including – in order to convince law enforcement officials about its commitment to its self-policing regime and its willingness to report their crime – all relevant details of the alleged crime. For the corporation, however, there is a trade-off between presenting evidence (in the hope of getting a substantial sanction rebate) and hiding as much evidence as possible (in the hope of avoiding charges). Given that no two cases are exactly the same and that prosecutors will have at least some discretion in the assessment of a corporate compliance system and the implications for a sanction rebate, the corporation is unlikely to know exactly what rebate to expect. In a setting where (1) an exchange of information happens, (2) the parties communicate, and (3) the information shared has implications for discretionary decisions, the corporation's 'collaboration' with prosecuting authorities and the criminal justice system will have the character of a negotiation. Regardless of what criminal procedural rules allow, which varies substantially across countries, such negotiations occur throughout the world, especially when the accused is a corporation.[46] The application of duty-based sanctions regimes intensifies the propensity to bargain, and while many legal scholars believe it is important to avoid any 'deals' between the accused and the prosecutor, economists take the likely bargain as a given, and focus instead on how the negotiations can be given a frame that promotes efficient law enforcement.

---

[46] See Garoupa and Stephen (2008) for an economic discussion. Makinwa (2014) discusses difficulties and gains based on case studies of settlement regimes in eight European countries.

Aspects that might become *items in such negotiations* include a confession from the accused, the contents of a charge (for example, a firm may provide evidence on one matter in exchange for prosecutors declining to investigate another matter), and the severity of a sentence (for example, how much sanction rebate and what form of sanction should be given). Other elements that may influence the negotiations are information provided about various players involved in the deal (for example, middlemen, information brokers, bank officials, and politicians), as well as collaboration for asset recovery and damage compensation. Also likely to be under discussion is the fate of the benefits that have been obtained through corruption. For example, should a contract secured through bribery be completed despite the corruption or should it be retendered no matter how much of the contract has been completed? The corporation will often declare its willingness to contribute to the investigation by hiring (expensive) private investigators and promise that, in the future, its compliance system will work far more efficiently. The accused are also likely to address the subject of which details should be released to the public, including the contents of the prosecutor's press release about the case.

Among the concerns associated with these law enforcement deals is a risk of reduced sanction predictability, which will have indirect consequences for prevention. Another concern is how the tendency to negotiate with the accused will harm the prosecutor's reputation and standing in the society at large. Especially if the contents of such negotiations are kept confidential, observers are likely to become suspicious that, for instance, prosecutors have been too lenient with politically well-connected corporations or have diluted charges to secure the offender's cooperation. Such suspicions are easier to allay when the main features of a case are addressed in open court.

A further problem with negotiated settlements is the risk of a biased result. Several factors justify this concern, one of them being the corporation's market power. The prospect of a severe sanction may create concern that the corporation will no longer be able to provide services that are valued by society as a whole, resulting in more lenient treatment for the corporation. Besides, the corporation's opportunity to inflate prices for its products or services in order to cover the penalty may (and perhaps should) influence the nature and severity of the sentence. Biases can also occur if lawyers, who negotiate on behalf of the entire corporation, have narrow interests. If representing the corporation's owners and/or shareholders, they might be eager to agree to place blame on certain individuals within the corporation's management. After all, if the CEO alone could be sacrificed and sent to prison, the corporation might be able to move on with its various operations without the burden of a huge fine. On the other hand, the lawyers representing the CEO might be willing to expose the firm to big penalties if only the CEO (and perhaps other members of top-level management) avoids personal liability and punishment.

As this brief discussion reveals, those who write the guidelines for this area of criminal procedural law face many challenges. Among the many questions with which they must wrestle are how to promote predictability and transparency around these negotiations while ensuring that offenders have strong incentives to come forward with their evidence. For the protection of the offender's rights, as well as the general public's claim for justice, there should be some form of ex ante or ex post control on negotiated deals. But what role should the courts and criminal justice judges play in exerting that control? How much weight should be placed on the importance of identifying individual offenders versus sanctioning the corporation as a whole? What should the bureaucratic structure for investigating cases and reaching compliance-based settlements be when the assessment of compliance regimes becomes essential for judging whether crime has occurred? How much resources should be devoted to independent fact-finding investigations when corporations have already provided evidence about a case? And, eventually, how far can the principles developed for criminal justice regulation of corporate crime apply to state institutions, such as license providers, tax offices, public hospitals, or police units? We return to these questions in Chapter 5.

4.6   CONCLUSION: ECONOMIC SOLUTIONS FOR MORE EFFICIENT CRIMINAL LAW ENFORCEMENT

Economists rarely spend much time trying to understand the world of law, even though they hope their arguments will be well received in that world. Economists are also generally poorly informed about the legal conditions for the use of criminal justice sanctions, the organization of criminal justice procedures, and the hierarchy of laws, and they tend to ignore whatever skepticism they encounter about the value of utilitarian approaches. Possibly because of (and not despite of) its distance from the world of legal scholars, economic reasoning around criminal justice responses can enrich legal debates and offer compelling ideas about efficient strategies. The following bullets summarize the main points made in this chapter about policy-relevant economic reasoning on crime and corruption.

4.6.1 Economic Reasoning on Crime and Corruption: Common Inferences for Policy

4.6.1.1 Toward more efficient criminal law enforcement

- Law enforcement efficiency implies crime prevention and a reduction in crime without wasting resources.
- Preventive effects require transparency and predictability in criminal law enforcement.
- The narrower the criminal law definition of 'corruption,' the less relevant the criminal justice system is in dealing with the problem.
- The more imprecise the crime definition is, the more difficult it is to enforce criminal justice strategies.
- The weaker the demand for evidence in corruption cases, the higher the risk of sanctioning an innocent.
- Efficient strategies against corruption and other crime committed with rational intent should emerge from an understanding of the offender's likely decision-making process.

4.6.1.2 The (simple) sanction principle with resource constraints

- A sanction set to deter crime must be sufficiently high to outweigh the offender's likely net benefit of crime.
- To match the gain obtained through crime, the optimal sanction is multiplied by the estimated risk of detection.
- For a certain expected deterrent effect, the trade-off between detection efforts and repression level should depend on the law enforcement strategies' relative marginal cost.
- While detection strategies are usually associated with substantial direct costs, a high repression level may have damaging indirect consequences.
- A sanction that is higher than it needs to be for the sake of deterrence implies a waste of productive resources and values.

4.6.1.3 The sanction principle extended, including insights from behavioral studies

- The higher the crime elasticity (offenders' sensitivity to criminal justice strategies), the lower the optimal sanctions, and vice versa.

- A repeat offense should imply a stricter sanction than a first-time offense.
- For the sake of marginal deterrence, sanctions must be scaled according to the consequences of different criminal acts.
- Sanctions may have a higher deterrent effect if they are imposed sooner rather than later.
- The moral cost of crime is higher in cases where the crime victims are easily imagined or geographically close.
- A high repression level may breed empathy with the wrongdoer, instead of encouraging condemnation of the criminal act, and may prevent whistle-blowers from speaking out.

4.6.1.4   Criminal justice systems and the control of corruption

- Law enforcement institutions must be able to operate independently of one another and of other state institutions, because no state institution is immune to corruption risks.
- The law enforcement value chain – from crime definition to enforcement to sanctions – is at risk of corrupt influence.
- Those in a position to prevent corruption from challenging the principle of equal criminal justice treatment may benefit personally from failing to do so.
- The risk of collusion between monitoring agencies and corrupt decision-makers challenges efficient law enforcement.
- Those in a position to react when corruption is observed are likely to remain silent if there are direct and indirect costs that outweigh the benefits associated with a reaction.

4.6.1.5   Corruption mechanisms

- A strategy against corruption should begin with an analysis of how authority within an organization is allocated, because this internal organization is essential for determining corruption risks.
- Detection of corruption is facilitated if institutional aims and performance targets are set so that it is possible to identify any departure from them.
- Corruption will often be adapted to monitoring efforts (such as controls on procedures) and this fact must be taken into account when developing control strategies.
- Transparency into decision-making processes and self-reporting rewards are factors that distort the trust required for corrupt deals.

- The more asymmetric the bargaining powers between those involved in corruption, the more likely they are to confess their crime.
- The benefit from crime is largely endogenous for those involved; it depends on the corrupt deal.
- If the bribe can be inflated with the size of the fine, the fine (alone) will have no or only a weak deterrent effect.
- Those in a position to benefit from honest decisions have incentives to report suspected corruption.

4.6.1.6 Corporate liability for corruption

- Crime committed on behalf of an organization should lead to a sanction even if the liable individual's identity is unknown.
- The stricter law enforcement's demand to know the guilty decision-maker's identity, the higher the risk of scapegoats.
- Sanctions on innocent members of an organization involved in corruption implies transactions costs and should be minimized.
- Duty-based sanctions regimes should replace the sanction principle when corruption has been committed on behalf of organizations.
- The 'duties' (in duty-based sanctions) must be stipulated explicitly and performance must be observable (that is, possible for investigators to evaluate).
- Strict residual liability, combined with a duty-based sanctions regime, reduces the risk of window-dressing.
- De facto negotiated settlements are unavoidable under a duty-based sanctions regime, and should be arranged under clear guidelines.
- Negotiated settlements are a (necessary) threat to the values of fairness, predictability, and deterrence, and explicit steps are necessary to reduce this threat.

How can such insights help generate practicable and effective strategies? Each argument is rational and reasonable – and addresses an aspect of efficient law enforcement. Considered in combination, however, the arguments appear fragmented and inconsistent, and therefore, they provide limited practical guidance on how to efficiently control corruption within the premises of the criminal justice system.

Some cross-cutting lessons can nevertheless be drawn. Transparency and predictability facilitate strategies against corruption in several important ways. In order to develop efficient criminal justice strategies, knowledge about the crime and the effect of former strategies is necessary. Incentive mechanisms can be used to motivate offenders to collaborate with law enforcement authorities. A high repression level intended to deter crime may have indirect consequences, which in the longer run make it more difficult to fight corruption. The position of the criminal justice system matters for its ability to enforce an anticorruption legislation. And eventually, the contents of an efficient criminal law approach will depend on factors outside the criminal justice system, which also implies that different societies require different law enforcement strategies.

Hence, while economic factors offer insights into many of the mechanisms that need to be understood in order to promote criminal justice efficiency, these insights must be combined with arguments in law in order to be found relevant for governments. However, when bringing the arguments together with law, their applicability is quickly challenged by other aims in the criminal justice system, and new questions emerge regarding trade-offs between values. Chapter 5 continues into that terrain, and begins by asking what constitutes efficiency, if the term is to be understood and acknowledged in both disciplines.

5. Principles versus pragmatism in law enforcement systems

Criminal justice systems are a natural target for criticism. They are entrusted with an impossible task (getting rid of crime), yet given the ultimate responsibility to control the problem. Their many objectives, the political ambitions with which others seek to burden them, and the fact that crime occurs for reasons outside their control, make it difficult to quantify and evaluate the many functions performed by these systems. As a consequence, the system's true performance is largely unobserved. It is much easier for critics to find fault with current criminal justice approaches than to agree on what criteria define a well-functioning criminal justice system – or, as I prefer to phrase it, what conceptualizes *efficiency* in the context of criminal law.

This is not to say, of course, that the complaints voiced about the criminal justice system are baseless. And the complaints expressed about how the system tackles corruption can seem particularly valid. Many of the legal reforms introduced to control corruption have looked good on paper in the form of new laws and procedures, but, as Chapter 3 makes clear, they have had limited impact in practice. This disappointing record is, or should be, a cause for great concern, because corruption is not a minor problem. As explained in Chapter 2, corruption distorts markets, prevents the fair allocation of benefits, and causes huge losses of state revenues; the problem challenges the very position of the state in society. Cross-border financial flows and rapid technological change foster new problems faster than our law enforcement systems manage to adapt; every time we manage to chop off one of the heads of the many-headed monster of corruption, new heads emerge. There is clearly a pressing need to identify *efficient* criminal justice approaches to the problem.

Economists have laid out a range of criteria for efficient solutions, as described in Chapter 4. But this very concern with efficiency makes legal scholars look skeptically at economic ideas. The economic efficiency concept is seen as too narrow to accommodate legal values and principles such as fairness and justice. If we want to do a better job of battling the corruption monster, we need to bridge this skeptical divide between economists and legal scholars and start building consensus about how best to change the criminal justice system so that it is both more efficient and no less attentive to principles of justice and fairness. We need to work together to determine the conditions under which a criminal justice system will contribute *efficiently* to controlling corruption.

The optimal law enforcement strategy is not something we can identify once and for all. How we use the criminal justice system to control corruption must be subject to continuous debate, because society itself is subject to continuous evolution. Nonetheless, there is an increasing amount of empirical and theoretical knowledge that helps us advance and promote the principles of criminal justice that can apply across decades, countries, and institutions. This chapter does not pretend to offer a complete answer to the question of how to create a more efficient system, but it does offer an approach to thinking about criminal justice efficiency while pinpointing essential functions and values. In practice, the multiple objectives in criminal law enforcement lead to challenging policy trade-offs between principles and practical considerations, and these must be addressed if we are to reach a consensus on what works. Among the challenges addressed in this chapter are:

(1)   achieving a balance between fairness and deterrence while keeping in mind cost-efficiency in strategic decisions;
(2)   holding corporations liable while taking into account a composite efficiency concept (a difficulty that is highlighted in attempts to incentivize compliance and self-reporting while recognizing the legal sanctions criteria); and
(3)   securing a solid position with law enforcement for the prosecutor – which is of particular importance for efficient responses to corruption.

The main arguments are summarized at the end of the chapter.

5.1   CRIMINAL JUSTICE EFFICIENCY

The criminal justice system has been established to meet the fundamental needs of safety and conflict resolution in the society of which it is part. The government is entrusted with exclusive power over the use of force for this purpose, a solution intended to reduce the risk of retribution, obviate the need for private enforcement, and prevent escalated conflict. As long as the criminal justice system acts as an unbiased decision-maker, its verdicts are expected to conciliate victims and inform citizens about the difference between acceptable behavior and crime. A criminal justice system that performs these functions efficiently will hold offenders responsible, promote moral values, and prevent future crime. These goals, however, are not necessarily interlinked, which complicates any attempt at reaching a consensus of what constitutes criminal justice *efficiency*.

5.1.1 The Efficiency Concept in the Context of Criminal Law

Efficiency is associated with the ways in which we achieve our aims. Efficiency does not demand solutions that are uncompromising, far-reaching, or swiftly achieved; efficiency is judged by how resources are used to reach the given aim. In this sense, 'efficiency' refers to functional performance – and how close some functions get to meeting the optimal target – and unless it is defined more precisely, 'efficient' can be understood to be synonymous with 'well-performing' or even with so vague a term as 'good.'

5.1.1.1 Why debate system efficiency
'Efficiency' is often discussed in the context of pursuing a short-term goal or a very narrow criminal justice reform, and, as such, 'efficiency' is often associated with matters such as the time spent investigating and prosecuting case, the proportion of cases that result in conviction, or the cost-savings that are achieved through, for example, the use of better surveillance technology. In these settings, the term has a clear meaning because it refers to a particular aim. The difficulty arises when one refers to a *system's* efficiency, especially when the system operates with several goals for crime control and vaguely defined conditions for system legitimacy. It is therefore tempting to restrict the matter of efficiency to specific sub-goals. Impact evaluation – which is necessary to assess whether a strategy works as intended – is already very difficult at the level of sub-goals, and the question of overall efficiency easily appears overwhelming.

The problem is that, unless one is able to assess various sub-goals associated with law enforcement in a broader context, achieving them will not necessarily contribute to *better* system performance. Dealing with cases quickly may well be desired, but what is the point if blame is erroneously placed? Cost savings are a good thing, but not if they imply ignorance of hidden forms of crime. For groups involved in law enforcement, the temptation to demonstrate the achievement of short-term or narrow goals may outweigh the desire to accomplish longer-term ambitions and to protect values, especially if career development or compensation is tied to narrow goals. Without a clear view of where one is heading, the pursuit of sub-goals may threaten overall system efficiency. The complexity of a criminal justice system's performance should not prevent the use of efficiency concepts. With recognition of the different elements associated with good performance, it is possible to carry out partial reforms that we can safely assume will improve the system as a whole. The challenge, therefore, is to identify what constitutes a *good* system.

The constant call for higher law enforcement efficiency is a further reason why the term should be used more precisely. The media's inclination to reveal law enforcement shortcomings (while paying less attention to what works well) creates the impression of an *inefficient* criminal justice system. Political candidates secure votes by promising law enforcement reforms: Crime will be controlled faster and more thoroughly and expenses will be cut, or so these candidates promise. The system will operate with more accountability and transparency than ever before, sanctions will be tougher while legitimacy of all sorts will be bolstered. Without a clear understanding of what constitutes an efficient criminal justice system, a jumble of conflicting political ambitions can seem to be a carefully conceived and attractive strategy. However, when horses pull in different directions, the direction is difficult to steer. Efforts to reach inconsistent goals will prevent law enforcement progress because decision-makers with different views will try to prioritize different functions.

At the same time, broad consensus on what constitutes a good system cannot be reached without accounting for the extent of cross-disciplinary collaboration and political dialogue. How to better enforce criminal law will always trigger ardent political debate. Nonetheless, the broader the common understanding of the fundamentals of criminal justice and law enforcement, the easier it will be for those who govern or work with these systems to collaborate and agree about strategic priorities.

This section describes a suggested simplification of the essential aspects of a well-functioning criminal justice system. This chapter's portrait of an efficient system, it should be emphasized, is heavily influenced by Nordic criminal law. Even so, it resonates with holistic ideas of what constitutes a good criminal justice system that have been articulated by a wide variety of judicial researchers and policy experts – and economists – in recent decades, and, indeed, by jurists, philosophers, and scholars in previous centuries. What I present here is a simplification of how I understand the matter, an understanding that informs my arguments about anticorruption.

5.1.1.2 Efficiency criteria associated with efficiency dimensions

Efficiency, we instinctively assume, should have something to do with *responses to crime*. After all, dealing with crime on behalf of society is the reason why criminal justice systems exist. As noted above, 'efficiency' refers to how things are done – in this case, to the process of enforcing laws. At the same time, like any system run by government institutions, a criminal justice system operates with budget constraints, and priorities should be set based on what seems to work best in pursuit of a certain aim. These main functions associated with criminal justice efficiency are included in Figure 5.1. Like the three sides of a triangle, the functions are connected, and it makes little sense to evaluate one without understanding the other two. Understanding criminal justice efficiency requires recognition of the performance and interaction of these different functions – or aims – which now will be discussed in turn.

Figure 5.1   Functions associated with criminal justice efficiency

5.1.2 Crime Deterrence

A criminal justice system that fails to prevent crime cannot be deemed to be efficient. Law enforcement consequences upon violation of the most basic rules in society confirm an internal agreement in society – that such acts are not acceptable – while demotivating those who are tempted by the benefits that can be obtained through crime. The intended law enforcement impact depends on the level of rationality among members of a society. As long as the members of the society are fairly rational, crime can be deterred through law enforcement actions, and citizens will perceive the signaled expectation of their responsible and moral conduct.

Addressing this expected rationality with the level of precision that economists prefer, the word 'rationality' implies some form of (rational) calculation of the net benefits of committing crime, a calculation that involves taking into account the risk of detection and penalties. The crime-preventing impact of the criminal justice system depends on how it manages to influence this assumed calculation. Exercising this influence is difficult, not only because crime is the result of a number of factors that are difficult to influence, but also because there are constraints on what the criminal justice system can do, including how far it can impose sanctions. The net benefit from a crime like corruption can be too substantial for sanctions to outweigh, and, therefore, the crime-preventing effect on rational decision-makers hinges very much on the system's impact on values in society and how it can add to potential offenders' 'moral burden' of committing crime. If their moral burden is sufficiently heavy, no benefit can tempt them to commit crime.

If this reasoning is correct, nurturing the moral caliber in society is equally important – or even more important – than the threatening effect of a heavy penalty, even from an economic perspective. For these reasons, in order to prevent crime, the criminal law reaction must perform a dual function: reinforcing moral values while taking tough action against unacceptable acts. A criminal justice system that aims primarily at only one of these functions can either gently encourage members of society to comply with the law, for example by stating the importance of honesty in public places, or threaten them, for example, by executing offenders, so that they are unlikely to dare to commit crime. But it will never prevent crime as efficiently as a system that performs a balance between both preventive functions.

Pursuing the two aims (reducing the net benefit of crime and increasing the moral burden of committing crime) requires different approaches. The legal scholars' concern with the economic arguments described in Chapter 4 is that they offer solutions pertinent to only one of the aims, namely, how to efficiently reduce the net gain from crime (taking into account various concerns relating to marginal deterrence and crime elasticity). The aim of enhancing the moral burden of committing crime, however, is associated with system legitimacy, a goal that is more difficult to specify, although it is generally associated with values such as fairness, democratic embeddedness in society, and recognition of, and respect for, human rights.

Despite their different solutions, the impacts of the two crime-deterring functions are difficult to disentangle. First, it is difficult to pinpoint exactly what deters crime in practice; and second, a system that efficiently reduces the net gains from crime may well be seen as legitimate and thus increase the moral burden of committing crime. However, there are also many choices made in a criminal justice system that increase the moral burden associated with crime, while having no intended impact on the net gain obtained through crime, and these are often associated with fairness.

5.1.3 Fair Process

In contrast to the economic reasoning, the legal criteria for imposing a criminal law penalty (as explained in Chapter 4, section 4.1) are associated with securing legitimacy through fairness; they are not established to reduce the net benefit from crime, and this is key to understanding the difference between economic and legal thinking (as discussed in Chapter 4, section 4.3). Recognizing these legal criteria, a criminal law sanction cannot be imposed unless a crime has occurred, the one responsible for the act (whether a human or legal person) is identified, and some element of guilt is confirmed. Arguments on good legal procedure are loaded with references to values: *Justice* must prevail. Members of society have a *right* to have their *autonomy* protected. The government must secure civilized channels for victims' demand for *retribution*. The evidence brought forward in court must be *valid* according to procedural law. The sanctions must be *proportional* in the sense that the severity of the penalty should match the crime, while the offender's human rights are respected. It is *reasonable* to physically prevent the offender from committing more criminal acts through incarceration or debarment from public office. It is considered *fair* to recover the assets gained from the crime and to *compensate* victims. The laws regarding criminal law procedure and sanctioning must be *rooted in society* and approved by a representative majority of citizens. And so the debate proceeds, using a value-laden language that is unlike that which is typically employed in economic analyses.

What is clear is that these values are associated with humans' fundamental needs and basic nature. Fairness, or procedural justice, is an 'inalienable right';[1] it cannot be written off as one among several alternative strategic law enforcement objectives. How to secure these values through the ways in which society is organized and governed has been debated for as long as there have been societies. These questions were addressed by ancient Greek philosophers and by China's Confucius, who claimed that laws must be based on people's 'natural morality.' More than two thousand years ago, he explained that the purpose of laws is to

---

[1] William of Ockham in *Work of Ninety Days* (1330), cited in Kenny (2010:328).

develop citizens' sense of duty, and that to have such effect in society, the government must lead by example and demonstrate virtue.[2] Such ancient ideas were met with resistance by the powerful, but they grew stronger throughout history. Marsilius of Padua and William of Ockham in the Middle Ages, for instance, maintained that the only form of rule that is legitimate is rule by consent of subjects.[3] Around 1650, Thomas Hobbes described how principles of rational interest would lead men to give up their liberty for the sake of a central power that would have to enforce laws and have the power to impose punishment.[4] In the same period, Baruch Spinoza pointed out how laws that fly in the face of public opinion merely irritate the upright without constraining criminals.[5] State legitimacy became a central theme for many of the most famous thinkers in the Age of Enlightenment, including Jean-Jacques Rousseau and John Locke, who emphasized the importance of separating the executive and legislative; Charles de Montesquieu underscored how government structures would have to secure the individual's autonomy.[6] Building on the work of such thinkers, Emmanuel Kant came to the conclusion that universality is essential to any viable moral philosophy; he also rejected the utilitarian idea of punishing citizens for the purpose of deterring offenders – which was the point at which legal scholars and economists really started to diverge on the matter of fairness.

Today, the spirit of past philosophers strongly influences the debate, and it is fascinating how we still struggle with the principles of governance that seem to have been unambiguous to thinkers who lived thousands of years ago. When it comes to current legal and economic debates, however, results in behavioral economics (which explores basic patterns of human decision-making) – seem to suggest some scope for consensus on the importance of legitimacy, as discussed in Chapter 4, section 4.3. A range of empirical studies, most of them experiments, confirm that humans are willing to give up other substantial benefits to

---

[2]   Presented primarily in *The Analects (475-221 BC)* by Confucius, who also maintained: 'If the people be led by laws, and uniformity sought to be given them by punishments, they will try to avoid the punishment, but have no sense of shame. If they be led by virtue, and uniformity sought to be given them by the rules of propriety, they will have the sense of the shame, and moreover will become good.' In the *Great Learning* (*The Analects* and *Great Learning* are two of 'The Four Books' in Confucianism). Translated by James Legge (1861).

[3]   *The Defender of the Peace* (1324), described by Kenny (2010:328).

[4]   *Leviathan* (1651), described by Kenny (2010:713).

[5]   *Ethics* (1677), cited by Kenny (2010:717).

[6]   *The Spirit of the Laws* (1748), cited by Kenny (2010:721).

preserve fairness. Increasingly, the value-laden terms mentioned at the beginning of this section are starting to influence economic analyses of crime and efficient law enforcement.

5.1.4 Value for Money

The more legitimate the contents of the criminal law, the more likely citizens are to comply with the law, and the lower the investment necessary to control crime.[7] For this reason, an evaluation of spending in the criminal justice sector can rarely be conducted as if the results of that investment are unrelated to the system's standing in society. However, a system associated with a waste of state resources will not be considered efficient, and for this reason, value for money in law enforcement investment is a separate criterion in the criminal justice efficiency concept.

From an economic perspective, it is reasonable to think of efficient spending as the level of investment that matches the gain on the margin. The law enforcement expenses are too high if the expenses associated with a small increase in crime control are higher than the value of what we think we obtain in terms of the reduction in crime achieved. When the expense for a purpose is higher than the expected return – for example, in terms of the results from investigation – resources should instead be allocated to purposes that have a higher rate of return. Of course, the values associated with crime control are hard to evaluate in purely monetary terms. These values include physical safety, protected property rights, and the feeling of living in a well-functioning society. The costs include the direct law enforcement expenses (for each part of the law enforcement value chain) and the indirect costs to society. For example, the cost of keeping an inmate in prison for one night is a direct expense, whereas the loss of his or her productive contribution to society and the consequences for his or her family are indirect costs. These are all relevant factors when considering value for money in law enforcement. In addition, the values and costs associated with law enforcement come to expression at different stages. For instance, the costs associated with evaluating the implementation of a new law or collaborating on law enforcement with other countries are expenses that are unlikely to generate returns in the near or mid-term.

---

[7] This, of course, depends on how members of society consider their role, responsibility, and influence in a society – a theme we will return to in Chapter 6.

In addition to securing value for money with each investment made, an efficient criminal law system will also undertake a comparison of alternative investments; in economic terms, the 'alternative costs' must be taken into account. Given resource constraints, efficient spending requires comparison of the values that can be obtained under alternative spending scenarios, which implies a need for solid knowledge about what alternative law enforcement strategies cost and what results they generate. Priorities for spending should depend on the consequences of different forms of crime and what crime prevention results are obtained from the law enforcement investments. Each Euro or dollar spent does not have to be the result of precise calculations and optimized strategies for efficiency to prevail. What matters is that those in charge of law enforcement are aware of what one obtains in law enforcement in return for what expense, and are committed to avoiding waste and directing efforts toward areas where high values for society are at stake. In order to reach that awareness, knowledge of efficiency concepts is necessary.

Whether the ambition relates to crime prevention, detection, rehabilitation, court procedures, or imprisonment, 'efficiency' involves *doing the right thing without wasting resources.* This principle is easy to support but difficult to put into practice, because doing so requires a lot of knowledge. We need to understand and evaluate not only the role and impact of the criminal justice system's various functions and strategies, but also the extent of various forms of crime and the impact of alternative strategies. Such knowledge requires insight about the entire law enforcement system, including alternative policy options and the factors that can (and cannot) explain causality between a certain policy and observed changes. For these reasons, law enforcement efficiency requires a combination of solid theoretical knowledge, understanding of the criminal justice system's functionality, the systematic collection of data over time, and close ties between policymaking and research.

5.1.5 Efficiency Trade-offs

General awareness of the complex values and objectives embedded in a criminal justice system will reduce tendencies toward populist or simplistic generalizations about the system's impact on crime. For those who seek to strengthen the system's role against corruption, however, such awareness alone is insufficient for the development of efficient solutions; they must also develop priorities in recognition of the different efficiency criteria, which in practice means to make priorities upon difficult trade-offs between objectives. Figure 5.2 elaborates on Figure 5.1 by including keywords representing relevant sub-goals, thereby illuminating the difficulty of achieving these trade-offs and making a system with multiple objectives perform efficiently.

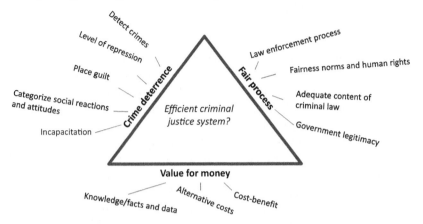

Figure 5.2   Functions associated with criminal justice efficiency, extended with keywords

Figure 5.2 is not meant to provide a complete picture of relevant objectives; many other aims are also associated with law enforcement. What should be noted, is that each of the keywords included is associated not only with the function it is attached to; but also each of the two other functions/sides of the triangle to which it is not attached. Detecting crime, for example, is important out of a fairness concern, and certainly, how it is done is subject to budget constraints. Government legitimacy, as another example, is essential for the norm-generating effects associated with a well-functioning criminal justice system, and as discussed, such effects have essential crime-deterring effects.

This multiplicity presents a challenge to policymakers, who must distinguish between fundamental values, main objectives, and secondary objectives, as well as between short-term goals and longer-term ambitions, and who must also deal with situations in which the focus on one objective obstructs the fulfillment of other important goals. On top of these difficulties, the sector is often a political battlefield. Different political parties, especially those with conflicting ideologies and agendas, can have different – sometimes strikingly different – views on what constitutes efficient law enforcement. In addition, within the administrative management of the sector, the views on how to efficiently curb corruption, and how high a priority to assign to this form of crime, may differ substantially.

Amid such a multiplicity of objectives and an array of competing priorities, policymakers are inevitably confronted with a variety of difficult trade-offs. Given the debate above, it is especially important to understand the following conflicting concerns.

5.1.5.1 Threat-based versus trust-based approaches

Striking the balance between taking tough action against crime and ensuring fairness is difficult in practice. The risk of considerable criminal justice sanctions may be exactly what deters the most cynical offenders. Comprehensive controls, a high risk of detection, and tough interrogations signal zero tolerance of crime, which might be highly appreciated by a majority of voters. At the same time, governments need to be trusted if citizens are to support and listen to them. A state administration that starts to violate citizens' rights, including their right to freedom, distorts and weakens the incumbent government's standing in society. The harsh penalties that seem needed to deter crime may delegitimize the state when they are actually imposed, making it seem brutal and repressive. A crime such as corruption may then seem a justifiable response to the illegitimacy of the state.[8]

A system that stimulates citizens to reach principled judgments will normally be cheaper financially and more sustainable than a system that relies primarily on threats. The problem for many criminal justice systems is that their governments fail to appear convincingly trustworthy to have the desired law-abiding impact on society. This problem is not a matter of criminal justice priorities; it is a question of government accountability and cross-cutting consistency. A regime that introduces a law against corruption one day, tortures suspected offenders (or critical journalists) another day, and allocates contracts to the president's own companies on yet another day cannot be expected to stimulate law-abiding norms in society. For such a regime, the trust-based strategy is not an option in the short run; it has to rely on *threat-based* alternatives: brutal force, heavy sanctions, and often human rights violations. These kinds of measures tend to precipitate a downward spiral into repression, with increasing law enforcement expenses, increasingly unhappy voters, and growing dependence of the regime on military allies, as described in Chapter 2, section 2.4. The law enforcement environment becomes hostile to the trust-based approach, a problem we return to in Chapter 6. Upon such reasoning, anticorruption strategies can hardly be developed and evaluated separately from government performance.

---

[8] This point is discussed by Søreide and Rose-Ackerman (2016) as well.

5.1.5.2 Detection versus deterrence

In its more entrenched or complex forms, corruption and some other forms of crime sometimes take on a character that clearly reveals a government's shortcomings in law enforcement. As discussed, corruption, organized crime, fraud, collusion, and money laundering are often kept hidden behind corporate structures, seemingly legitimate transactions, and international financial markets offering plenty of opportunities for concealing the proceeds of crime. Even with abundant resources for law enforcement, there are limits to what the law enforcement system can manage to control. This problem calls for the rethinking of strategies and competencies, above all, for bringing cases to light. Options available to policymakers include adopting a strategy for encouraging self-reporting – for example, through lenient treatment of those who report their own crime, as discussed in Chapter 4. While this strategy will enhance the rate of detection, however, it may weaken the intended deterrence associated with predictable sanctions. Of course, to some extent, detection *is* deterrence. Regardless of how the crime is revealed, a higher likelihood that it will be revealed – and will elicit some reaction – will deter some offenders. Which combination of leniency for self-reporting and predictable sanctions will have the strongest crime prevention effect is nonetheless difficult to tell. Moreover, predictable leniency (introduced to reveal more cases of crime) will come at the cost of predictable and consistent criminal law responses (maintained to enhance system legitimacy and deterrence). It is difficult to see how these aims can be reconciled unless there is a high degree of transparency and confidence in the criminal justice system.

5.1.5.3 Determining guilt versus incentivizing responsibility

Another trade-off involves striking a balance between placing blame correctly and incentivizing responsibility. Policymakers may be understandably tempted by the idea of introducing the kind of vicarious liability associated with corporate criminal liability (which we turn to in the next section of this chapter), because it places criminal liability on those in a position to know about and act to prevent crime, such as the leaders of organizations and their expert advisers, such as lawyers, financial consultants, and accountants. Clearly, such responsibility intensifies their risk awareness, and thus it might successfully induce decision-makers in exposed positions to increase their efforts to prevent crime. Even if the accomplice is as guilty as the offender, however, as discussed in Chapter 3, section 3.2, a wider criminal liability comes into conflict with the fundamental conditions for criminal justice sanctions, described in Chapter 4, section 4.1. The blame must be placed correctly, which means that the identity of the offender must be known. A system that demands rational decision-makers will strive to prevent responsible individuals from hiding behind a bureaucracy, or the excuse that they were dutifully obeying orders, or pursuing goals as stipulated by a manager or expert adviser. All decision-makers, leaders, and expert advisers share some of the responsibility, and in principle (at least by administrative law) the blame could be allocated according to their position and role – while out of fairness concerns, the more uncertainty there is regarding guilt, the lower the penalty should be. The problem with this reasoning is its failure to secure a certain deterrent effect. If a law enforcement action results in a situation where no decision-maker has been given a sharp penalty that matches the gains from the corruption, the system is de facto resigning to the too soft approach discussed above, in section 1.2, where law compliance is only encouraged, while offenses are not punished. In corruption cases, it is difficult to imagine how crime deterrence can be secured, while offenders are persuaded to self-report their crime, without a combination of leniency to those who speak out and an unabridged sanction for those who are found guilty.

5.2 PRACTICAL IMPLICATIONS: HOLDING ORGANIZATIONS LIABLE

So far, in this chapter, we have seen how enhanced clarity regarding efficiency in criminal law enforcement forces us to consider trade-offs between important values and aims. With this three-dimensional efficiency concept in mind, we now turn to practical implications. How can these ideas help us improve law enforcement reactions vis-à-vis organizations – an area of criminal law where principles are disputed while efficient solutions are truly needed?

As described in Chapter 3, corporate criminal liability is one of the major challenges in the enforcement of the criminal law on corruption. The development of efficient international capital markets has not been accompanied by sufficient control mechanisms, and most criminal justice systems are now unable to prevent offenders from profiting from corruption and other forms of crime without their facing serious risk of criminal sanctions. This section addresses the question of efficient solutions by focusing, first, on the liability problem, second, on the sanctions, third, on negotiated settlements, and fourth, on the applicability of efficiency principles, when the organization accused of corruption is not a private sector corporation but a state institution or state-owned entity.

5.2.1   Toward Vicarious Liability for Corporations

In recognition of the legal sanction principles listed in Chapter 4, section 4.1, which require a guilty rational individual, sanctioning corporations involved in criminal law violations has generally been impossible or very difficult to do. The insistence that reactions on criminal law violations are reserved for circumstances in which the identity of the offender is known has resulted in a market system where firms and their owners can profit from crime but not be held responsible. The criminal justice ambition of legitimacy and fairness – operationalized with personal guilt as a prime condition for penalty – has been exploited by those who seek impunity.

5.2.1.1   Justifying criminal liability

Over the course of the twentieth century, the problem of crime hidden behind corporations intensified as trade across borders increased, corporate structures grew more complex, and opportunities to operate in financial markets with a hidden identity proliferated. The higher frequency of cases in which corporations obviously had been involved in crime, together with the impossibility of identifying the responsible individuals, fueled calls for more pragmatic solutions regarding the criminal liability issue. In most criminal justice systems today, corporations are recognized as capable of committing offenses, yet the conflict with the fundamental criminal law criteria for imposing penalties still generates significant controversy. Therefore, while the economic solutions for efficient regulation are quite clear, as discussed in Chapter 4, section 4.5, the rules regarding corporate criminal liability are still evolving. The debate about what criminal law solutions should look like is far from over.

The path toward corporate criminal liability and the current status is well described by Mark Pieth and Radha Ivory (2011). They explain how governments have taken different routes toward defending criminal law liability. The core question of *personal* guilt in criminal law has led some judiciaries to take a bodily view on corporate entities. In a debate that appears ridiculous from all perspectives but the legal one, the different parts of a corporation have been referred to as 'limbs,' 'nerves,' and the 'brain center,' and efforts have been made to determine the organization's personality or 'mental state' (Pieth and Ivory, 2011, Chapter 1). In other jurisdictions, corporate liability is defended with a negligence-based approach in the sense of placing criminal liability on a corporation because it could and should have prevented the incident, almost regardless of the question of guilt. This practice started in the United States more than hundred years ago, with a doctrine referred to as 'respondent superior,' which allowed courts to impose sanctions on a corporation for the misconduct of employees acting within the scope of their responsibilities and for the intended benefit of the company (Oded, 2013:106-116). Even when employees had been instructed by the management to comply with the law, the corporation could be held liable when the employee nevertheless violated the rules. While this rule has been much modified in the United States with an increasing recognition that there are degrees of corporate negligence, the idea of vicarious liability – that is, criminal responsibility placed on the corporations for what employees have done – has gained ground internationally. As became clear in Chapter 3, however, huge gaps can exist between the law and law enforcement, and while the world as a whole is moving in the direction of vicarious liability, many countries remain hesitant to impose criminal sanctions on corporations.[9]

5.2.1.2   Strict liability with compliance-based defense

Regardless of each judiciary's underlying logic that defends its regulatory status, most countries today have formal rules that ensure that an entity should be held liable if all the following criteria are met:

(1)   an act of corruption has taken place and the organization is involved;
(2)   the individuals involved operate on behalf of the entity;
(3)   the organization or a division of it benefits from the crime; and
(4)   the entity could have prevented the crime with clear signals and internal controls.

However, while some countries – including Germany, France, and the Netherlands – include all forms of crime under this liability, many countries – among them Spain, Italy, and Portugal – limit corporate liability to specific forms of crime. Chapter 3, section 3.2 provided examples of how some corruption cases, upon discretionary interpretation of the rules, have been categorized as being outside the limits of

---

[9]   For example, in Portugal, criminal liability for a company can be fully avoided if the company shows that the bribe was not made on behalf of the company and is not in its interest, and that there was no lack of control by the company's responsible person. The same applies to a company that can prove that the person 'acted against orders or express instructions' from the responsible persons in the company. Similar rules apply, for example, in Italy and Brazil (among other countries) – where a range of mitigating factors reduce corporations' chances of being punished for corruption.

corporate liability, and thus, even if all the four criteria appeared to be met, the corporations suspected of corruption were not subject to a criminal law procedure. Besides, in some countries, corporate liability is second to individual liability and thus relevant only when the individuals involved cannot be identified, an approach that may encourage companies to find scapegoats so as to avoid paying huge fines. Other countries apply both corporate liability *and* individual liability irrespective of each other.[10]

While there are important cross-country variations as to how these rules function, the four common denominators (that is, the four criteria that most judiciaries seem to accept) can be understood as defining a strict liability for corruption that decreases in relation to the extent to which attempts were made to prevent the crime. The extent to which the leaders of an organization choose to let the corruption happen influences this judgment, and because this choice is difficult to observe, the degree of criminal negligence is now seen to depend on characteristics of the corporate culture, often reflected in the nature and robustness of a company compliance program. To various degrees, such programs regulate the corporation's compliance with the duties described in Chapter 4 (see the section 'Duty-Based Liability'), and thus the legal developments appear to converge toward the principles considered efficient from an economic perspective. However, in several countries, criminal liability can be fully avoided if the entity had internal compliance systems in place intended to prevent the act from happening. Currently, the evaluation of a 'corporate culture' has become the essential question when defining corporate liability from a legal perspective.

From an economic perspective, a compliance-based defense presents obvious weaknesses, because it implies a highly discretionary judgment of what is essentially unobserved behavior. Even if the number of standards, rules, and methods for assessing a corporate's culture (or its 'personality') is increasing, the risk of window-dressing remains (as described in Chapter 4). The increasing presence of ethics in management studies syllabi around the world can be expected to reduce business leaders' inclination to take part in corruption, but basic profit-seeking incentives still draw managers and executives in the opposite direction. Corporations can profit enormously by gaining an oligopoly position in a new market, and, in some settings, a bribe is what allows them to assume

---

[10] As happened in the Norwegian case against Yara, described in Chapter 3, section 3.3, where the corporation first accepted a (criminal) fine and secondly, the four leaders were prosecuted and found guilty (the verdict from July 2015 is appealed).

that position. If the bribe is transferred and detected, however, a convincing compliance system is what they need to reduce (or eliminate) the risk of criminal justice consequences and diminish their scope.[11]

As discussed in Chapter 4, economic theories of regulation are driven, in large part, by the search for a solution to the problem of asymmetric information, and one of the main messages from that literature is that subjects should be regulated on the basis of observable facts. Evaluation of criminal negligence should, as far as possible, be kept to reliable performance indicators, and response should follow predictably upon observed crime. Instead of trying to assess a corporation's (real) willingness to comply – many evaluations seek to determine if a corporation is really committed to maintaining a robust internal compliance system, undertaking due diligence efforts, and other self-policing measures – prosecutors should try to determine negligence based on facts, thereby making law enforcement more predictable for both subjects and the general public. The criminal law principle that leads to a criminal charge against an individual who drives on an icy road in the middle of the night, even if nobody is hit, would, if applied to corporate liability, imply a higher risk of liability on those companies that choose to operate in high-risk corruption zones. The increasing amount of data on how corruption seems to vary across markets, sectors, and countries could be used as indicators of what risk level would be acceptable from a criminal law perspective. The amount a corporation gains from acting corruptly – to the extent that this is possible to estimate – is another relevant factor for the judgment of liability, because it indicates the level of disincentive for leaders to prevent the crime.

5.2.1.3   The applicability of criminal law and organization
The more a judiciary departs from the question of guilt and the moral caliber of the accused, the more it deviates from the fundamental principles of criminal law. Instead of altering these principles, it is relevant to ask if criminal law is the right tool for regulating corporate misconduct. Would law enforcement function more efficiently if under purely administrative law, outside the scope of criminal law? Economists have tended to distance themselves from this legal discourse by proposing mechanisms that incentivize compliance and by pragmatically claiming that what matters is that corporations are held liable. In practice,

---

[11]   For example, in the United Kingdom, under Clause 7 of The Bribery Act of 2010, there is a defense for a company if it had 'adequate procedures' against bribery.

however, it is the relationships between fundamental principles, judicial organization, and legal definitions, and the space for interpretation, that determine what law enforcement actually takes place in a society.

Many academics have called for more administrative solutions for the sake of a simplified law enforcement procedure when it comes to corporate crime. With a specific focus on corruption, John Hatchard (2014) finds that the use of civil law remedies instead of criminal proceedings might be a 'key factor in reducing crime,' especially because it will 'require a lower standard of proof' (Hatchard, 2014:339–340). In foreign bribery cases, the criminal proceedings can be 'a notoriously difficult exercise' and, according to Hatchard, 'persuasive threats' such as debarment give 'a potentially effective alternative than resorting to the criminal law' (Hatchard, 2014:262–267). Pieth and Ivory (2011:5) address the efficiency trade-off, arguing that 'the stigma and sanctions of criminal law promise greater deterrence from corporate misconduct and more opportunities for asset recovery, compensation, and mandatory corporate reform. At the same time, the peculiarities of corporate personality and the restraints posed by the principles of fair procedure may limit the ability of lawmakers to check corporate power through the criminal law.'

While some procedural benefits clearly stem from corruption being defined as a crime (such a definition makes asset recovery easier, for instance), and may counterbalance the benefits of an administrative solution, the answer to the question of legal organization needs to be anchored in recognition of what crime is. If criminal law applies to acts that cause the most severe damage to society (as discussed in Chapter 1), and corruption causes damage as described in Chapter 2, then corruption does seem to belong within the reach of criminal law, whether or not the corrupt acts were conducted by organizations. What signal would policy-makers be giving society if acts are considered crime when conducted by individuals, but not if organizations are known to be involved and the individual decision-makers cannot be identified? As Lawrence Friedman (2000) puts it, such a solution would ultimately 'diminish the moral authority of the criminal law as a guide to rational behavior.'[12]

The best solution may lie in the middle ground, with corruption being defined as a crime and thus subject to the high procedural standards associated with criminal law, but with the assessment of compliance

---

[12]   Cited by Christina De Maglie (2011:269), who reviews the regulation of corporate crime in Italy, a country where the question of criminalization is much debated.

systems and operational performance subject to regulation of a more administrative character. Organizations could be monitored regularly to assess their compliance systems (in the same way that oil and gas production companies are regularly monitored for safety), including their ability to deal with corruption risks. Information about this performance (monitored systematically with facts collected over time) could then be used if and when a company is suspected of corruption. With such a system – which seems to be emerging in several jurisdictions – the question of negligence-based liability could be determined by reference to facts and observations, which would make law enforcement in the case of corruption more predictable.

5.2.2 Criminal Corporate Sanctions and Procedure

The high procedural standards associated with criminal law lead to the question of how these standards apply to corporations. To what extent can an organization have human rights? Is there any reason to consider the risk of self-incrimination? And are such strict rules regarding evidence necessary? After all, the relevant penalties are not targeted at specific individuals, and a more relaxed application of procedural law would speed up many law enforcement actions.

The three sides of the efficiency triangle help illuminate these questions. Yes, there can be cost-savings in speedier law enforcement, and more processed cases will increase the deterrent effect. However, what will it do to transaction costs in society if corporations are held criminally liable on weak evidence? What kind of added investments will be made or markets avoided if they are held liable when no offense has been committed? Corruption is regulated by criminal law because of the gravity of the act, and this is supposed to be reflected in a significant penalty. Out of fairness concerns, however, the more severe the sanction imposed, the more important strict procedural rules are. A sanction that is proportional to the crime in terms of the gain obtained and scaled to the low risk of detection (in line with the economic principles discussed in Chapter 4, section 4.2) *will* be severe for the organization in question. Even if no individual is imprisoned, a severe penalty can eliminate a corporation,[13] leaving its staff unemployed and its investors out of pocket. This is what happened to the multinational accounting company Arthur Andersen, a firm that had 85,000 staff. As discussed above, a

---

[13] Discussed by Nanda (2011:72–73).

government that is answerable to the people cannot impose such penalties unless the decision follows due process (that is, procedural rules seen as legitimate by society).

In the longer perspective, a fair criminal law regulation protects society as much as it protects the accused from being subject to a violation of rights, because such violations undermine the criminal justice system's position in society – and can even undermine the government's power to deal with corruption (as discussed in Chapter 2, section 2.2 and Chapter 6, section 6.1). The specific rights accruing to organizations, however, can be modified and provision made for their reasonable needs for protection (which do *not* overlap completely with those accruing to individuals and that are stipulated as internationally recognized human rights).

Which sanctions are applicable to organizations – from an efficiency perspective – may follow from the principle of duty-based sanctions with residual liability, described in Chapter 4, section 4.5. As the law has developed in that direction, however, the application of the principle has become subject to substantial discretion, and what is supposed to be efficient has come with the added cost of lower sanction predictability. Organizations cannot be expected to self-report when they have no chance to predict what awaits them.[14]

Administrative monitoring combined with fact-based criminal law judgment might curb the discretionary character of such sanctions. Penalties would then result from the same sanction principle, with similar calculations made for similar crimes, and the sanction rebates would depend predictably on observable facts.

For the economic incentive mechanism (that is, the one associated with the duty-based sanctions) to work, the principle must be applied with a *steep sanction ladder* – in other words, a clearly established benchmark sanction would apply if there is no reason for a sanction rebate, along with substantial predictable effects of each (stipulated) reason for a rebate.[15] In the case of Arthur Andersen, the penalty was too large for the

---

[14]   See Healey and Serafeim (2014) for a business survey where firms reveal hesitance to approach the prosecutors with evidence while the consequences are uncertain (with regard to settlement, debarment/procurement and double jeopardy).

[15]   Many judiciaries apply this principle, and, in some, liability can be fully evaded upon a confession and/or self-reporting. See, for example, Hungary, Poland, Romania, Russia, Spain, and Ukraine in the CMS Guide (used for the Chapter 3 review of law enforcement challenges). Regarding the United Kingdom the OECD describes the rules as follows: 'If the offender pleads guilty, the

company to bear. There appeared to be few reasons for reducing the sanction in this case, as apparently, the firm was unable to perform its basic accounting services. As discussed in Chapter 4, section 4.5, an international corporation that commits crime and offers legitimate services can be difficult to distinguish from organized crime (that also commits crime and offers legitimate services), which raises the question of why we would want to protect the existence of the former while we want to eradicate the latter? An organization that seems to insist on continuing its corrupt and other illegal practices should not have the right to continue its business, and criminal law can and should be used to protect society in cases of high risk of continued crime and future harm. However, in many instances, when the organization provides legitimate and demanded services, the individuals involved in committing the crime can be identified and thus prosecuted, which will likely reduce the penalty imposed on the whole corporation, allowing it to continue to operate.

Regarding the sanction ladder and *the residual liability* – which, as explained in Chapter 4, section 4.5, is the minimum penalty imposed if a case of corruption occurs and is intended to avoid window-dressing – it is important to keep this law enforcement action to a sufficiently low level so that the organization sees a clear benefit in reporting the incident, instead of risking the far more serious benchmark sanction.

While the principle of duty-based sanctions with strict residual liability has been developed with the aim of promoting deterrence, the principle is consistent with other sanction objectives. Pure retribution vis-à-vis an organization becomes less effectual the more unclear the matter of individual guilt. Rehabilitation, however, is very relevant. Implementation of the principle with monitoring of compliance will influence the corporate culture, and corporations seeking to avoid sanctions will have to establish a functional compliance system that works over time. The principle is also consistent with the aim of victim compensation. Some judiciaries reduce the penalty imposed on a corporation if the corporation makes restitution to victims or in other ways attempts to remedy the consequences of the offense. In Italy, for example, the fine can be cut by up to half if such victim compensation schemes are in place. This is an element in the calculation of sanctions in the United States as well, where

---

sanctions imposed upon him/her can be reduced, the length of the reduction depends on when in the process of investigation/prosecution the plea is given. For example, if a plea is given 'at the first reasonable opportunity,' 1/3 of the 'sentence should be discounted,' but if the case has gone to court, only 1/10, according to guidelines. Phase 3 Report on the UK, p. 19.

the court also takes into account what the accused organization has done to prevent the risk of future offenses.[16]

5.2.3 Legitimate Negotiations on Evidence and Sanctions

A further practical difficulty regarding corporate criminal liability, for which the question of more efficient solutions is highly relevant, is the 'creeping spread of negotiated settlements' – that is, the increasingly common bargains struck between corporations and prosecutors regarding the contents of a charge and sanction (as discussed in Chapter 4, section 4.5.3).[17] Economists tend to think of such negotiations as a welcome tool for cutting costs in law enforcement and increasing the number of law enforcement actions, although economists do not claim to have the solutions to problems regarding the relevant rules and associated institutional structures. Many legal scholars, by contrast, frown at the idea of an offender having the opportunity to negotiate his or her penalty, a practice that is seen as highly inconsistent with the aims of a fair and predictable sentencing process.

Negotiated settlements involve some challenging efficiency trade-offs, which different countries have tackled with different law enforcement solutions. Some countries have formalized rules regarding these settlements, which include strict procedural rules and most details of the result being made public. Some have wide prosecutorial discretion in these matters and apply them with limited transparency. Some countries accept negotiations only upon a confession, while others do not see the point in such a condition. Others again reject formally introducing negotiated settlements as a formal law enforcement solution, yet it happens regardless, for example, by stretching the rule about sanction rebate when the accused has confessed to the crime. Abiola Makinwa (2015), who initiated and coordinated a study to map the rules and practices associated with negotiated settlements in eight European countries, explains how substantial cross-country 'differences in the foundation, process and administration of these arrangements result in a lack of regulatory

---

[16]   See Nanda (2011).

[17]   Regarding trends in the United States, see Nanda (2011). See also the OECD WGB Phase 3 Report on the United States which finds (on p. 32) that: 'Most foreign bribery cases are solved through plea agreements, deferred prosecution agreements and non-prosecution agreements.'

consistency and an uneven playing field.'[18] A more coordinated regulation is necessary to secure the intended benefits associated with self-reporting and faster law enforcement proceedings. Sharon Oded (2015) sees a clear value in moving in such a direction, as he underscores how such arrangements enable prosecuting systems to process more corruption cases and raise the risk of detection. Another benefit of negotiated settlements, compared with ordinary court proceedings, is that they can be combined with organizational restructuring, monitoring, and taking steps to encourage future compliance. Negotiations are unlikely to be an *inefficient* solution if the negotiated settlement is aligned with the criminal law sanction criteria (listed in Chapter 4, section 4.1), and such alignment should be achievable as long as the risk of a court process looms in the background – and becomes a reality if negotiations fail to come to a conclusion that both parties (and preferably also a third party) can accept or the terms of the agreement are broken ex post negotiations (Oded 2015:203–209). And while the idea of highly discretionary offers of leniency for corrupt corporations might be difficult for legal scholars to accept, Makinwa explains how an arrangement 'that encourages self-reporting and voluntary disclosure, lessens the information asymmetry faced by prosecutors' (Makinwa 2015:9). The alternative to a bargain is not necessarily a fair but expensive court process; in many cases, the alternative is that *no* law enforcement action takes place.

Considering the mechanisms discussed in Chapter 4 and this chapter's criteria for criminal justice efficiency, discussed above, negotiated settlements would seem to strengthen law enforcement performance when it comes to both deterrence and value for money. In terms of legitimacy, however, such arrangements pose a clear risk of diminishing citizens' belief in the fairness of the criminal justice system. It is very difficult to create a fair system unless competing versions of the truth are considered by a neutral party, and this is often absent in negotiated solutions. Karin Van Wingerde and Gerben Smid (2015:119–20) explain how the Netherlands has taken significant steps toward securing efficiency gains with formal rules allowing plea bargaining without ex post court approval. According to Van Wingerde and Smid, however, the arrangement 'seems not to be very effective for two reasons': first, few details are published

---

[18]   Makinwa (2015:14). The volume cited is edited by her and includes the eight country reports (The Netherlands, France, Sweden, Germany, Poland, the United Kingdom, Italy, and Norway) as well as reports by experts providing different perspectives on the cross-cutting challenges associated with negotiated settlements.

about the deals, so 'we know little about the reasons for the settlement, the nature and extent of the offences, and the content of the agreement'; and second, the arrangement is seen as having significant advantages for firms and may well benefit them 'more than the public interest.'

The arrangement obviously reduces sanction predictability, because the outcome of a bargain depends on the parties' bargaining powers. Whether the settlement is the result of a negotiation or a de facto imposition can be impossible for outsiders to tell, depending on what information is released, if any at all. Rules may exist that are intended to govern which details to make public, but it can be hard to ascertain if these rules are followed in practice, because the supply and demand of confidentiality regarding the details of the crime might be one of the strongest cards in the bargain – that is, the accused will often go far in admitting to crime if the facts of the case can be kept secret. Other risks include a too biased representation of the accused, as discussed in Chapter 4 (that is, favoring either the management *or* the owners), and biases on the side of the prosecutor (including the risk of corruption).

Therefore, in order to secure the tempting efficiency gains associated with negotiated settlements, governments must be sure to protect legitimacy when they develop rules intended to regulate such practice.

Governments should introduce guidelines regarding the foundation for entering into negotiations, which bargaining chips to bring to the table, and the procedure to be used in the bargaining process. Guidelines, though, will be insufficient to secure fair outcome and protect the prosecutor's legitimacy in circumstances in which the prosecutor is given considerable discretion in negotiations. As a minimum, the reasons for entering into negotiations must be made known to the public and the sanction result must be defended explicitly by the criminal justice system so that citizens can compare the outcome of one case with the results of similar cases. Accountability mechanisms might involve institutional changes as well, including some form of ex post formal control of the bargain outcome. Despite endangering the efficiency gains associated with enforcement costs and cases processed, prosecutors or judges – or some other third-party player in charge of approving the outcome of negotiations – should have the ex post option of opening court proceedings if the details of the deal are not sufficiently convincing in terms of the ratio between evidence and the eventual penalty.[19]

---

[19] These views are also presented in Søreide (2015:138–146). For further economic arguments, see Garoupa and Stephen (2008).

5.2.4   Criminal Liability for State Institutions

To what extent is the principle associated with duty-based sanctions regimes (with residual liability) relevant for organizations in general, not only privately owned corporations? State institutions – such as a utility regulator, a hospital, or a police unit – are all organizations expected to obey criminal law, and thus the matter of ownership should not determine criminal law enforcement. Besides, duty-based sanctions regimes accentuate leaders' responsibilities and induce efficient implementation of ethical guidelines, whistle-blower programs, and monitoring systems.

For several reasons, this sanction regime may *appear* less relevant for state institutions.[20] Civil servants are often entrusted with huge discretion which complicates law enforcement in general, because it is difficult to determine if corruption has taken place unless it is clearly evident that a bribe transaction has taken place. And, if a bribe transaction is known, the public sector decision-maker is likely to be known as well, which reduces the relevance of a sanction imposed on the organization as a whole. Such sanctions may be seen as more applicable in cases of bribery by private sector organizations, because the whole organization profits from the crime, making it easier to claim that the individuals involved acted on behalf of the organization and not necessarily for personal gain.

The main reason why corporate liability principles are nevertheless applicable for state institutions is the problem of entrenched corruption, where a corrupt culture has developed and many civil servants appear to be involved while they collaborate to keep the facts secret.[21] In these circumstances, duty-based sanctions may strengthen detection and prevention, improve fairness, while keeping law enforcement costs within limits, which becomes evident if only the sanctions applied are adapted for the fact that the offender is a public institution.

A fine will have different effects in private and public institutions. In the private sector, a heavy fine harms those who supposedly have profited from the corruption, especially the owners of a company and those individuals who have received bonuses to reward them for participating, directly or indirectly, in a corrupt deal. In the public sector, where the owner is the state, imposing a heavy fine on a public elementary school or police office inflicts harm on taxpayers in general or the clients for the services provided by the state in particular – in these examples, the

---

[20]   This discussion draws heavily on Søreide and Rose-Ackerman (2016).

[21]   The characteristic differences between public and private institutions and the role of duty-based sanctions regimes in public institutions are described also in Søreide and Rose-Ackerman (2016).

children attending a school riddled with a corrupt culture or the victims of crime who may receive less attention from the police. Imposing a small fine, on the other hand, is no satisfactory solution. An investigation and law enforcement process vis-à-vis a state institution must be expected to have some impact on the given institution and its leaders – regardless of the size of the fine. However, a reaction that neither reflects the graveness of the harm caused, nor affects the institution's operations in any significant way, may rely on too high expectations regarding symbolic effects, and citizens are not so easily convinced that criminal law is being enforced.

For these reasons, when it comes to public institutions, it is necessary to impose penalties *other* than fines.

At least three categories of sanctions are relevant for corrupt state institutions:

(1) *Intensified monitoring:* for example, external controllers are tasked not only to investigate acts in the past but also to oversee the institution's daily work moving forward – a penalty likely to be given to leaders of the sanctioned institution and to prove expensive for the government, yet seen as reasonable, given the gravity of the problems.

(2) *Reorganization of authority:* for example, responsibilities are taken away from the institution, leaders and some staff members are relocated, and the entity is restructured.

(3) *Victim compensation:* for example, the institution is given the responsibility for identifying the victims of the corruption and finding ways of compensating them through monetary or nonmonetary means.[22]

Given explicit guidance in recognition of the duty-based sanction principle, including a sanction ladder reflecting the degree of negligence (as discussed above), state institutions would be able to predict the type and severity of a nonmonetary sanction for corruption, and thus the law enforcement reactions would be predictable and would serve as corruption deterrents while unmistakably signaling expected compliance. Similar to liability vis-à-vis private corporations, the duty-based sanction regime should be combined with the principle of residual liability in public institutions as well: an organization should face sanctions under

---

[22] Such compensation is possible both in cases of pulverized consequences (many victims that have faced limited costs) and more serious consequences for a fewer number victims.

any circumstance in which collusive corruption is known to have developed (that is, in any case in which the liability goes beyond those who are knowingly involved). Organizations would be sanctioned according to how they have handled the corruption, whether they have a culture that fosters or prevents corruption, and which tools they have in place to avoid corruption in the future. A (residual) sanction imposed whenever the organization appears to have been corrupt reduces the risk of window-dressing; the leaders cannot avoid a sanction by pointing at their solid compliance system.

The major concern regarding sanctions imposed on state institutions relates to the administration of such law enforcement: How can the state punish itself? What should the position of the prosecutor be vis-à-vis the accused when the accused is a state institution? This is one of the challenges addressed in the next section.

5.3 THE PROSECUTOR'S STANDING ON EFFICIENT LAW ENFORCEMENT

Chapter 3's review of obstacles to efficient law enforcement leaves no doubt that law enforcement requires the prosecutor (as an institution) to have the authority to perform its duties independently. In order to efficiently investigate a case, secure evidence, interrogate suspects, hear witnesses, and charge an offender, the prosecutor must have certain competencies and resources. With a composite efficiency concept in mind, this section considers both the prosecutor's traditional and new responsibilities, the difficulty of maintaining independence, and the importance of public access to law enforcement information.

5.3.1 Competencies for Efficient Law Enforcement

What are the minimum tools for efficient law enforcement? Certainly, the presence of an international infrastructure for hiding corruption, with bribes often paid by multinationals via complex corporate structures and third parties, while bribe-recipients might be protected by politically steered institutions, has created new challenges – with a scope far beyond the circumstances that criminal law was developed for. Prosecutors around the world evolve, and with different pace, they seek to adapt to new challenges, and still, there is much uncertainty around their roles and efficient performance. What are the required competencies that follow on directly from the prosecutor's functions, as discussed in this and previous chapters?

The answers depend on which roles the prosecutor is expected to perform: the 'classic' role, the role of negotiator, and the role of regulator.

(1) *The 'classic' prosecutor:* Regardless of which incentives for self-reporting are introduced, most criminals will try to keep their crimes secret. Consequently, the criminal justice system must retain its functions of investigating suspected crimes and charging those whom the evidence suggests are guilty. An efficient law enforcement organization needs to have its expenses for these functions (for example, staff salaries, and the cost of using increasingly advanced technology for processing complex cases) covered by the state. Insufficient resources are frequently cited as the largest obstacle to law enforcement, including in high-income countries. Securing the resources necessary for the prosecutor to execute the prime functions, including leadership sufficiently committed and competent to carry the responsibility, is a political responsibility. Failure to secure these basic government services is easily taken as a sign of weak political commitment to the anticorruption agenda (as discussed in Chapter 3, section 3.1).

(2) *The negotiating prosecutor:* The more or less formalized function of a negotiator in dialogue with the suspect or accused requires specialized competence. The formal or informal opportunity for such negotiations expands the prosecutor's power – indeed, to some extent, the prosecutor takes on the role of a court. However, an investigator is not trained to perform as a judge. Investigators are not supposed to act neutrally in the sense of balancing a sanction against both the circumstances of the accused and the gravity of the offense. They cannot be expected to hold an unbiased view regarding the validity of the evidence they present or the information given by the accused. Facing prosecutors with almost monopoly powers (for example, 'Confess and accept this sanction, or I will eliminate your business with a heavy fine!') and whose careers may well depend on the number of cases they win, the accused is at a clear risk of self-incrimination,[23] even in the case of corporations with expert defense lawyers. Enhanced authority should be matched with strategies to strengthen accountability, which might be especially relevant in cases of negotiations that take place on a discretionary basis with offenders who have already demonstrated their propensity to take or offer

---

[23] In the sense of admitting more than the committed crime in order to secure for oneself what appears to be the best possible of all undesired law enforcement outcomes.

bribes. Strengthened accountability, however, will not necessarily solve the fundamental difficulties of allowing prosecutors to act as negotiating judges.

(3) *The prosecutor as a regulator*: As the question of criminal negligence is tied to an assessment of corporate culture, the prosecutor needs reliable information about the inner life of the organization it suspects of corruption. Of course, an organization accused of committing a crime will prefer to decide for itself what information is relevant, if necessary in collaboration with private investigatory consultants. As discussed above, however, this information should be as fact-based as possible. The mere existence of a compliance program is not evidence of sincere compliance. A promise of better conduct in the future is of little interest to prosecutors when they are assessing a criminal act.[24] Furthermore, the nature of an organization's corporate culture cannot be accurately identified by investigators who visit that organization to investigate a crime. Monitoring of corporate culture is, or should be, a regulatory task, like monitoring of safety standards, and regulatory institutions should be established to undertake such work. Like environmental or health care regulation, monitoring of corporate culture should look at the factors listed as 'duties' in Chapter 4, section 4.5 (self-policing, self-reporting, a whistle-blower system, and so forth). Mandatory reporting in compliance with the law – something that many firms have to do in many areas, including reporting on issues of relevance to corruption risks – can be subject to randomized controls; over time, the regulator will generate a substantial amount of information on how firms appear to comply with the law. What is not so clear, however, is whether this regulatory function should be carried out by the criminal law prosecutor.[25]

---

[24]   Although several jurisdictions consider the risk of future breach of laws when calculating sanction rebates.

[25]   The monitoring of compliance systems will not necessarily require added state bureaucracy. Private solutions have emerged – such as the British BS 10500, which is used as a model for the proposed ISO 37001 (see http://www.iso.org/iso/home.html for details), which are standards on which corporations can be accredited by auditors or other certifying agencies. Stephen Matthews warns, however, that: 'the auditing bodies performing these evaluations do so for a fee, and may not have the requisite expertise to make the fine-grained, risk-based, case-by-case assessments that law enforcement agencies (including the US Department of Justice and the UK Ministry of Justice), as well as the more competent and reputable private certification firms, routinely emphasize as necessary.' See *The Global Anti-Corruption Blog* on 5 February 2015, http://globalanticorruptionblog.com/

It is not unreasonable to expect a prosecutor to operate with several competencies and responsibilities. After all, most business leaders and professionals manage a range of different functions; with the necessary training, prosecutors – in the sense of institutions with highly competent staff – can operate in different roles. The pertinent question is whether these multiple functions have conflicting objectives, and thus create incentive problems that prevent the efficient performance of each role. There is also a risk that the introduction of new roles (as a negotiating judge and regulator of compliance) means that too much power is concentrated in one law enforcement institution. If so, structural changes might promote better solutions in consideration of the three pillars of efficiency discussed above: fairness, prevention, and value for money. For example, could it be that judges in courts would be in a better position than the prosecutor to reach fair settlement results? After all, judges are trained to consider how a criminal justice sanction should be decreased upon a confession and collaboration with the prosecutor. Such a solution, however, raises the question of who should provide a check on the settlement result. One candidate might be the appeal courts. However, by removing the negotiating function from the prosecutor, we remove the whole basis for the intended efficiency gain. Every solution we might consider presents challenges to be solved.

When it comes to the prosecutor's regulatory function, it makes sense to remove the evaluation of organizations' compliance systems from the duties of the prosecutor (or the investigator), because an accused organization's expected performance in the future easily distorts the judgment (or the charge) of a criminal law enforcement action, which should center around the offense that happened in the *past*. The law enforcement institutions should be structured in ways that help to avoid this difficulty. Exactly how is difficult to establish because the evaluation of compliance systems is tied to the question of criminal liability, which is the basis for the prosecutor's criminal charge.

There are more reasons why a reorganization of responsibilities may be necessary for more efficient prosecution of cases. As mentioned above, one of the reasons why organizations prefer not to self-report is the uncertainty regarding the consequences of a law enforcement process. The calculation of a sanction can be made more predictable inside the criminal justice system. What concerns many corporations, however, are the risks of indirect consequences such as debarment from public tenders

2015/02/05/dear-governments-please-dont-make-private-certification-the-touch
stone-of-adequate-anti-bribery-program/#more-3069 (retrieved November 2015).

or exclusion from operations and markets for other reasons. Some of these added consequences can be handled through better coordination and collaboration across institutions. And, if the corporate culture is to be assessed for the sake of determining the degree of negligence, this evaluation is also applicable for those who need to know if a corporation is 'morally qualified' to participate in a public tender. The debarment procedures in public procurement do not function very well in their current design,[26] and by moving the authority and competence for deciding on debarment to the criminal justice system, or to a regulatory body entrusted with monitoring corporate conduct, one could coordinate the effect of total sanctions and thereby increase the predictability for the accused. Such steps, combined with the principles discussed above, might induce more corporations to self-report their corruption, without any substantial loss of fairness or state revenues.

5.3.2 Prosecutor Independence and Accountability

Considering the prosecutor's functions and performance, it is essential to keep in mind the problems addressed in Chapter 3, section 3.5, namely, that the prosecuting authority itself can be corrupted. This difficulty has a constitutional character as it reflects the trade-off between ensuring independent criminal law enforcement – in the sense of preserving the prosecutor's ability to place a charge without the consent of other government institutions – and securing political control of the implementation of criminal justice policy decisions. On the one hand, any attempt by external actors (especially from the political level) to influence or control the criminal justice system will clearly jeopardize the system's standing in society and its legitimacy. On the other hand, elected political leaders are representatives of the people. A criminal justice system embedded in the society where criminal law enforcement is to take place should not be completely isolated from democratic forces.

5.3.2.1 The risk of a corrupted judiciary
Considering this trade-off with respect to corruption, it is necessary to keep in mind the distinction between, on the one side, corruption risks related to the lack of independence of the judiciary from the rest of the government and, on the other side, the risks that arise within the criminal

---

[26] A crime does not have to be detected for a corporation to be dishonest and some corporations experience corruption but are nevertheless trustworthy. Problems with debarment in public procurement are described by Hjelmeng and Søreide (2014), and Auriol and Søreide (2015).

justice system when the judiciary exerts its independence.[27] Factors related to *lack of independence* include the organization of the judicial system (in particular, the existence of a constitutional court and the position of prosecutors vis-à-vis the government), procedures for making budget decisions for the judiciary (including pay scales), the selection of individual judges (as well as their judicial tenure and career path), whether or not judges have immunity from prosecution, and the level of protection they receive from threats and intimidation.

Factors related to the risk of corruption *within* the judiciary are completely different. They include the decision-making process regarding which cases to investigate (and who is involved in making these decisions), asset disclosure rules, caseload per judge and associated delays, working conditions (especially vis-à-vis lawyers in the private sector), revolving-door concerns, the performance of a whistle-blower system within the criminal justice system, the extent to which court proceedings are open to the public, and general rules for documenting opinions and dissents in court.

Outside observers will often find it hard to tell whether biased criminal justice outcomes are the consequence of corruption within the judiciary or of undue influence being exerted by corrupt decision-makers elsewhere in the government system. What matters for the general public are the mechanisms that secure a certain level of accountability in the performance of law enforcement, regardless of whether the system is subject to internal or external pressures. Unless the system is trustworthy, people will soon turn to private solutions in the form of informal conflict resolution, mafia-style protection rackets and enforcement of their own law, and commercial arbitration outside formal legal systems.

Which mechanisms will secure accountable criminal law enforcement? Empirical studies designed to throw light on this question face the challenge of distinguishing between de jure criminal law enforcement and its de facto counterpart.[28] This distinction is nevertheless made in a study by Anne van Aaken, Lars P. Feld, and Stefan Voigt (2010), who investigated the relationship between the extent of corruption and prosecutorial independence. They found that de facto prosecutorial independence substantially reduces the magnitude of corruption in society. As discussed with reference to Figure 3.1 in Chapter 3 (and more generally in Chapter 2), proving causality in studies of the relationship between

---

[27] This point is elaborated by Rose-Ackerman (2007).
[28] Ríos-Figueroa and Staton (2014) provide a review and assessment of law enforcement indicators.

corruption and institutional or societal factors is usually problematic, if not impossible in this case, because societies with low levels of corruption may also be more inclined to accept prosecutorial independence. Nonetheless, the strong correlation is a clear pointer to the relevance of prosecutorial independence in the fight against corruption, as well as the importance of assessing accountability mechanisms with respect to their actual performance. In another study, this time with Jerg Gutmann, Stefan Voigt dug deeper into the role of prosecutorial independence and found that judicial accountability mechanisms have little effect on a judiciary's appetite for corruption unless the judiciary is independent, whereas prosecutorial independence without efficient accountability checks 'can have adverse effects' (that is, if a culture of corruption emerges in an unchecked judiciary, the executive has few opportunities to deal with the problem).[29] In summary, prosecutors should be subject to accountability mechanisms that are compatible with the independence sufficient to function without the government's interference in cases.

5.3.2.2 The independence spectrum: two contrasting cases

Despite the correlation between performance and independence, a quick comparison of two neighboring European countries – both old civilizations with highly competent legal scholars and a public that is well educated and aware of legal and democratic values – easily makes one realize that it might be difficult to draw conclusions regarding the optimal prosecutor position.

In Italy, policymakers have deemed it of utmost importance to give the judiciary the powers it needs to efficiently address problems of political corruption and mafia networks; the Italian constitution also grants magistrates considerable independence. While the government has no authority to interfere in judicial proceedings, the prosecutor operates under *the legality principle*, namely, to secure law and order, prosecutors must respond to all cases of crime. However, as Carlo Rosetti (2000) and Alberto Vannucci (2009) explain, despite such powers and principles, the Italian criminal law system has not improved its performance against political corruption. The famous *mani pulite* ('clean hands') operations in the 1990s resulted in as many as four thousand indictments against politicians and public administrators, including six former prime ministers and more than five hundred members of Parliament. Nevertheless, in terms of law enforcement, the operation was a disaster, because it created an enormous overload of cases in a system that was already sluggish. For

---

[29] Voigt and Gutmann (2014).

the accused, the delays amounted to denial of due process, and given the difficulty of dealing with the backlog, the government, with parliamentary support, introduced a deadline for the disposal of cases. If not brought before a judge within a certain number of years, the proceedings are cancelled and the case is dismissed. Combined with the right to appeal to a higher court, and the fact that no sanction is imposed until a final verdict has been reached, this 'solution' resulted in de facto impunity for many state officers, government ministers, and party leaders (Rosetti, 2000:173). Frequent allegations of corruption within the Italian judiciary add to the difficulty of determining a workable reform strategy. The politicians, however, who introduced the deadline for the disposal of cases that resulted in de facto impunity for many of those accused of corruption, cannot necessarily be trusted to solve the task.

In France, the judiciary stands at the opposite end of the spectrum from the Italian judiciary in terms of independence. But France, too, suffers from law enforcement shortcomings. French prosecutors represent the state, not the people, and the government (citing executive supremacy) can interfere with ongoing investigations. This lack of judicial independence was evident in a case involving the bank Crédit Lyonnais. This huge financial scandal 'led to the discovery of a system of interlocking networks of secret interrelationships among ministers, the Crédit Lyonnais presidents, chief financial and executive officials, the public administration, the French and Italian Socialist Parties, and leading businessmen with alleged Mafia ties' (Rosetti:175). Rather than encourage the prosecutors to root out those involved in the scandal, the government interfered to prevent the magistrates from 'reaching the upper ranks of the government system implicated in a conspiracy to defraud the state' (Rosetti:174). The subordination of the prosecutor to the executive was exploited to cover up corruption and collaboration with international organized crime; clearly, the incumbent regime and its allies were put above the law. Parts of this complex case have subsequently been pursued in France and abroad, but the most powerful players have faced no consequences for their crimes.[30]

The independence to freely investigate and prosecute offenders is essential to avoid improper influence on law enforcement, and the criminal justice system itself must, like other public institutions, be subject to checks and balances. Prosecutorial independence, however, is

---

[30] See, for example, the investigation of IMF President Christine Lagarde, starting in 2014, and FBI press release on 18 December 2003: 'Credit Lyonnais and Others to Plead Guilty and Pay $771 Million in Executive Life Affair.'

not sufficient by itself to secure these two aims. When one considers the cases of Italy and France, however, democratic performance appears no less important for efficient and unbiased law enforcement than the way in which the judiciary is organized. Most societies have more mechanisms for holding politicians accountable than they have for controlling prosecutors, however, and as David Johnson points out in a study of prosecutorial powers, 'in democratic countries, elections, the media, and public opinion constrain and restrain politicians' behavior, and no one argues that politicians should be 'independent' of the citizens they represent' (Johnson, 2003:274).[31]

5.3.2.3 Access to law enforcement information

Regardless of whether the main risks are associated with political influence or internal corruption of the judiciary, access to law enforcement information may strengthen the pressure from the public for judicial integrity and promote efficient monitoring of the judiciary's performance in criminal law enforcement. While performance data for the judiciary as a whole should be gathered, analyzed with statistical tools, and made available to the public, the details of specific cases should also be released. Access to information about the accused, the offense, the evidence, the sanction, and its justification (including factors that modified the sanction, as well as the actual enforcement of the sanction) is necessary to build and preserve public confidence in the judiciary. For this reason, most developed countries have strict rules regarding which details to make public.

Despite such rules, however, governments can be tempted to keep such law enforcement details hidden. Confidentiality protects both the criminal justice system and the incumbent political leadership against criticism. These institutions could be inclined to collude in developing plausible excuses for keeping information secret. In parallel, influential offenders will call for confidentiality to protect their reputations. Firms accused of bribery request confidentiality for the sake of avoiding what they consider unreasonable additional law enforcement reactions and administrative consequences (such as debarment from public procurement, demands for compensation, or refiled criminal law charges in countries that do not recognize double jeopardy principles).

---

[31] Transparency International (2007) provides a useful introduction to the problem of a corrupted judiciary, practical accountability mechanisms, and constitutional challenges – with examples from many countries.

Offenders accused of corruption are inclined to collaborate with investigators and provide a confession in exchange for a cloak of secrecy to be drawn around the details of the crime and around the confession. The trade-off between transparency and the benefits of collaboration is not straightforward, and arguments must be weighed from the perspective of all three sides of the efficiency triangle. A reduced case load (following the concealment of some of the facts of cases) is a weighty argument against openness, but can fairness be guaranteed without the release of at least some details about the law enforcement action, including the identity of the accused, the criminal law violation, the evidence, and a justification for the sanction?[32] One way of solving these sorts of dilemmas is to deny requests for opacity but to mitigate the risk of added consequences that may come on top of the law enforcement burden. Better coordination between criminal and administrative law enforcers could avoid (what, for the indicted, appears to be) extra punishment[33] and help produce clearer rules on double jeopardy internationally. As discussed above, the question of debarment from public procurement should be decided by the criminal justice system, rather than by procurement agents.

Taking a broader perspective, we must recognize that criminal justice systems differ substantially across countries in terms of their organization, competencies, capacities, and accountability. Yet, while each country must find its own solution for securing judicial integrity and avoiding undue influence on law enforcement, the risk of conflicting motivations, biased results, and human rights violations cannot be ignored. Deals hatched in backrooms for lenient sanctions in exchange for offenders providing evidence of past corrupt acts and promises of future compliance can substantially boost the number of cases processed, encouraging private sector leaders to applaud the law enforcement system's flexibility and understanding, and the government to trumpet

---

[32] Regarding this matter on openness, the OECD WGB Phase 3 Report on the Czech Republic maintains on p. 33 (with reference to articles 1, 2, 3 and 5 in the OECD convention): If 'agreements on guilt and punishment' have been made, it is recommended that these are made public, with 'as much information as possible' on the reasons behind the agreement, the convicted natural or legal persons and which sanctions/terms that are agreed.

[33] For an economic discussion on double punishment, see Garoupa and Gomez-Pomar (2004). According to them, double punishment is a cost on society, and should be avoided (that is, if one form of penalty is imposed, the next should be barred). Among arguments in favor of double punishment are the risk of legal error and collusion between law enforcers and the accused.

'a more efficient law enforcement system.' Voters, however, must be wary of tendencies among powerful elites to steer the criminal justice system in the direction of de facto impunity for profitable but very damaging forms of crime. Unless all three efficiency pillars are taken into account when designing reforms of the criminal justice system, those reforms will not necessarily be 'more efficient.'

5.4 SUMMARY: EFFICIENCY AND LAW ENFORCEMENT PRINCIPLES

Consensus around what constitutes efficiency in criminal justice approaches to corruption is essential for finding and implementing workable strategies. This chapter has discussed the importance of understanding efficiency in light of several objectives, including crime control and detection, promoting fairness, and value for money. The waste of monetary and nonmonetary resources is not compatible with efficiency, and moral development through criminal justice requires fairness and transparency. While law enforcement strategies may well be developed with 'smaller' sub-goals in mind, the recognition of a broader efficiency concept is necessary if efficiency successes are not to come at the expense of other goals.

In this chapter, I have briefly touched on some of the trade-offs that must be considered and I have explained why brutal law enforcement strategies may stifle a criminal justice system's ability to nurture the moral capacity of potential offenders. I have discussed the importance of promoting self-reporting in corruption cases, but warned about the temptation of ignoring transparency. I have argued in favor of keeping the prosecution of corruption under criminal law, rather than administrative law, including in cases involving organizations, but argued for rethinking law enforcement responsibilities when organizations are being prosecuted. One change in particular would be very helpful: distinguishing between the different prosecuting functions in these cases, notably, the roles of 'compliance regulator' and 'prosecuting judge.'

I have argued in favor of negotiated settlements as a necessary law enforcement action in cases of corporate crime, yet I have also urged that the negotiating process be subject to ex post monitoring and that court proceedings should be retained as a fallback option. Facts about the case and the settlement result should be publicly available. Transparency brings with it the risk of reducing the inclination among offenders to self-report, but the main problem for many of those who remain silent is the unpredictability associated with law enforcement consequences, and predictability can be bolstered by extending the criminal justice system's authority over some of the possible consequences and improving coordination with other law enforcement and/or administrative institutions at the national and international level. Debarment from public procurement, for example, could be determined as part of settlement processes, and double jeopardy risks can be reduced by extending current international agreements. I have also made the point that duty-based sanctions regimes (with strict residual liability) are highly relevant for state institutions as long as the sanctions imposed are adapted to these cases (fines imposed on a public institution is not an efficient solution if it harms taxpayers or clients).

Ultimately, I have pointed out the importance of the prosecuting institution's ability to operate without undue influence from other government institutions. Constitutional independence, however, is far from sufficient to secure this goal. Besides, the risk of corruption within prosecuting bodies is especially high in cases of corruption where the accused has already confirmed his or her inclination to revert to bribery when facing temptations or problems.

6. The law enforcement environment at the national and international level

Every government has a responsibility for developing efficient strategies against domestic crime, and for that purpose the mechanisms discussed in Chapters 4 and 5 might well be useful. When it comes to entrenched corruption, however, the crime is both a source and a reflection of government weakness. Many civil servants may want to combat corruption, but significant parts of the state administration cannot be trusted to do so. The bigger the problem is, the less reason there is to believe that the government will find an efficient law enforcement solution to the problem. This means that the magnitude of this form of crime reflects the government's standing in society, and thus a strategy to tackle corruption cannot be separated from a strategy to strengthen that standing, whether through strengthened governance capacity, adherence to checks and balances, or the holding of free and fair elections. At the same time, corruption is subject to international factors and forces that are beyond the control of individual national governments. For these reasons, efficient solutions require governments to join forces at the international level.

This chapter addresses why criminal law strategies must depend on the given society's law enforcement environment, why the coordinated action so urgently needed at the international level is so difficult to achieve, and why some law enforcement instruments may nevertheless come to play a powerful role in the fight against corruption.

6.1 CONTEXTUAL UNDERSTANDING OF THE LAW ENFORCEMENT CHALLENGE

The previous chapters have addressed the mechanisms of criminal law responses to corruption as if those responses are subject to universal principles. But the same enforcement strategy is likely to work differently in, say, Mexico than in Denmark. As this book has underscored, the organization and functioning of the criminal justice system cannot be detached from the broader system of government in a country. The more trusted, legitimate, and fair the overall government system appears to be, the more likely it is that crime detection efforts and criminal justice processes will keep levels of crime generally, and corruption specifically, low. This is why many low-crime societies need invest only modest amounts in crime control while having few worries about the risk of crime escalation. Most societies, however, face much sterner challenges. For them, debates about optimal strategies for law enforcement are of little interest unless they can help produce concrete, if modest and incremental, improvements in practice.

6.1.1   Heaven and Hell: Different Law Enforcement Equilibria

The extent of corruption differs across sectors, regions, cities, and institutions, and across countries with similar geographic characteristics. The concept of *crime control equilibria* helps us understand these differences.

Figure 6.1 is inspired by a model by Jens Andvig and Kalle Moene (1990) that describes how the profitability of corruption may depend on the extent of the problem. The horizontal axis is the extent of corruption in the previous period while the vertical axis shows the current extent of corruption as a function of the level of corruption in the previous period. The figure illustrates a dynamic multiple equilibrium model with two stable equilibria, A and C, and an unstable equilibrium, C. One argument this figure illustrates is that the impact of crime control varies across different levels of government accountability, and once a stable equilibrium is reached, good or bad, it is difficult to get out of it. In short, any country will need to work very hard, or perform very poorly, to change its level of corruption.

Think of A as the *good equilibrium* (or *low equilibrium*) where crime control is efficient because the government is trusted and its laws are quickly melded with norms in society in a highly transparent process of a two-way dialogue. Proposing a bribe transaction in this situation is hazardous because there is normally a high risk that the counterpart might be honest. For the highly trusted politicians and civil servants, the scale of the damage to their reputations that being caught acting corruptly would inflict is too huge for most of them to dare to participate in a corrupt deal. In addition, low-corruption societies have better monitoring systems, a more welcoming environment for whistle-blowers, and more reliable criminal justice systems. Citizens expect law compliance, and not grabbing, and group pressures in various settings tend to favor honesty. Compared to other countries, the national law enforcement strategies appear efficient, although, in reality, the level of crime would be low no

corruption period t

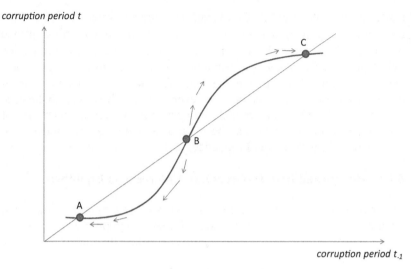

corruption period t.₁

Figure 6.1   The notion of multiple corruption law enforcement equilibria

matter which enforcement strategies were chosen – as long as they are consistent with the overall impression of a fair and just government.

In the C-equilibrium, the situation is the complete opposite; whatever the government tries to achieve, a large majority of citizens oppose it, and instead of adjusting their moral views to come into line with law enforcement needs, they grab what they can when in a position to do so, well aware that 'everybody else' would do exactly the same. The more problems with corruption a society faces, the weaker the government's position is to deal with the problem. The more corruption, the easier it is to bribe one's way out of trouble if detected. Losing one's formal wage if caught may not be a big problem if the wage level is very low; bribes may constitute the main revenues and motivate the work. The more extensive the corruption problem, the easier it is to ask for or offer bribes, and the lower the social stigma associated with such acts.[1]

When corruption levels are high and the state has lost its legitimacy, the average citizen has little reason to abide by anticorruption laws. The state cannot be relied upon to provide essential services, so individuals obtain them in other ways, turning to a network of allies, informal rules, and private conflict resolution to get what they need. These informal

---

[1]   Along the lines spelled out here, Andvig and Moene (1990) explain how corruption increases in its own extent and why there might be good and bad equilibria.

solutions and rules become more reliable in regulating society and thus more important than whatever services the government can offer. The formal powers associated with state structures still offer rent-seeking opportunities, and talented individuals may well prefer a job in the public sector with opportunities for corrupt benefits, instead of honest production. Bureaucratic decisions continue to be sold in exchange for bribes and the government continues to be strongly mistrusted, but most citizens somehow manage in this situation because they know the rules of the game. A majority of citizens would probably prefer a reliable and honest state administration, but demanding such reform would involve risks.

These mechanisms associated with high corruption circumstances suggest that different forces in society keep the level of corruption high; once it reaches a certain level, corruption easily stabilizes in a *high equilibrium* (or *bad equilibrium*). Even if a government tries to tackle the problem with increasing resources for law enforcement, strengthening controls, and imposing heavier penalties, the high equilibrium may seem virtually unmovable. This is why the same countries are high-corruption countries year after year. The darker colored countries on Transparency International's Corruption Perceptions map for 2015 (included in Chapter 2) are almost the same ones that are dark on the 2005 map. Not only are they perceived to be more corrupt, but they are also far more likely to see themselves in a bad law enforcement equilibrium.

Point B in Figure 6.1 is an *unstable* equilibrium – it is at a tipping point. A society on the move toward B swiftly ends up in another stable equilibrium; which means a shift from a low-corruption situation to a high-corruption situation, or vice versa. Such a shift may begin gradually, by a more relaxed (or strict) attitude to checks and balances, or an increasingly more brutalized (or safe and just) society. Or it may be triggered by a certain event – for example, the result of the outbreak of violent conflict, an abrupt change from an autocratic to a more democratic regime, or the launch of a comprehensive 'big push' reform program.[2] As point B is unstable, society in change will easily result in one of the two stable corruption equilibria.

6.1.2 Threat-based Enforcement or Trust-based Compliance

An efficient criminal justice strategy will either have to protect a good, or low, crime equilibrium *or* contribute to the forces in society that are pushing in the direction of a good equilibrium.

---

[2] See Easterly (2006).

Protecting the status quo makes sense only for societies that consider themselves to be in a good equilibrium. If, as argued in Chapter 5, the state's position in society determines its ability to influence citizens' moral burden of committing a crime, then a criminal justice strategy should strive to protect the image of the state as a fair law enforcer that works for the benefit of society. Such a strategy is more likely to keep corruption levels low than a strategy that involves a tough and comprehensive crackdown on corruption, where the main goal is for the state to be *seen as acting* to curb the problem while showing little mercy toward those who violate the law. The latter type of strategy is likely to violate procedural laws and fairness principles while brutalizing society and unnecessarily alienating law enforcers from potential law violators.[3] For these reasons, governments must carefully consider their level of toughness/brutality; short-term gains tend to come at the cost of dealing with longer-term challenges.

Despite the value of harmonized criminal law responses across countries, a society should embrace a criminal law enforcement strategy that matches its equilibrium position. For countries with low levels of corruption, it will not be *efficient* to let law enforcement practices take a form that distorts the government's standing in society, if that reduces the government's ability to influence citizens' attitudes toward crime. Influencing their moral cost is a far cheaper deterrent than imposing criminal justice penalties.

For many governments, however, such a trust-based strategy is not an option. Societies at point C in Figure 6.1, a bad equilibrium, cannot protect a legitimacy that does not exist. Policymakers in such situations typically resort to a purely threat-based approach, much in line with the classic economic prescriptions described in Chapter 4, acting on the assumption that a visibly stern criminal law approach is exactly what the society needs to spur development and climb out of the bad equilibrium quagmire. To what extent can such threat-based strategy be expected to succeed?

The equilibrium theory discussed in this section suggests that incentives at the individual level – which explain aggregated forces in society

---

[3]   A comprehensive cost-cutting strategy may have similar consequences. A downsized state administration easily reduces the confidence in government decisions while violations of various laws result in few consequences since civil servants no longer have the capacity to follow up. The government's risk of being perceived as unfair is intensified, of course, if criminal law enforcers appear to discriminate between ethnic groups, skin color, income level, or status in other ways.

– can sustain an adverse status quo. Unfortunately, this logic can swiftly lead one to the mistaken conclusion that any anticorruption agenda is bound to fail because the forces pull in the opposite direction to what one wants to achieve. Many strategies against corruption have, indeed, been failures, often because they have been too modest in their ambitions and too restricted in their scope – entrenched corruption requires a political and social earthquake, not a legal nudge, to dislodge it.[4] However, recognizing the mechanisms that perpetuate corruption in a society is not the same as saying that the destiny of societies is preordained by the institutions they have inherited through historical accident, as also Raghuram G. Rajan and Luigi Zingales (2006:1) underscore. What is important is that policymakers and citizens understand what it takes to make institutions function; there are limits to what can be achieved through very partial reforms.

As discussed in Chapter 2, the likelihood of succeeding with policy choices depends on the given society's economic progress, the extent or absence of conflict within that society, and the society's democratic mechanisms. There is broad consensus in the literature, however, that – notwithstanding differences in the circumstances facing countries – it is possible to curb corruption and promote development with 'better institutions,' including criminal law enforcement institutions. Rajan and Zingales nevertheless question commonly assumed causalities about the role of institutions, because there are so many examples of very *similar* institutions (such as constitutions) across countries with very *different* levels of development and perceived corruption. What is important, claim Rajan and Zingales (2006:40) after undertaking an empirical study of these factors, is to understand where the demand for institutional change comes from: 'Changing explicit institutions without changing the constituencies backing them is likely to be a futile exercise, for the constituencies against change will find a way around the constraints imposed by the institutions.' Reforms have found it hard to take root in Africa and Latin America, because: 'a relatively small, educated urban middle class has often sided with a small ruling clique in opposing wider, deeper reform.'[5]

---

[4] For a recent OECD report, Robert Klitgard (2015) attempted to collect anticorruption success stories, yet experts in the field struggled to come up with good examples. Many countries can point to progress on this agenda. Whether this progress is the result of specific anticorruption initiatives is not so certain, however, as they coincide with larger societal changes.

[5] Moene and Søreide (2016) explain a government's supply of integrity mechanisms as a function of the state's main source of state revenues.

This reality seems difficult for reformers to grasp. At least, there is no lack of warnings in the literature. As discussed in Chapter 5, philosophers have understood for centuries how development is hindered if there are no robust integrity mechanisms to control an incumbent elite. At regular intervals, this old insight about governance is presented anew. A few decades ago, Gordon Tullock (1967) and Anne Kruger (1974) added to this line of reasoning by describing the importance of understanding the mechanisms of a rent-oriented society; everything one tries to achieve by introducing new laws and institutions can be undermined if a crony network of an elite controls the performance of government institutions. However, even if their arguments were presented in the most cited publications, it did not prevent optimism from sweeping through the ranks of development advisers about the potential for new laws and institutions to create social change. This wave has hit different social science disciplines differently, as Kevin Davies (2004) explains,[6] and while many economists seek to disentangle various institution-development hypotheses, there is an increasing recognition of the difference between real and façade reforms and why partial reforms might be useless unless followed by more substantial change.[7] In parallel, we see an increasing demand for robust evaluation of reform initiatives and development programs; a new law, academics and practitioners now aver, is not a success until changes have occurred on the ground.

Like the fate of other partial reform strategies, the prospect of eradicating entrenched corruption through a criminal justice strategy depends on which other developments take place at the same time. As discussed in Chapter 5, a government's ability to influence citizens' views about right and wrong depends on its standing in society. Even in societies with high levels of corruption, the adoption of a deterrence-based approach should therefore be accompanied by the introduction or enhancement of fair procedures, a demonstrated commitment to securing value for money in public spending, and a strategy to cultivate public support for the chosen repression level. In other words, the most brutal law enforcement – in the sense of being '*seen as acting*' as the main law enforcement goal (with strict supervision, life-long imprisonment sentences and low recognition of the accused's procedural rights) may

---

[6] See also Davies and Trebilcock (2001).

[7] Moene and Søreide (2015) explain why incumbents can sometimes secure higher personal revenues through corruption behind façade institutions, backing the point that many laws and new institutions do not deliver change because they were never intended to by those in power to decide. See also Baland, Moene, and Robinson (2010).

threaten citizens into obeying the laws, but it is not a sustainable solution in any country.

6.2 FIGHTING EACH COUNTRY'S CORRUPTION INTERNATIONALLY

A major problem for governments that want to eradicate corruption – and to do so by making their criminal justice response more efficient – is that many of the hurdles that they have to cope with are outside their control.

6.2.1 The International Character of Law Enforcement Obstacles

Many law enforcement obstacles have an international character. This is a challenge for law enforcement in any country. The countries struggling the most with corruption, however, are typically low-income countries with a number of capacity problems, and these weaknesses are easily exploited by those who are interested only in maximizing profits, and who are largely or entirely indifferent to the impact of their actions on developing countries.

6.2.1.1 The allure of bribery in challenged societies

For some international players, transnational companies among them, access to a country's nonrenewable resources, or the opportunity to sell defense systems, seems to justify whatever form and level of influence they exercise.[8] Besides, countries moving away from entrenched corruption, beyond the Figure 6.1 tipping point and toward corruption control, are often emerging markets. Those who can secure a strong market position in these countries, at the expense of well-functioning competition, may profit substantially in a growing economy. If such positions are secured through bribes, then the country's escape from the bad equilibrium quagmire may be imperiled. Bribes – so often justified as 'part of the culture' and paid 'because it was the only way to enter the market' – can cause tremendous damage.[9]

---

[8] Numerous reports from researchers and civil society organizations draw attention to the many facets of this problem, including country case studies.

[9] See, for example, the accused's explanation in the case: 'Ex SAP executive admits paying 'necessary' Panama bribes' by Richard L. Cassin at the FCPA Blog on 12 August 2015: http://www.fcpablog.com/blog/2015/8/12/ex-sap-executive-admits-paying-necessary-panama-bribes.html#sthash.GXpTRPxC.dpuf.

The international players in a position to benefit from a strong market position or a specific contract with a 'corrupt regime' are inclined to turn a blind eye to these consequences. A contract obtained through bribery will often be more rewarding than other comparable contracts, because the price-quality combination is not necessarily what matters for decision-makers' intent chiefly on securing bribes for themselves. The bribe transactions can be arranged secretly and smoothly, so that even the main beneficiaries from the corruption do not appear to know what is going on. Sophisticated bribery approaches combined with a large geographical distance between the official being bribed and the headquarters of the briber, make it extremely difficult for domestic law enforcers to detect the crime, let alone prosecute it.

For these different reasons, an emerging market country's most important contracts and regulatory decisions are often at a high risk of being subject to corrupt influence by foreign companies and to pressure from their home governments.[10] Tempting bribes dangled before its high-ranking civil servants are not what a pro-development government needs. Yet that same government's inability (because of a lack of law enforcement capacity and international cooperation) to investigate suspected corruption can be misinterpreted as a cultural inclination to condone the crime and a lack of political willingness to deal with the problem.

The easier it is for decision-makers to hide the bribes they receive in secret bank accounts, the easier it is for them to take part in corruption, and the harder it is for governments to control corruption with a (domestic) criminal law approach. Many emerging markets confront a combination of entrenched corruption and huge flows of capital out of the country, and this combination prevents governments from securing the tax revenues they need to establish an institutional framework

---

[10]   See arguments in *The Economist* on 1 February 1997: 'Don't be salesmen.' Since 1999 Transparency International has gathered perceptions-based data on foreign bribery (in total five reports, see http://www.transparency.org/research/bpi/overview – retrieved in July 2015). The two first surveys included questions on governments' inclination to support their commercial sectors through various forms of diplomatic pressure, including the use of tied aid, diplomatic pressures, threats of reduced foreign aid, financial pressure in other ways, commercial pricing, tied defense/arms deals, tied scholarships, and gifts. Some governments were found to use such pressures frequently, while others were less inclined – or in a weaker position – to influence foreign contract allocations.

sufficiently solid to deal with corruption.[11] Many decision-makers not only hide their corrupt revenues; they also hide their identity when offering or demanding bribes. Those who can hide behind a corporation, a bank account, or a trust[12] are virtually safe from criminal justice prosecution, especially in countries that still do not have in place automated systems to control information about personal income and other details that would raise red flags in more developed countries.

The infrastructure for corruption is international, and was originally established for the sake of facilitating trade and capital markets. Many of the hiding places for personal revenues and corporate profits are offered by financial service providers outside the countries where the corruption has taken place. Furthermore, financial transactions can be done in seconds and leave few traces, making the task of investigation even harder. The kinds of arrangements and systems that might help governments in their efforts to eradicate corruption – such as financial transparency, ownership registries, and agreements to deny market access to companies that fail to disclose required information – are difficult to establish. The obstacles are not primarily of a technical or legal character; the problem is rather that many governments have chosen not to embrace the measures that do exist. Some of these governments are located in OECD countries, as Guttorm Schjelderup (2015) explains. And indeed, the governments that publicly throw their support behind development initiatives and contribute to the international anticorruption agenda are sometimes the very same governments that allow their financial markets to offer the type of financial secrecy that facilitates capital flight and corruption.[13]

6.2.1.2 The role of other governments

By no means all governments are guilty of behaving in this fashion, however. Directly, through their own development agencies, or indirectly, through their contributions to multinational endeavors, OECD governments make important contributions in terms of finance and expertise to

---

[11] For useful reports and attempts of quantifying the problems, see Tax Justice Network at: http://www.taxjustice.net and Global Financial Integrity at: http://www.gfintegrity.org/.

[12] A trust is an arrangement where a property or fund is held and managed by one party for the benefit of another, often applied for tax avoidance and evasion, and for keeping the beneficiaries' identity hidden.

[13] See Shaxson (2011) for an eye-opener on this inconsistency. Nicholas Shaxson, other investigative journalists and many civil society organizations – as mentioned – assist in mapping the problem in important ways.

developing governments seeking to control corruption more efficiently. Unfortunately, the manner in which developed countries provide help in low-income countries with substantial corruption problems sometimes reduces these governments' ability to deal with those problems.

Eager to see results, some development policy advisers may press governments in low-income countries too hard for reforms in line with what the advisers claim is international best practice. The problem often lies not in the quality of the advice itself (the suggested reforms typically are exactly what the society needs); the problem is the government's lack of ownership of the new laws and institutions it is pressed to introduce. The development partners involved might applaud the reforms it has helped to initiate, but they might well have been designed and implemented without the significant involvement of government administrative institutions, which then end up lacking both the competence and the motivation to use, maintain, and develop the reforms.

Laws and institutions that are implemented without the necessary backing from state administrators and politicians are likely to be neglected or disdained by society at large. If this pattern repeats itself, the good intentions behind a development partnership may generate *law fatigue* – that is, citizens see little reason to take notice of another law if most previous laws are poorly enforced. The reforms not only fail to deliver; their failure also makes it more difficult for the incumbent regime to develop an efficient anticorruption strategy. The risk of such unintended consequences might be reduced if conditionality[14] on integrity in development lending and aid is tied to evaluations of the results of reforms, instead of letting financial support depend on the introduction of reforms dictated by the lenders.

6.2.1.3   The unintended consequences of collaborating with a corrupt regime

A further problem associated with lending tied to the implementation of preordained reforms, instead of to the attainment of concrete results, is the risk of stabilizing and perpetuating an exploitative regime of the sort described in Chapter 2, section 2.2. A reform program that is both approved by development partners and a condition for financial transfers

---

[14]   That is, the use of conditions attached to the provision of benefits such as loans, debt relief or bilateral aid. Conditionality on integrity refers to the set of control, transparency, and oversight mechanisms a country should have in place as a condition for financial support. In this context the concern is not the integrity of the management of the loans, but about what impact such conditions may have on governance.

makes it easier for the incumbent regime to appear more legitimate than it really is, which hampers those political and social forces that are pressing for change.

Although development organizations are established to provide support to the most challenged economies, they seem unable to combine the demand for a legitimate government with the need to protect the active dialogue with the regime that is vital for political collaboration.[15] The same difficulty applies to multilateral corporations operating in a country ruled by an exploitative regime, especially those corporations (such as arms and defense suppliers, utility providers, and producers of nonrenewable resources) that rely on contracts and close collaboration with government institutions. The fact that they have negotiated deals with the incumbent regime may incentivize them to support the regime in the various choices they make instead of opposing the regime. Closer dialogue between a corporation and the incumbent leaders is likely to help the corporation navigate smoothly through the numerous practical state administrative issues that inevitably arise. This mutually productive arrangement might be disrupted, though, were the political opposition to oust the incumbent regime. Coups d'état create even more uncertainty than election defeats for large multilateral corporations, because (regardless of international treaties and stabilization clauses, discussed below in section 3) they more likely threaten the deals the corporations have negotiated with the former regime. Well aware of cases in which the opposition has secured popular votes by promising to reconsider the government's contracts with large foreign enterprises (contracts that, for example, might offer low tax rates for mineral producers), corporations may prefer to avoid steps that could be interpreted as disapproval of the incumbent regime.

Some large corporations have the power to exert substantial political influence in the countries in which they operate.[16] Like development partners, they defend their presence with the argument that they themselves violate no laws. Such arguments are either naïve or cynical. Not only will their (legal) financial transfers to the government support the incumbent regime; they may also stabilize an exploitative regime with their presence, collaboration, and disincentive to demand change.

---

[15] These fundamental difficulties associated with development lending are extensively described in the literature on the political economy of aid – addressed also by Søreide, Gröning, and Wandall (2016).

[16] For an example of a large corporation with its own foreign affairs strategy, see Coll (2013) on Exxon Mobile.

Withdrawal from the country is not necessarily the most 'responsible' solution for an international corporation because its investments, presence, technical and administrative expertise, and the employment opportunities it may offer, are all needed for economic development. How can it be present without contributing to stabilizing a corrupt regime? Corporations that want to promote less corrupt, more democratic governments may jeopardize their business operations. If they speak out against corruption within the existing regime, they run the risk of being thrown out and replaced by a corruption-condoning competitor – a fate that nearly befell the oil company BP when it tried to operate transparently in Angola.[17] Even for large organizations, it is difficult to be the only player that voices a concern. While many international players would like to influence host societies for the better, they quickly face some form of coordination problem.

6.2.2   Coordination Failure in Anticorruption

International strategies against corruption are motivated by the need for countries to solve problems together. At the same time, some countries may have to give up benefits to make the agreement work, and political tension might develop around the trade-off between pursuing national benefits and protecting the international agreement. This subsection addresses how the failure to coordinate anticorruption strategies across countries might be rooted in competition, mistrust, lack of information, and lack of enforcement opportunities.

Coordination failure, a much studied problem in economics,[18] occurs when a group of decision- makers/players could achieve a more desirable outcome but fail to do so because they do not coordinate their decision-making.[19] This failure occurs if each player understands:

(1)   that an optimal result depends on all the other players deciding to give up a second-best result in order to reach the optimal outcome, but

(2)   that their second-best outcome is lost if one player chooses *not* to pursue the optimal result.

---

[17]   *The Guardian*: 'Scramble for Africa: Fear of corruption and chaos in oil rush' by Charlotte Denny on 17 June 2003: http://www.theguardian.com/world/2003/jun/17/usa.oil.

[18]   The Prisoners' Dilemma is among the more familiar terms from the literature. See Kreps et al. (1982).

[19]   For explanation, see Cooper and John (1991).

With reference to our corruption dilemma, the players must give up the benefits of corruption for law compliance, even if they stand to lose a lot if others continue their corrupt practices. A situation where the optimal result is beneficial primarily for a society's majority, while the player that deviates from the optimal decision-making strategy secures narrow benefits that go far beyond what the other players in that case obtain, can easily assume the character of a competition.

Coordinated action for compliance is a substantial challenge when it comes to international enforcement of laws against corruption. Chapter 4, section 4.4 addressed the problem of coordination failure on the side of state institutions: even if everybody sees the benefit of a well-functioning state administration, no one addresses the problem of corrupt officials and institutions because of the expected personal cost, also referred to as a collective action problem. In international bidding for state contracts, some players may want to make a bribe payment simply because of the risk that other players might deviate from the rules and pay a bribe to secure unfair benefits. The risk of losing benefits because other players are corrupt incentivizes corruption. Even the risk of speaking out about the problem of contracts lost in unfair competition brings the added risk of losing benefits, and thus a victimized player may choose to stay silent about the problem.[20] These are all coordination problems *if* the players would be better off if none of them were involved in corruption. For countries, and their populations, this is almost always the case.

6.2.2.1 The difficulty of joint action against foreign bribery

There is a high risk of coordination failure for any international agreement that stipulates that each country should investigate and prosecute foreign bribery. The most important international agreement of this sort is the OECD Anti-bribery Convention, referred to in Chapters 1 and 3. Although the principles behind this convention can be violated in many ways, we focus here on governments' responsibility to prosecute firms attached to their society if found responsible for bribe transfers abroad. Acting in compliance with this agreement when others do not *may* lead to commercial losses if:

(1) host countries allocate business benefits to those who make bribe payments, and
(2) the risk of detection and prosecution at home prevents firms from taking part in corruption.

---

[20] These specific circumstances are described by Søreide (2008, 2009).

None of the players can know for certain the extent to which these conditions hold, and, therefore, governments take into account the fact that they may *perhaps* hold. And thus, while each government understands that markets free of corruption would benefit international development, the risk of losing out in the competition for commercial benefits is felt more directly by their domestic societies.

The difference between the possible gains from corruption and the outcome of a situation without corruption is what each country will lose (or gain) if the agreement is recognized by all countries. As we know from Chapter 3, the Anti-bribery Convention is much lauded rhetorically but largely ignored in practice. Some countries are highly committed to making the agreement work, but most do not seem to enforce it, even if it has been incorporated into their criminal law. Instead, most signatories continue to celebrate contracts obtained abroad regardless of how they are obtained and they seem to have no intention of pursuing their firms upon suspected violation of the competition rules. After all, tolerating foreign bribery reduces the risk that one's firms will lose out because others pay bribes. How much bribery actually happens is impossible to know. A firm that won a contract because it paid a bribe does not proclaim that fact. And the firms that did not win do not know for sure whether they lost because of corruption or because of some legitimate reason. This lack of information spawns suspicions, which can quickly hatch into allegations. Some firms may find it easier to put the blame for a lost contract on unconfirmed corruption instead of on their inability to win in a fair competition, and that inclination sustains the notion of a risk associated with compliance with the agreement.

Securing contracts or other commercial benefits by bribing officials implies a gain at the expense of those who might win in a fair competition. This is cheating, and, of course, cheating usually leads to quick wins when there is no mechanism to enforce the rules. Our aim here is to understand governments' role in anticorruption coordination failure, and so use the word 'cheating' to refer to a country's failure to comply with the international agreement, in the sense that suspected corruption is ignored by the criminal justice system for the sake of the benefits obtained abroad.[21] Cheating obviously limits the Anti-bribery

---

[21]   As Gordon Tullock has laid out in his studies of warfare and disarmament agreements, the difficulty of trusting other societies under international conditions is the main reason why many international agreements are weakly enforced. See Tullock (2005) – a volume of his relevant publications (edited by C.K. Rowling). Several of this section's arguments on cheating versus complying with the agreement are much inspired by that volume's part 5 – *The Economics of War.*

Convention's impact on corruption problems internationally. If cheating is rewarding and there is no enforcement mechanism, each player will have strong incentives to cheat and little confidence that the other players will abide by the rules.

What can explain a government's inclination to cheat? One obvious factor is the risk of commercial losses if a government complies with the agreement. The commercial loss will depend on how the competition is distorted by corruption. After all, corrupt decision-makers who allocate commercial benefits (such as a license or a contract) are not corrupt all the time, and when they are corrupt, there is a limit to what extent a bribe will be allowed to distort contract or regulatory decisions. Some firms will gain in honest competition, others will lose. The more tempting the possible gain from bribery, the higher the willingness may be to pay a bribe, but some firms are less inclined to pay a bribe because their home country enforces the international antibribery agreement. For those who enter into the competition with a willingness to pay bribes, we can think of the bribe as the (personal and informal) price that has to be paid to secure a beneficial deviation from the decision that would otherwise be made (as discussed in Chapter 1). However, a large contract in, say, the agriculture sector or a license in the petroleum sector will usually require the bidder to possess a certain level of technology in order to perform at a level that will not embarrass the government, which is supposed to be intent on getting value for its taxpayers' money. Even very large bribes may not be sufficient to change this condition. Therefore, a corrupt decision-maker typically faces a trade-off between accepting bribes and recruiting the most appropriate technology. Under this circumstance, the competition between firms is not about the price-quality combination alone; it is also a competition between bribery and technology, especially if the most technologically advanced firm is prevented from offering bribes: One firm tries to win by offering large bribes, while another firm competes by offering superior technology. The result of this competition will depend on how the decision-maker weighs large bribes against the benefits of the best technology. The more the decision-maker values technology, the larger the bribe necessary to secure the contract – if, indeed, it can be secured through corruption.[22] Equally, the more myopic the decision-maker's focus on corruption, the more likely the briber is to win the contract – and, assuming no other factors affected the decision,

---

[22] The more the decision-maker appreciates the best price-quality solution, the more it takes to compensate her for making a decision that deviates from the superior option. A decision-maker with a myopic focus on bribes will be more easily pleased – because there are no competing values.

the smaller the bribe necessary to secure the contract.[23] According to this logic, countries with a commercial sector that performs strongly in fair competition might be more motivated to comply with the international agreement, simply because their firms will win contracts more easily if competitors compete by the rules.

This is not the whole story, however. A government considers the benefits associated with the international agreement across many sectors of its economy – with different degrees of comparative advantage in technology – as well as its possible influence on other governments and their likelihood of complying with the agreement. The size of a country's economy can also play a part. Compared to a country with a small economy, a country with a large economy will often have more influence on the fulfillment of an international agreement, as well as more influence on its contents. It will typically have more opportunities to secure benefits in alternative ways and greater ability to impose consequences on a player that deviates from an agreement. There is a huge difference between, for example, the United States and the Netherlands, or between China and Malaysia in these respects. Large countries can choose to use this power for the benefit of an international agreement, as we see the United States seek to do with its active enforcement of its antibribery law.

In addition to the matter of commercial losses, an essential factor in understanding the extent of cheating of international agreements is, as Gordon Tullock (2005) explains, the opportunity to conceal the cheating. The easier it is for a country to hide its cheating, the more likely cheating is to occur. Of course, this is something that each government knows before it enters into an agreement. Assuming that there are costs associated with the agreement (such as the costs associated with the risk of losing foreign commercial benefits), the ease with which cheating can occur is likely to influence governments' inclination to enter into an agreement in the first place. The international conventions against corruption have gained substantial political support. Voters around the world are happy that corruption is finally being taken seriously (or at least finally *seems* to be taken seriously). UNCAC is signed and implemented by most countries, and the OECD Anti-bribery Convention is signed by many countries that are not members of the OECD. This apparent success might be understood in light of what characterizes the coordination problem. The difficulty of observing a country's true

---

[23] For further explanation, see Bjorvatn and Søreide (2013) where these arguments are analyzed with an economic model.

enforcement practice creates an opportunity for a government to gain politically by entering into the agreement, while few benefits are abandoned as the agreement does not need to be upheld.[24]

Hence, while it makes little sense for a government to enter into an agreement one knows most other signatory governments will deviate from (in addition to oneself), the level of popular support for anticorruption initiatives might outweigh the costs associated with entering into the deal, including the nonsense. For these reasons, international agreements on anticorruption may have little anticorruption effect on the ground.

6.2.2.2 Toward enforcement substitutes

How to deal with a government that is known to have cheated is a difficult question to answer. There are no substantial formal consequences for countries that knowingly have cheated the OECD Anti-bribery Convention. Besides, it is difficult to tell if a specific case of cheating is a rare exception or is one among many similar cases where foreign bribery is condoned. A government may also point at obstacles (which may be real or invented) that stand in the way of it investigating and prosecuting the specific case of corruption that has been revealed, which complicates the task of determining if a case of suspected corruption really is an instance of cheating within the international agreement. Leaving that matter aside, what is more challenging still in terms of imposing formal consequences on a cheating government is the lack of an international enforcement mechanism. International anticorruption agreements rely on governments to enforce a rule they are highly inclined to ignore. Ideally, violations would be brought before an international court; this might even be a practicable solution among countries where governments already collaborate closely on such matters. Many governments, however, would prefer not to give up authority to a third party; they would be unlikely to recognize such a court and would not enforce its verdicts.[25]

What they might be more ready to accept is a solution whereby governments would not have to give authority to others to enforce on

---

[24] Aloysius Llamzon (2014) explains why many international conventions fail to make any substantial difference in the fight against corruption. He points specifically at the vagueness with which the rules are stipulated – which implies interpretation that is both costly and time-consuming, thus in many cases preventing enforcement – as also pointed out in Chapter 3.

[25] The idea of an international court should not be dismissed, however. At present it seems difficult to establish, but as more law enforcement processes are solved at the international level, it may well be a possible solution in the future.

their behalf (and possibly against their interests), and instead would be given some form of performance oversight mechanism. The governments would keep their (de facto) opportunity to cheat on the agreement (as discussed above) but would nevertheless accept international enforcement pressure. After all, every country risks being the victim of others' cheating, and a move toward more pressure for enforcement would be preferred by many countries and strongly promoted by governments that think their firms might well win more contracts in a fair competition. An international reduction in cheating as the result of enhanced enforcement pressure is likely to depend on political recognition of the mechanism, the availability of information that reveals a country's cheating, and public attention to the cases that are revealed.

Unfortunately, the OECD Working Group on Bribery, despite being widely considered to function better than most entities that evaluate country performance,[26] illustrates the kinds of shortcomings that such a mechanism is likely to possess. The WGB is fraught with inefficiencies; governments insist on keeping their veto power on proposed group decisions (which hampers any attempt of introducing more forceful mechanisms); and data collected on each country's failure to pursue suspected corruption is not made public. The WGB seems to confirm the assumption that governments protect their right to enter into international agreements that they have no or only weak intentions to respect. After all, they already have a common benefit in protecting their reputation by declaring commitment, and enforcement is not 'necessary' to defend the investment of time spent in the process.

With no real enforcement mechanism, the international anticorruption agenda is in the hands of the most powerful governments and dependent on their level of interest in using their influence for the sake of securing markets free of corruption for the international public good. Democratic governments, one might intuitively assume, are most likely to support an international agreement for fair markets free of corruption. Their voters, however, being concerned by multiple domestic policy choices, cannot be relied upon to replace their leaders because they condone corruption abroad. Moreover, when it comes to democracies' propensity to punish deviation from important international agreements, Gordon Tullock remarks that: 'democracies have notoriously short memories, and in all

---

[26] The procedures are referred to as 'the gold standard' of evaluation of conventions (OECD 2013).

Western democracies the public tends to think that international agreements are a good thing, per se' (Tullock, 2005:349).[27]

Ultimately, the reputational effect of an international convention is in itself a political asset, even for those who have no intention of respecting the terms of the convention. For the sake of international peace, it might be a good thing that democracies sometimes prefer to ignore other countries' inclination to disregard some of our common treaties.[28] However, if there are no consequences for those who choose to deviate from an international agreement, such agreements are of little use in solving our common problems.

6.3 LAW ENFORCEMENT IN CASES OF INTERNATIONAL CORRUPTION

So far, this chapter has depicted a gloomy de facto international anticorruption situation. Three reasons account for this bleak outlook. First, the most challenged countries cannot be expected to solve their corruption problems on their own. Second, it is nearly impossible to thwart the international financial infrastructure that facilitates corruption. And third, governments are unlikely to accept international criminal law enforcement that targets firms in their own countries.

Fortunately, the current situation is not as dismal as this chapter may have made it seem. As Chapter 3 confirms, various forms of international collaboration are taking place to evaluate countries' criminal law enforcement performance; the resulting reports contain sharp messages of shortcomings, and because these reports are made public, governments can be pushed to act. While there is an infrastructure for hiding corrupt transactions, there is also an expanding infrastructure for finding them. Besides, many countries are now evaluated by international organizations, not only on how they perform on corruption control and on which laws they have implemented, but also on their de facto implementation of international agreements for tighter financial regulation. Viewed as a whole, the environment for criminal law enforcement is improving, *especially* at the international level.

---

[27] Of course, the general public may be skeptical of some international agreements; the point is that the general public – when endorsing the contents of an agreement – is easily pleased by the very fact that the agreement has been signed.
[28] There is substantial variation in the extent to which international treaties are respected; not all agreements can be cheated as easily as those on corruption.

Corruption can never be solved once and for all, however. Positive steps need to be sustained and expanded. The problem evolves as society evolves, and as the tools to counter corruption are devised, applied, and fine-tuned. The kinds of international cooperation spearheaded by the World Bank, the OECD, the United Nations, and regional bodies have played a crucial role in putting anticorruption on the world's agenda, but theirs is a moving target. The particular facets of corruption with which they wrestle this year will not be the same next year. International initiatives need to be continually monitored, evaluated, adjusted, bolstered, and supplemented by new measures. We must always ask how many of these initiatives are actually working; to what extent are they really addressing corruption as opposed to merely seeming to be doing so; what are the risks that new tools will prompt corruption to take new forms?

In this perspective, we now turn to two examples of areas where law enforcement progress occurs, irrespective of international conventions: global settlements and investment arbitration. Are they tools against corruption or are we on the wrong track? Impunity for the corrupt – as is addressed at the end of this section – is an abiding problem. The test for any new and creative international criminal justice strategy against corruption lies in its impact on impunity.

6.3.1 Law Enforcement Collaboration in Complex Cases: Global Settlements

Internationally, a number of cases have come to light of multinational corporations being involved in bribery in several countries and prosecuted in several countries where the corporation operates. In the absence of an international court that could consider all aspects of the case and enforce one criminal law reaction, law enforcement actions need to be coordinated across countries with the aim of signaling assertive law enforcement and incentivizing compliance with common anticorruption rules. If coordination cannot be achieved, corporations face the risk of double jeopardy (with penalties being imposed for the same crime by several jurisdictions),[29] multiple demands for asset recovery and victim compensation, and profound uncertainty about when the law enforcement

---

[29] There are international agreements against double jeopardy, and these are respected by many jurisdictions. However, there are shortcomings in these agreements because the firm is usually protected against multiple penalties only when a penalty is imposed by court, and not as a negotiated settlement.

process might end, as well as debarment from public procurement for an unknown period of time.

In addition to the risk of overly severe total penalties, a firm faces the danger that the sum of law enforcement actions might damage its market performance. This is a critical concern, because large international enterprises often operate in oligopolies; they have substantial market power. Law enforcement actions that reduce competitive pressure in markets may harm society more than it helps by reducing corruption.[30] Most multinational enterprises provide services that are demanded because they are needed. An enforcement action vis-à-vis the supplier of essential services or products is unlikely to be carried out if it harms the supply. Therefore, an aggregated penalty should take a form that makes it possible for suppliers to stay in operation, unless the consequences of their criminal activities overshadow the benefits associated with their production (as discussed in Chapter 5).[31]

Any attempt to devise efficient solutions in terms of the composite concept discussed in Chapter 5 is difficult to imagine unless we find a coordinated solution to these international law enforcement difficulties. Multiple reactions imply not only inflated total penalties but also expanded total expenses. Even if the law enforcement expenses are covered by different jurisdictions, resources are wasted if the same case is pursued in multiple jurisdictions, and an uncoordinated solution would thus be very far from cost-efficient. Not only might the sum of penalties aggregate to a level far beyond what is reasonable, but also the unknown number of law enforcement reactions creates an unpredictable aggregate sanction. In the absence of international law enforcement coordination, the offender is given no incentive to report its own crime. This is a huge problem in law enforcement if self-reporting is essentially the most important way to detect illegal activities by multinational corporations, which rightly have a reputation for performing peerless financial acrobatics to conceal illegal revenue. A multinational corporation is a large organization, and it will typically have on its staff at least some managers who are inclined to collaborate with governments to find a law enforcement solution – but only if they expect the solution to be reasonable.[32]

---

[30] Auriol and Søreide (2015), Søreide et al. (2016).

[31] Of course, enhanced competition is a goal in oligopoly markets, yet not a main concern in criminal law.

[32] Healy and Serafeim (2013) provide data on private sector managers' perspectives on these matters.

Since the establishment of the UN and OECD conventions as a legal platform for acting against corruption, collaboration in investigation and prosecution has increased, and coordinated law enforcement actions have become more common, especially among some jurisdictions. Yet, there is still no predictable system or set of clear international rules regarding coordinated approaches; the jurisdictions involved have to come to an agreement on a case-by-case basis. The private sector is usually highly uncertain about what to expect from the collaboration, and even if the principle of lenient treatment of those who self-report is generally recognized by jurisdictions around the world, self-reporting remains sufficiently risky that the management of a corporation may well decide to stay silent about bribery detected within the organization. And if silence is the preferred solution, the bribery may well continue if it benefits the firm.

In the search for workable solutions, Richard Alderman (2014) has proposed in a study for the B20[33] the use of 'global settlements' – that is, law enforcement actions where a company can resolve all outstanding issues with all jurisdictions at the same time and achieve a closure of the case. Each case would still be solved in agreement with the jurisdictions involved, but the process of doing so would follow clearer rules and principles, making law enforcement reactions more predictable.

Putting the idea of global settlements into practice requires tackling many tricky issues, such as deciding who takes the lead on investigations, what forms collaboration should take, which aspects of a case can be negotiated, when to end investigations (whether several settlements should be accepted if the case appears endless), how to share the expenses, how to share recovered assets, which victims to compensate, and how to administer the collaborative system. Nonetheless, given the growing current of international collaboration on anticorruption, and in recognition of the difficulties of reaching more formal international criminal law enforcement solutions, the global settlements are a realistic option.

The B20 and Alderman underscore that such coordinated actions are not meant to replace existing criminal law enforcement at the national level. Coordinated action with negotiated settlements is an option primarily when clear law enforcement shortcomings are associated with a purely national action. Besides, in a case in which the corporation

---

[33]   B20 is a collaboration between the largest business organizations. See the B20 Task Force's recommendations on anticorruption: http://www.b20 australia.info/Pages/Anti-Corruption.aspx.

appears to have no intention of changing its corrupt business strategy, the law enforcement institutions involved have little reason to negotiate a settlement, and the case should be handled by a court process at the national level. It would be unfair to the many corporations that make substantial efforts to avoid corruption to treat notorious bribers leniently.

Many questions need to be answered in order to establish a practice of global settlements, and the trade-offs associated with negotiated settlements are no easier to calculate at the international level than at the national level. As discussed in Chapter 5, these procedures should secure fairness, a sufficiently strict penalty, transparency and some form of control or appeal option. Such values will often be protected more forcefully within a criminal justice system than outside these institutions.

Despite the second-best character of global (as well as national) settlements, the pressure for more coordinated action gives hope that better solutions will be found. For many years, multinational government-steered organizations (like the World Bank, the OECD and the United Nations) have promoted law enforcement collaboration on anticorruption more generally, and they could come to play a key role in developing the necessary political agreement around the rules for 'criminal justice global settlements' as well.

6.3.2   The Role of International Investment Arbitration

A good deal of international commercial activity is associated with multinationals entering a country via foreign direct investments. While these investments are associated with economic development, they are also exposed to various forms of corruption problems. The regulatory terms of the investments are often negotiated directly with high-ranking civil servants or politicians, a situation that often encourages and certainly facilitates bribery.

As part of the deal, the investor can dispute the host government's compliance with the agreement with the help of arbitration, meaning that arbitrators representing each party plus a neutral institution consider the dispute and reach a conclusion outside the formal legal system of the host or home countries of the parties. These arbitration agreements are often referred to as 'investment arbitration' or 'investor-state dispute settlement' (ISDS). The disputes are addressed within the framework of either a bilateral investment treaty (BIP) between the host state and the investor's state or a multilateral treaty. Apart from the terms of the contract and relevant national law or public international law, the specific sources of law used when resolving a dispute over compliance are largely for the parties to decide.

Arbitration to resolve investment-related disputes is a recognized instrument of public international law. From a development perspective, it is seen as a tool that protect investors from political risk, including populist political moves that lead to the takeover of the investor's sunk capital or alterations in tax rates once the investor starts to profit from the investment. With this tool in place, new potential investors might be less hesitant to enter a developing country's market, and this is a key to highly needed economic growth. Moreover, Aloysius Llamzon, who has analysed the role of investment arbitration in the fight against corruption, claims that arbitration has the potential to play an important role in law enforcement, especially in societies where the criminal justice system is too inefficient or too riddled with corruption to address the problem efficiently.[34]

A fundamental concern with arbitration agreements, however, is that those representing the incumbent regime accept the terms of the deal on behalf of their country for a very long period, while they themselves may have a much shorter time period in mind, being concerned above all to stay in power, possibly by negotiating deals that look better for their country than they actually are and that involve the payment of bribes. An international enterprise may be willing to offer bribes for a variety of reasons, such as obtaining more market power, paying lower taxes, and being allowed to ignore labor rights, human rights, and environmental concerns. If the incumbent regime is corrupt, a society is likely to end up with deals on its most important economic activities that shortchange the country but are cemented for decades. The fact that some of the terms of a deal are often kept confidential, even when the deal is brought to arbitration, adds to popular suspicion of deals between governments and multilateral enterprises.[35]

Traditionally, those involved in investment arbitration have not exploited the opportunity to use the instrument as a tool for solving corruption problems. Some arbitrators, according to Llamzon (2014:214), even act permissively when they encounter corruption, which they see as part of the business landscape in some countries. Given this attitude, they find it 'unfair to penalize selected investors' that are only part of a larger system of 'endemic, entrenched, and institutionalized corruption.' Even in

---

[34]   This point is also made by Meyer (2013) – who emphasizes the importance of transparency in these proceedings.

[35]   Yet the secrecy surrounding arbitration is more strongly associated with *commercial arbitration*, where private parties in secret can dispute the contents of a deal. Over the last decade there has been substantial pressure for more transparency into arbitration procedures.

cases where corruption evidently has taken place, the 'arbitrators have mostly exhibited real reluctance to deal with [corruption] directly,' Llamzon (2014:202) claims. Corruption is seen as a 'highly complex issue to tackle,' as it can raise 'questions of equity and fairness as to the relative culpability of the parties.' 'The parties and tribunals alike are more comfortable' with the kinds 'of illegality that are committed unilaterally,' such as fraud, and are more visible than corruption. Llamzon suggests that many cases that address fraud are, in reality, cases about corruption.

One of the challenges arbitrators must tackle arises when a host state with a regime different from the one that entered into the deal alleges that the deal was negotiated corruptly, even though the new regime has not prosecuted the same corruption nationally. In most of these cases, arbitrators do not seem to demand that those who seek to invoke corruption must have tried to combat it. In the case of *World Duty Free vs. Kenya*,[36] for instance, Kenya sought to cancel an investment contract due to corruption, but failed to prosecute the country's former president, Daniel arap Moi, for the same corrupt actions. Llamzon (2014) finds that the failure of the state to prosecute corruption nationally has been an argument that tribunals have considered in their refusal to take into account corruption allegations. Arbitrators' reluctance to entertain such allegations is encouraged by the fact that international instruments in this area of law are 'almost entirely silent on rules concerning burdens of proof, evidentiary weight, and appropriate degrees of sanction' (Llamzon, 2014:11). Matters of corruption are therefore handled inconsistently.

Somewhat surprisingly, considerations of fairness seem to prevent many arbitrators from ruling on issues of corruption, Llamzon (2014:220–21) finds. Many governments accuse the investor of contributing to the corruption, and if such corruption was actually proved, the investor's entire investment might be nullified. In most cases, in the view of many arbitrators, such a consequence would not be fair for investors, as governments are usually guilty of serious violations of investor protections under investment treaties. If the investors were found guilty of bribery, the state would be 'excused' for its own violations as long as corruption was present. Arbitrators may therefore sometimes view corruption allegations – even if true – as somehow unfair and choose not to act on them.[37]

---

[36]   Case reference: ICSID (2006) Case No.ARB/00/7.
[37]   Llamzon (2014:221).

A further problem is that, in cases of corruption, sanctions are typically imposed on the investors alone, with no consequences for the government representatives who have participated in the illegal schemes. Hence, while allegations on foreign bribery can be pursued both through the arbitration mechanisms and by the home countries of the investors, so far no arbitration cases have led to host governments being held responsible for the participation of their officials in the corrupt act.[38]

In order to strengthen investment arbitration as a tool against corruption, the procedures should abide by principles that make it more likely that governments will be held responsible for corruption in which their officials were complicit. Abiola Makinwa (2013:276) suggests the establishment of a 'socially responsible arbitration tribunal,' in which the primary obligation of the international arbitrator is not to the parties that made the deal but to the larger society. The arbitration agreements should also contain an expectation that a government, if it alleges corruption in a given case, must also pursue that case through its national criminal justice system, if the government is to receive support from the arbitration tribunal. Governments that fail to do so may well be suspected of giving impunity to their influential decision-makers; if such suspicions endure or even deepen, the legitimacy of those governments, in the eyes of the international community, should diminish appreciably.

6.3.3 Collaboration for Reduced Impunity

This book has focused on how criminal law enforcement systems are used and might be used to combat corruption. It has reached the conclusion that efficient solutions require an understanding of several efficiency dimensions, because otherwise multiple objectives will be pursued at the expense of one another. Considering the dire situation in many countries, however, this is a highly abstract debate. A nuanced strategy seems, to many societies, to be too feeble or too sophisticated an approach to have any impact on their corruption problems. Such societies look instead for less subtle, more hard-hitting approaches – for anything that will make even a marginal improvement and reduce the impunity that their leaders and officials currently enjoy.

Changing the widespread belief that the corrupt have virtual or even total impunity from the criminal law is one of the biggest and most

---

[38] This problem is also debated by Pauwelyn (2013), who compares the potential anti-corruption impact of investment arbitration with the role of the WTO's conflict resolution processes.

important tasks facing law enforcement, both within the countries victimized by the problem and within the international community at large. A perception that corruption will yield benefits at any or all levels of government is extremely dangerous, because it pushes countries toward a high corruption equilibrium and prevents countries already in that situation from escaping it. The only way of avoiding such consequences is to combat impunity – a task that domestic players cannot accomplish without the support of an international community. For this reason, impunity should not be traded against other political goals, including military ambitions and commercial deals. No leader should get away with corruption. Even those officials who have formal immunity because they occupy a particular position should lose that immunity once they have left that office, at which point they can be held liable for acts committed before or after their tenure.

None of the arguments presented in this book should be regarded as a reason to treat the corrupt indulgently. The negotiated settlements discussed in several chapters must not be a way of smuggling impunity into the criminal law process, whether at the national or international level. This is why transparency in negotiated settlements is so important. The general public must be confident that all offenses provoke a criminal law reaction. For law enforcers, transparency might be annoying because they find it easier to reach a settlement if the option of keeping the facts of the crime confidential is on the negotiating table as a bargaining chip. Negotiated settlements, however, must not be allowed to obstruct or disrupt the clear signal from the criminal law system that impunity is impermissible. Over the long term, even those who negotiate settlements may come to appreciate the value of transparency in making law enforcement more efficient.

Likewise, this book's emphasis on legitimate solutions must not be misinterpreted as a call for the overly lenient treatment of criminals. Corruption can never be defeated through the criminal justice system unless enforcement actions take place in a way that enhances the moral burden associated with such crime. Moral values of the kind that militate against corruption cannot develop in society unless those involved in corruption are met with a clear law enforcement reaction. At the same time, those values can be influenced only by a criminal justice system that is embedded in society; a society's criminal justice system must be seen by the members of that society as fair, effective, and resonant within that society's culture, norms, and institutions. Legitimacy, therefore, cannot be detached from the efficiency concept discussed in Chapter 5. A government is not legitimate unless it seeks to efficiently enforce its criminal law in corruption cases, and to do so in ways that are cost-efficient, fair, and predictable.

A government that condones corruption within the ranks of its civil servants and politicians cannot be treated as legitimate because it *is* not legitimate. Politically, however, most governments around the world are treated with respect, regardless of how far they condone corruption. The benefits of silently accepting this fact far outweigh the values of speaking up against it, it seems. At the political level, however, inaction against corruption is almost as damaging as the corruption itself. An authoritative voice must be raised against not only governments that accept corruption among their own politicians and civil servants, but also governments that cheat on their international commitments to enforce their antibribery laws.

Internationally, we can trust civil society leaders to voice concerns clearly and cleverly. NGOs and investigative centers dedicated to protecting society against unreliable politicians – and hackers committed to protecting citizens' fundamental rights – increasingly contribute decisively to make the world aware of corruption.[39] Where governments fail to secure the transparency necessary for these organizations to act, other players – such as Wikileaks and the International Consortium of Investigative Journalists – put revealing information into the public domain. When access to information laws and press freedom meets resistance, which occurs even in the most developed countries,[40] social media replaces formal transmission channels for information. Thanks to these activities, the most oppressive and corrupt leaders cannot avoid being aware of their society's demand for accountability.

Voicing concerns is not only something civil society leaders need to do, however. When coming from political leaders abroad, the statements

---

[39] For an example of an investigative center, see the Organized Crime and Corruption Reporting Project (OCCRP) https://www.occrp.org/ – which is a non-profit center. There are also private investigators who offer their services when the criminal justice systems fail or need support. A hacker group known to voice concerns about corruption and promote citizens' rights is Anonymous – see https://www.facebook.com/ArmyAnonymous. Like Edward Snowden, many activists find it right to violate a law to protect more fundamental values. While such acts distort law and order, the activists receive broader support the more governments fail to demonstrate their accountability.

[40] Some governments even try to control their academics' research results and the contents in what they publish – consider, for example, how researchers in Canada seek to prevent government interference in their research – see *The Independent New Foundland & Labrador* on 25 April 2014: 'Getting science wrong, with dire consequences' (by Hans Rollman).

make a different impact, but unfortunately there is much unhelpful 'politeness' at this level. In 1996, when James Wolfensohn was president of the World Bank, he made a famous speech in which he described corruption as a cancer that destroys societies and hinders development; thereafter, it became somewhat easier to address corruption in diplomatic circles, but it never became easy.[41] Confronting corruption in a diplomatic setting is perceived as accusing a government of a crime and branding its politicians as being unable or unwilling to deal with the problem. Such forthrightness rarely nurtures a productive dialogue on other important matters. Those in a position to be listened to (because, for example, of the size of their economy or the market power of their corporations) nevertheless know that they have a choice: they can maintain a friendly tone and collaborate with corrupt regimes, or they can condemn corruption and, in that way, support the movements that demand change and an end to impunity. President Obama's call in July 2015 for African presidents to step down after their terms in office are over is an example of how concerns can be raised politically.[42] If making statements alone is considered too risky, concerns can be raised in collaboration with other players – for example, as a signatory to a multilateral anticorruption agreement or a member of a group of countries ready to protest instances of impunity.

The most important tool for reducing impunity, however, is to strengthen criminal justice efficiency at the national and international level. If criminal justice systems work well and collaborate closely with one another, they will bolster a large range of other integrity mechanisms and make it possible for corrupt societies to move from a high corruption equilibrium toward efficient law enforcement.

6.4 CONCLUSION: CONTROLLING CORRUPTION IN THE MOST CHALLENGED SOCIETIES

The previous chapters of this book addressed the role of national criminal justice systems in controlling corruption domestically and bribery abroad. Chapters 1 and 2 described the nature of the corruption problem and explained why it is so important to find better solutions than we currently have, and Chapter 3 explained what law enforcement obstacles look like

---

[41] See Sebastian Mallaby's (2005) biography on James Wolfensohn's role as the President of the World Bank, Chapter 7.

[42] See BBC News on 28 July 2015: 'Obama warns on Africa leaders refusing to step down.'

in practice. Chapter 4 gave an introduction to the economic reasoning about how criminal law can efficiently curb corruption, yet it also underlined the basic premise for a law enforcement reaction, which, out of concerns for fairness, restrict the range of criminal law reactions a government can employ. In Chapter 5 it became clear why dialogue between economists and legal scholars is necessary to help strengthen strategies against corruption. This dialogue can help us not only to do a better job of matching law enforcement solutions to law enforcement problems, but also to develop a concept of criminal law efficiency that is built on both economic and legal reasoning around optimal strategies. Given the many trade-offs that must be considered, however, this cross-disciplinary dialogue is only a starting point for developing practical policy solutions; each criminal law system must weigh the different efficiency criteria (crime control and detection, fairness, and value for money) against one another and within the unique context of the society of which that system is a part. These efficiency criteria are not, or should not be, surprising – they have been articulated in one way or another since Confucius – but the concept of a holistic approach to criminal law efficiency is by no means trivial, because the failure to embrace such comprehensive reasoning appears to be exactly the reason why corruption is so hard to curb with a criminal law approach.

This final chapter has emphasized the importance of understanding why the impact of criminal justice strategies will depend on the larger law enforcement environment and on factors that are outside the control of the criminal justice system. Societies are in different crime control equilibria, some enjoying low corruption but others mired in high corruption. Social forces (which themselves depend on many different factors and mechanisms) tend either to work against corruption or to cement the problem. A cemented problem – entrenched corruption – means that essential checks and balances are absent or functioning poorly, and thus the greater the need to deal with corruption, the more difficult it is to make anticorruption strategies work. In international relations, the absence of an uncompromising, unambiguous condemnation of governments that condone corruption helps to keep such regimes in power, and this is not what the victimized populations of, for example, Angola, Ukraine, Venezuela, Haiti, or Kenya need.[43]

---

[43] These countries are selected arbitrarily as examples because they score poorly on corruption indices – and I am concerned about their specific corruption-related challenges.

A criminal law strategy is not sufficient to solve the problem in the most challenged societies, but it can be a key component of the solution. Everything that the criminal justice system tries to achieve in this respect, however, is achieved more easily if the government operates fairly and accountably, and the brutal crackdowns which sound convincing may not be what delivers success in the longer run.

What this chapter has also pointed out, however, is why accountability alone is not enough for those societies that face the greatest corruption challenges. In different ways, their corruption problem takes on an international character, and they need the active support of international players and governments to fight against those who exploit their institutional weaknesses, condone their corruption problems, or strengthen the international infrastructure for hiding corrupt transactions. For several reasons, governments find it hard to live up to the commitments they have made in international agreements and conventions to combat corruption. Therefore, it is necessary to develop the law enforcement tools that can make a difference at the international arena, especially for the most challenged societies. Pragmatic second-best solutions should not be rejected as illegitimate if criminal justice principles are fairly well protected. This chapter addressed the potential value of tools such as global settlements in complex cases and investment arbitration. Fortunately, these are just some of an increasing range of developments in international law enforcement that promise to help us devise and implement more efficient strategies against corruption. These are interesting times; and for those who want to be part of the solution, instead of part of the problem, there is reason for optimism.

References

Abbink, C. 2006. Laboratory experiments on corruption. In S. Rose-Ackerman (Ed.) *International Handbook on the Economics of Corruption*. Cheltenham, UK, and Northampton, MA: Edward Elgar.

Abed, G. T. and S. Gupta (Eds). 2002. *Governance, Corruption and Economic Performance*. Washington, DC: International Monetary Fund.

Acemoglu, D. and M. O. Jackson. 2014. Social norms and the enforcement of laws. Working Paper w20369. National Bureau of Economic Research.

Acemoglu, D., S. Johnson and J. A. Robinson. 2001. The colonial origins of comparative development: An empirical investigation. *American Economic Review*, 91(5): 1369–1401.

Acemoglu, D., S. Johnson and J. A. Robinson. 2005. Institutions as a fundamental cause of long-run growth. In P. Aghion and S. Durlauf (Eds) *USA Handbook of Economic Growth*, 1: 385–472, Elsevier.

Aidt, T. S. 2003. Economic analysis of corruption: A survey. *The Economic Journal*, 113(491): 632–652.

Alderman, R. 2014. B20 Task Force on Improving Transparency and Corruption: Development of a Preliminary Study on Possible Regulatory Developments to Enhance the Private Sector Role in the Fight against Corruption in a Global Business Context. Report prepared for B20. Available at http://www.ethic-intelligence.com/wp-content/uploads/2014_B20_report.pdf.

Al-Kasim, F., T. Søreide and A. Williams. 2008. Grand corruption in the regulation of oil. *U4 Issue, 2008*(2). Bergen: Chr. Michelsen Institute.

Al-Kasim, F., T. Søreide and A. Williams. 2013. Corruption and reduced oil production: An additional resource curse factor? *Energy Policy*, 54: 137–147.

Allingham, M. G. and A. Sandmo. 1972. Income tax evasion: a theoretical analysis. *Journal of Public Economics*, 1:323–338.

Anderson, L. 2011. Demystifying the Arab Spring. *Foreign Affairs*, 90(3): 2–7.

Andvig, J. C. 2005. A house of straw, sticks or bricks? Some notes on corruption empirics. Prepared for The IV Global Forum on Fighting Corruption and Safeguarding Integrity. NUPI Working Paper 678. Oslo: Norwegian Institute of International Affairs.

Andvig, J. C. and K. O. Moene. 1990. How corruption may corrupt. *Journal of Economic Behavior and Organization*, 13: 63–76.

Andvig, J. and T. Barasa. 2014. Grabbing by strangers: crime and policing in Kenya. In T. Søreide and A. Williams (Eds) *Corruption, Grabbing and Development: Real World Challenges*. Cheltenham, UK, and Northampton, MA: Edward Elgar.

Arlen, J. 2012. Corporate criminal liability: theory and evidence. In A. Harel and K. N. Hylton (Eds) *Research Handbook on the Economics of Criminal Law*. Cheltenham, UK, and Northampton, MA: Edward Elgar.

Arlen, J. (Ed.). 2013. *Research Handbook on the Economics of Torts*. Cheltenham, UK, and Northampton, MA: Edward Elgar.

Arlen, J. and R. Kraakman. 1997. Controlling corporate misconduct: An analysis of corporate liability regimes. *New York University Law Review*, 72: 687–779.

Arrow, K. J. 1959. Rational choice functions and orderings. *Economica*, 26: 121–127.

Ashworth, A. 2005. *Sentencing and Criminal Justice*. Cambridge, UK: Cambridge University Press.

Aspinall, E. and G. van Klinken (Eds). 2010. *The State and Illegality in Indonesia*. Leiden: KITLV Press.

Auriol, E. 2014. Capture for the rich, extortion for the poor. Paper presented at Public Procurement and Concessions Design Conference in Brazil, February 2014.

Auriol, E. and A. Blanc. 2009. Capture and corruption in public utilities: The cases of water and electricity in Sub-Saharan Africa. *Utilities Policy*, 17(2): 203–216.

Auriol, E. and S. Straub. 2011. Privatization of rent-generating industries and corruption. In S. Rose-Ackerman and T. Søreide (Eds) *International Handbook on the Economics of Corruption*, Vol. 2. Cheltenham, UK, and Northampton, MA: Edward Elgar.

Auriol, E. and T. Søreide. 2015. An economic analysis of debarment. NHH Working Paper 2015–2019. Bergen: Norwegian School of Economics.

Baland, J. M, K. O. Moene and J. A. Robinson. 2010. Governance and development. *Handbook of Development Economics*, 5, 4597–4656. Elsevier.

Basu, K., K. Basu and T. Cordella. 2014. Asymmetric punishment as an instrument of corruption control. *World Bank Policy Research Working Paper*, 6933. Washington, DC: The World Bank.

Becker, G. S. 1968. Crime and punishment: An economic approach. *Journal of Political Economy*, 76: 169.

Bel, G., A. Estache and R. Foucart. 2014. Transport infrastructure failures in Spain: mismanagement and incompetence, or political capture? In T. Søreide and A. Williams (Eds) *Corruption, Grabbing and Development: Real World Challenges*. Cheltenham, UK, and Northampton, MA: Edward Elgar.

Bénabou, R. and J. Tirole. 2011. Identity, morals, and taboos: beliefs as assets. *The Quarterly Journal of Economics*, 126(2): 805–855.

Benitez, D. A., A. Estache and T. Søreide. 2012. Infrastructure policy and governance failures. CMI Working Paper 5. Bergen: Chr. Michelsen Institute.

Benson, M. L. and S. S. Simpson. 2015. *Understanding White-Collar Crime: An Opportunity Perspective*. NY, New York: Routledge.

Bertrand, M., S. Djankov, R. Hanna and S. Mullainathan. 2006. Does corruption produce unsafe drivers? NBER Working Paper 12274. Cambridge, MA: National Bureau of Economic Research.

Besley, T. 2006. *Principled Agents? The Political Economy of Good Government*. Lindahl Lectures Series. Oxford, UK: Oxford University Press.

Bjorvatn, K. and T. Søreide. Corruption and competition for resources. *International Tax and Public Finance*, 21: 997–1011.

Bjorvatn, K., G. Torsvik and B. Tungodden. 2005. How middle-men can undermine anti-corruption reforms. CMI Working Paper. Bergen: Chr. Michelsen Institute.

Black, B., R. Kraakman and A. Tarassova. 2000. Russian privatization and corporate governance: What went wrong? *Stanford Law Review*, 52: 1731–1808.

Blount, J. and S. Markel. 2012. The end of the internal compliance world as we know it, or an enhancement of the effectiveness of securities law enforcement? Bounty hunting under the Dodd-Frank Act's Whistleblower Provisions. *Fordham Journal of Corporate and Financial Law*, 17: 1023–1061.

Bonner, R. C. 2012. Cartel Crackdown: winning the drug war and rebuilding Mexico in the process. *The Foreign Affairs*, 91:12.

Bowles, R. and N. Garoupa. 1997. Casual police corruption and the economics of crime. *International Review of Law and Economics*, 17(1): 75–87.

Bussel, J. 2015. Typologies of corruption: a pragmatic approach. In S. Rose-Ackerman and P. Lagunes (Eds) *Greed, Corruption, and the Modern State: Essays in Political Economy*. Cheltenham, UK, and Northampton, MA: Edward Elgar.

Campos, J. E. L. and S. Pradhan (Eds). 2007. *The Many Faces of Corruption: Tracking Vulnerabilities at the Sector Level*. Washington, DC: World Bank.

Cargill, T. F. 2014. The role of the state in finance and money: implications for economic stability. *Journal of Private Enterprise*, 29(3): 29.

Carranza, R. 2012. Anticipating the past: transitional justice and socio-economic wrongs. *Social Legal Studies*, 21(2): 171–186.

Chassang, S. and J. Ortner. 2014. Making collusion hard: asymmetric information as a counter-corruption measure. Working Paper. Princeton, NJ: Princeton University and Boston, MA: Boston University.

Chayes, S. 2015. *Thieves of State: Why Corruption Threatens Global Security*. New York and London: W. W. Norton & Company.

CMS. 2014. *CMS Guide to Anti-bribery and Corruption Laws. Anti-Corruption Zone*. Available at: http://www.cms-lawnow.com/aczone.

Cohn, A., E. Fehr and M. A. Maréchal. 2014. Business culture and dishonesty in the banking industry. *Nature*.

Coll, S. 2013. *Private Empire: ExxonMobil and American Power*. London: Penguin Books.

Cooper, R. and A. John. 1991. Coordinating coordination failures. In G. N. Mankiw and D. Romer (Eds) *New Keynesian Economics*. Cambridge, MA: MIT Press.

Dal Bo, E. 2006. Regulatory capture: A review. *Oxford Review of Economic Policy*, 22(2): 203–225.

Davies, K. 2004. What can the rule of law variable tell us about rule of law reforms? *Michigan Journal of International Law*, 26: 141–161.

Davies, K. and M. J. Trebilcock. 2001. Legal reforms and development. *Third World Quarterly*, 22(1): 21–36.

Della Porta, D. 2001. A judges' revolution? Political corruption and the judiciary in Italy. *European Journal of Political Research*, 39(1): 1–21.

Dufwenberg, M. and G. Spagnolo. 2015. Legalizing bribe giving. *Economic Inquiry*, 53(2): 836–853.

Easterly, W. 2006. Reliving the 1950s: The big push, poverty traps, and takeoffs in economic development. *Journal of Economic Growth*, 11(4): 289–318.

Eigen, P. 2003. *The Web of Corruption: How a Global Movement Fights Graft*. Frankfurt/Main: Campus Verlag GmbH.

Estache, A. (Ed.). 2011. *Emerging Issues in Competition, Collusion, and Regulation of Network Industries*. London: Centre for Economic Policy Research.

Feldman, Y. and O. Lobel. 2009. Incentives matrix: the comparative effectiveness of rewards, liabilities, duties, and protections for reporting illegality. *Tex. L. Rev.*, 88: 1151.

Fisman, R. 2015. Political connections and commerce: a global perspective. In S. Rose-Ackerman and P. Lagunes (Eds) *Greed, Corruption, and the Modern State: Essays in Political Economy.* Cheltenham, UK, and Northampton, MA: Edward Elgar.

Fisman, R. and E. Miguel. 2010. *Economic Gangsters: Corruption, Violence, and the Poverty of Nations.* Princeton, NJ: Princeton University Press.

Foster, J. E., A. W. Horowitz and F. Méndez. 2012. An axiomatic approach to the measurement of corruption: Theory and applications. *The World Bank Economic Review*, 26(2): 217–235.

Freedom House. 2014. *Combating Impunity: Transitional Justice and Anti-Corruption.* Prepared by Sanja Pesek. New York, NY and Washington, DC: Freedom House.

Frey, B. 2009. Punishment – and beyond. CESifo Working Paper 2706. Munich: Center for Economic Studies (CES); Ifo Institute; and Munich Society for the Promotion of Economic Research.

Friedman, L. 2000. In defence of corporate criminal liability. *Harvard Journal of Law and Public Policy*, 23(3).

Gamu, J., P. Le Billon and S. Spiegel. 2015. Extractive industries and poverty: A review of recent findings and linkage mechanisms. *The Extractive Industries and Society*, 2(1): 162–176.

Garoupa, N. 1997. The theory of optimal law enforcement. *Journal of Economic Surveys*, 11(3): 267–295.

Garoupa, N. and F. Gomez-Pomar. 2004. Punish once or punish twice: a theory of the use of criminal sanctions in addition to regulatory penalties. *American Law and Economics Review*, 6(2): 410–433.

Garoupa, N. and F. H. Stephen. 2008. Why plea-bargaining fails to achieve results in so many criminal justice systems: a new framework for assessment. *Maastricht J. Eur. & Comp. L.*, 15: 323.

Gilberthorpe, E. and E. Papyrakis. 2015. The extractive industries and development: the resource curse at the micro, meso and macro levels. *The Extractive Industries and Society*, 2(2): 381–390.

Gloppen, S. 2013. Courts, corruption and judicial independence. In T. Søreide and A. Williams (Eds) *Corruption, Grabbing and Development: Real World Challenges.* Cheltenham, UK, and Northampton, MA: Edward Elgar.

Groenendijk, N. 1997. A principal-agent model of corruption. *Crime, Law and Social Change*, 27(3–4): 207–229.

Harel, A. 2012. Economic analysis of criminal law: a survey. In I. A. Harel and K. N. Hylton (Eds) *Research Handbook on the Economics of Criminal Law.* Cheltenham, UK, and Northampton, MA: Edward Elgar.

Harel, A. 2014. Behavioural analysis of criminal law: a survey. *Bergen Journal of Criminal Law & Criminal Justice*, 2(1): 32–55.

Harsanyi, J. C. 1977. *Advances in Understanding National Behavior.* Netherlands: Springer.

Hasker K. and C. Okten. 2008. Intermediaries and corruption. *Journal of Economic Behavior & Organization*, 67(1): 103–115.

Hatchard, J. 2014. *Combating Corruption: Legal Approaches to Supporting Good Governance and Integrity in Africa*. Cheltenham, UK, and Northampton, MA: Edward Elgar.

Healey, P. and G. Serafeim. 2014. An analysis of firms' self-reported anticorruption efforts. Working Paper 12-077. Boston, MA: Harvard Business School.

Hjelmeng, E. and T. Søreide. 2014. Debarment in public procurement: rationales and realization. In G. M. Racca and C. R. Yukins (Eds) *Integrity and Efficiency in Sustainable Public Contracts*. Brussels: Bruylant.

Hough, M., J. Jackson, B. Bradford, A. Myhill and P. Quinton. 2010. Procedural justice, trust, and institutional legitimacy. *Policing* 4(3): 203–210.

Høyland, B., K. Moene and F. Willumsen. 2012. The tyranny of international index rankings. *Journal of Development Economics*, 97(1): 1–14.

Hume, D. and T. L. Beauchamp. 2007. *A Dissertation on the Passions: The Natural History of Religion: A Critical Edition* (Vol. 5). Oxford, UK: Oxford University Press.

Ivory, R. 2014. *Corruption, Asset Recovery, and the Protection of Property in Public International Law: The Human Rights of Bad Guys*. Cambridge, UK: Cambridge University Press.

Jøhnson, J. and T. Søreide. 2013. Methods for learning what works and why in anticorruption. U4 Issue 2013:8, Chr. Michelsen Institute (CMI): U4 Anticorruption Resource Center.

Joly, E. 2003. *Er det en slik verden vi vil ha?* (Norwegian version. Orginal title: *Est-ce dans ce monde-là que nous voulons vivre*). Oslo: Aschehoug.

Kabur, D. and R. Webb. 2000. *Governance-Related Conditionalities of the International Financial Institutions*. United Nations Conference on Trade and Development.

Kahneman, D. 2011. *Thinking, Fast and Slow*. New York: Farrar, Straus and Giroux.

Kahneman, D. and A. Tversky. 1979. Prospect theory: an analysis of decision-making under risk. *Econometrica*, 47: 263–291.

Kahneman, D. and A. Tversky. 1986. Rational choice and the framing of decisions. *Journal of Business*, 59: 251–278.

Karl, T. L. 1997. *The Paradox of Plenty: Oil Booms and Petro-States*. Oakland, CA: University of California Press.

Kaufmann, D. and P. C. Vicente. 2011. Legal corruption. *Economics & Politics*, 23(2): 195–219.

Kenny, C. and T. Søreide. 2008. Grand corruption in utilities. World Bank Policy Research Working Paper Series. Washington, DC: World Bank.

Klaes, M. 2000. The birth of the concept of transaction costs: issues and controversies. *Industrial and Corporate Change*, 9(4): 567–593.

Klitgard, R. 2015. *Addressing Corruption Together.* Paris: OECD.

Kolstad, I. and T. Søreide. 2009. Corruption in natural resource management: implications for policy makers. *Resources Policy*, 34: 214–226.

Kreps, D. M., P. Milgrom, J. Roberts and R. Wilson. 1982. Rational cooperation in the finitely-repeated prisoners' dilemma (No. TR-375). Stanford University of California: Institute for Mathematical Studies in the Social Sciences.

Krueger, A. O. 1974. The political economy of the rent-seeking society. *The American Economic Review*, 291–303.

Laffont, J. J. and J. Tirole. 1991. The politics of government decision-making: a theory of regulatory capture. *The Quarterly Journal of Economics*, 1089–1127.

Lambsdorff, J. G. 2002. Making corrupt deals: contracting in the shadow of the law. *Journal of Economic Behavior & Organization*, 48(3): 221–241.

Lambsdorff, J. G. 2007. *The Institutional Economics of Corruption and Reform: Theory, Evidence and Policy.* Cambridge, UK: Cambridge University Press.

Lambsdorff, J. G. 2012. Behaviorial and experimental economics as a guide to anticorruption. In S. Serra and L. Wantchekon (Eds) *New Advances in Experimental Research on Corruption. Research in Experimental Economics*, Vol. 15. Bingley, UK: Emerald Insight.

Lambsdorff, J. G. 2015. What can we know about corruption? A very short history of corruption research and a list of what we should aim for. *Jahrbücher für Nationalökonomie und Statistik.* Bd, 235(2).

Legge, J. 1861. *The Chinese Classics: With a Translation, Critical and Exegetical Notes, Prolegomena, and Copious Indexes, 5 vols.* (A revised second edition was released in 1893 (Oxford: Clarendon Press), and reprinted by Cosimo in 2006).

Lin, M. W. and C. Yu. 2014. Can corruption be measured? Comparing global versus local perceptions of corruption in East and Southeast Asia. *Journal of Comparative Policy Analysis: Research and Practice,* 16(2): 140–157.

Llamzon, A. P. 2014. *Corruption in International Investment Arbitration.* Oxford University Press.

Mahdavi, P. 2014. Extortion in the oil states: nationalization, regulatory structure, and corruption. UCLA manuscript.

Mallaby, S. 2005. *The World's Banker: A Story of Failed States, Financial Crises, and the Wealth and Poverty of Nations.* New Haven: Yale University Press.

Manzetti, L. 1999. *Privatization South American Style.* New York: Oxford University Press.

Marjit, S. and H. Shi. 1998. On controlling crime with corrupt officials. *Journal of Economic Behavior & Organization*, 34(1): 163–172.

Martimort, D. and S. Straub. 2009. Infrastructure privatization and changes in corruption patterns: the roots of public discontent. *Journal of Development Economics*, 90(1): 69–84.

Mauro, P. 1995. Corruption and growth. *The Quarterly Journal of Economics*, 681–712.

McCarty, N., K. Poole and H. Rosenthal. 2013. *Political Bubbles: Financial Crises and the Failure of American Democracy.* Princeton University Press.

Mehlum, H., K. Moene and R. Torvik. 2003. Predator or Prey? Parasitic Enterprises in Economic Development. *European Economic Review*, 47: 275–94.

Messick, R. and S. Schutte. 2015. *Corruption risks in the criminal justice chain and tools for assessment.* U4 Issue No. 6 U4. Bergen, Norway: Anti-Corruption Resource Centre, CMI.

Meyer, O. 2013. The formation of a transnational *ordre public* against corruption: lessons for and from arbitration tribunals. In S. Rose-Ackerman and P. Carrington (Eds) *Anticorruption Policy: Can International Actors Play a Constructive Role.* Durham, NC: Carolina Academic Press.

Miceli, T. J. 1991. Optimal criminal procedure: fairness and deterrence. *International Review of Law and Economics*, 11(1): 3–10.

Miceli, T. J. 2009. *The Economic Approach to Law.* Stanford University Press.

Mitchell, A. V. and P. Sikka. 2011. *The Pin-Stripe Mafia: How Accountancy Firms Destroy Societies.* Basildon: Association for Accountancy & Business Affairs.

Moene, K. and T. Søreide. 2015. Good governance facades. In S. Rose-Ackerman and P. Lagunes (Eds) *Greed, Corruption, and the Modern State: Essays in Political Economy.* Cheltenham, UK, and Northampton, MA: Edward Elgar.

Moene, K. and T. Søreide. 2016. Prospects of corruption control: a cross-country perspective. *Corruption Control.* (forthcoming).

Mookherjee, D. and I. P. L. Png. 1995. Corruptible law enforcers: how should they be compensated? *The Economic Journal*, 145–159.

Moore, M. S. 2010. *Placing Blame: A General Theory of the Criminal Law.* Oxford University Press.

Mungiu-Pippidi, A. 2015. *The Quest for Good Governance: How Societies Develop Control of Corruption.* Cambridge, UK: Cambridge University Press.

Myerson, R. B. 1986. Multistage games with communication. *Econometrica: Journal of the Econometric Society,* 323–358.

Myerson, R. B. 1999. Nash equilibrium and the history of economic theory. *Journal of Economic Literature,* Sept., 1067–1082.

Niehans, J. 1987. Transaction costs. *The New Palgrave: A Dictionary of Economics,* v. 4: 677–680.

Norwegian Official Reports (NOU). 2009. *Tax Havens and Development.* Report from the Government Commission on Capital Flight from Poor Countries. Official Norwegian Reports 2009:19. Oslo: Ministry of Foreign Affairs.

Nucifora, A., E. Churchill and B. Rijkers. 2015. Cronyism, corruption, and the Arab Spring: the case of Tunisia. In *2015 Index of Economic Freedom.* Washington, DC: The Heritage Foundation.

Oded, S. 2013. *Corporate Compliance: New Approaches to Regulatory Enforcement.* Cheltenham, UK, and Northampton, MA: Edward Elgar.

Oded, S. 2015. Expert opinion: the efficiency viewpoint. Ih A. O. Makinwa (Ed.) *Negotiated Settlements for Corruption Offences, A European Perspective.* The Hague: Eleven Publishing.

OECD. 2013. *OECD Working Group of Bribery Annual Report.* Paris: OECD Publishing.

OECD. 2014a. *OECD Foreign Bribery Report: An Analysis of the Crime of Bribery of Foreign Public Officials.* Paris: OECD Publishing.

OECD. 2014b. *Lobbyists, Governments and Public Trust, Volume 3: Implementing the OECD Principles for Transparency and Integrity in Lobbying.* Paris: OECD Publishing.

OECD. 2015. *Consequences of Corruption at the Sector Level and Implications for Economic Growth and Development.* Paris: OECD Publishing.

Olken, B. A. and R. Pande. 2012. Corruption in developing countries. *Annual Reviews of Economics,* 41(1): 479–509.

Ortner, J. and S. Chassang. 2014. Making collusion hard: asymmetric information as a counter-corruption measure. *Princeton University William S. Dietrich II Economic Theory Center Research Paper,* 064-2014.

Pauwelyn, J. 2013. Different means, same end. The contribution of trade and investment treaties to anti-corruption policy. In S. Rose-Ackerman and P. Carrington (Eds) *Anticorruption Policy: Can International Actors Play a Constructive Role.* Durham, NC: Carolina Academic Press.

Peisakhin, L. V. 2011. Field experimentation and the study of corruption. In S. Rose-Ackerman and T. Søreide (Eds) *The International Handbook on the Economics of Corruption. Vol. 2.* Cheltenham, UK, and Northampton, MA: Edward Elgar.

Pena, A. M. N. 2014. Corporate criminal liability: tool or obstacle to prosecution? In D. Brodowski, M. E. de la Parra, K. Tiedemann and J. Vogel (Eds) *Regulating Corporate Criminal Liability* (pp. 197–210). Switzerland: Springer International Publishing.

Persson, A., B. Rothstein and J. Teorell. 2013. Why anticorruption reforms fail: systemic corruption as a collective action problem. *Governance,* 26(3): 449–471.

Pieth, M. and R. Ivory. 2011. *Corporate Criminal Liability: Emergence, Convergence, and Risk.* Springer Netherlands.

Pieth, M., L. Low and N. Bonucci (Eds). 2013. *The OECD Convention on Bribery: A Commentary.* Cambridge University Press.

Piketty, T. 2014. *Capital in the 21st Century.* Cambridge, MA: Harvard University.

Poisson, M. 2014. Grabbing in the education sector. In T. Søreide and A. Williams (Eds) *Corruption, Grabbing and Development: Real World Challenges.* Cheltenham, UK, and Northampton, MA: Edward Elgar.

Polinsky, A. M. and S. Shavell. 2000. The fairness of sanctions: some implications for optimal enforcement policy. *American Law and Economics Review,* 2(2): 223–237.

Polinsky, A. M. and S. Shavell. 2001. Corruption and optimal law enforcement. *Journal of Public Economics,* 81(1): 1–24.

Polinsky, A. M. and S. Shavell. 2007. The theory of public enforcement of law. In M. Polinsky and S. Shavell (Eds) *Handbook of Law and Economics, Volume 1,* 403–454. Elsevier.

Posner, R. A. 1985. An economic theory of the criminal law. *Columbia Law Review,* 1193–1231.

Prado, M. M. and L. D. Carson. 2014. Brazilian anti-corruption legislation and its enforcement: Potential lessons for institutional design. IRIBA Working Paper 09. Manchester: International Research Initiative on Brazil and Africa.

Rahman, D. 2012. But who will monitor the monitor? *The American Economic Review,* 102(6): 2767–2797.

Rajan, R. and L. Zingales. 2006. The persistence of underdevelopment: institutions, human capital or constituencies (October 2006). CEPR Discussion Paper No. 5867.

Ríos-Figueroa, J. 2007. Fragmentation of power and the emergence of an effective judiciary in Mexico, 1994–2002. *Latin American Politics and Society,* 49(1): 31–57.

Ríos-Figueroa, J. and J. K. Staton. 2014. An evaluation of cross-national measures of judicial independence. *Journal of Law, Economics, and Organization*, 30(1): 104–137.

Robertson, A. F. (Sandy). 2006. Misunderstanding corruption. *Anthropology Today*. 22(2): 8–11.

Robinson, J. A., R. Torvik and T. Verdier. 2006. Political foundations of the resource curse. *Journal of Development Economics*, 79: 447–468.

Rose, J. and P. M. Heywood. 2013. Political science approaches to integrity and corruption. *Human Affairs*, 23(2): 148–159.

Rose-Ackerman, S. 1975. The economics of corruption. *Journal of Public Economics*, 4(2): 187–203.

Rose-Ackerman, S. 1978. *Corruption: A Study in Political Economy*. New York: Academic Press.

Rose-Ackerman, S. 1999. *Corruption and Government. Causes, Consequences and Reform*. Cambridge: Cambridge University Press.

Rose-Ackerman, S. 2014. Corruption and conflicts of interest. In *Corruption and Conflicts of Interest: A Comparative Law Approach*.

Rose-Ackerman, S. and P. L. Lindseth (Eds). 2010. *Comparative Administrative Law*. Cheltenham, UK, and Northampton, MA: Edward Elgar.

Rose-Ackerman, S. and P. Carrington (Eds). 2013. *Anticorruption Policy: Can International Actors Play a Constructive Role*. Durham, NC: Carolina Academic Press.

Rose-Ackerman, S. and B. J. Palifka. 2016. *Corruption and Government: Causes, Consequences and Reform*. (forthcoming: late 2015 or early 2016). Cambridge: Cambridge University Press.

Ross, M. 2012. *The Oil Curse: How Petroleum Shapes the Wealth of Nations*. Princeton University Press.

Rossetti, C. 2000. The prosecution of political corruption: France, Italy and the USA – A comparative view. *Innovation: The European Journal of Social Science Research*, 13(2): 169–181.

Rothstein, B. 2011. *The Quality of Government: Corruption, Social Trust, and Inequality in International Perspective*. Chicago: University of Chicago Press.

Saisana, M. and A. Saltelli. 2012. Corruption Perceptions Index 2012 Statistical Assessment. *JRC Scientific and Policy Reports*.

Samuelson, P. A. 1947. *Foundations of Economic Analysis*. Cambridge, MA: Harvard University Press.

Sappington, D. 1991. Incentives in principal–agent relationships. *Journal of Economic Perspectives*, 5(2): 45–66.

Sarsfield, R. 2012. The bribe game: microfoundations of corruption in Mexico. *Justice System Journal*, 33(2): 215–234.

Schjelderup, G. 2015. Secrecy jurisdictions. *International Tax and Public Finance*, 1–22.

Sen, A. 2001. *Development as Freedom*. Oxford University Press.

Sen, A. 2011. *The Idea of Justice*. Harvard University Press.

Shafir, E. (Ed). 2012. The *Behavioral Foundations for Public Policy*. Princeton, NJ: Princeton University Press.

Shaxson, N. 2007. *Poisoned Wells: The Dirty Politics of African Oil*. PalgraveMacmillan.

Shaxson, N. 2011. *Treasure Islands: Tax Havens and the Men Who Stole the World*. London: Bodley Head.

Shelley, L. I. 2014. *Dirty Entanglements: Corruption, Crime, and Terrorism*. Cambridge University Press.

Søreide, T. 2005. Is it right to rank. Paper presented at the *IV Global Forum on Fighting Corruption and Safeguarding Integrity*, Session Measuring Integrity. Brasilia, Brazil, 7–10 June 2005.

Søreide, T. 2008. Beaten by bribery: why not blow the whistle? *Journal of Institutional and Theoretical Economics*, 164(3): 407–428.

Søreide, T. 2009. Too risk averse to stay honest? Business corruption, uncertainty and attitudes toward risk. *International Review of Law and Economics*, 29: 388–395.

Søreide, T. 2011. Ten Challenges in Public Construction: CEIC-CMI Public Sector Transparency Study. Vol. 1 No. 19. Bergen: Chr. Michelsen Institute (CMI).

Søreide, T. 2013a. Democracy's shortcomings in anti-corruption. In S. Rose-Ackerman and P. Carrington (Eds). *Anticorruption Policy: Can International Actors Play a Constructive Role*. Durham, NC: Carolina Academic Press.

Søreide, T. 2013b. *Korrupsjon: Mekanismer og Mottiltak* (Textbook. Translated: *Corruption: Mechanisms and Counter-Measures*). Oslo: CappelenDamm.

Søreide, T. 2014a. *Drivers of Corruption: A Brief Review*. Washington, DC: The World Bank.

Søreide, T. 2014b. Corruption and competition: fair markets as an anticorruption device. *Nagoya Journal of Law and Politics*, 258: 237–262.

Søreide, T. 2015. Negotiated settlements for corruption offences: position in Norway. In A. O. Makinwa (Ed.) *Negotiated Settlements for Corruption Offences: A European Perspective*. The Hague: Eleven Publishing.

Søreide, T. and A. Williams. 2014. *Corruption, Grabbing and Development: Real World Challenges*. Cheltenham, UK, and Northampton, MA: Edward Elgar.

Søreide, T. and S. Rose-Ackerman. 2016. Corruption in state administration. In J. Arlen (Ed.) *The Research Handbook on Corporate Crime and Financial Misdealing*. Cheltenham, UK, and Northampton, MA: Edward Elgar.

Søreide, T., A. Tostensen and I. A. Skage. 2012. *Hunting for Per Diem: The Uses and Abuses of Travel Compensation in Three Developing Countries.* Norad Report no. 2/2012. Oslo: Norad.

Søreide, T., L. Gröning and R. Wandall. 2016. An efficient anticorruption sanctions regime? The case of the World Bank. *The Chicago Journal of International Law.* (forthcoming).

StAR. 2013. *Left out of the Bargain: Settlements in Foreign Bribery Cases and Implications for Asset Recovery.* Prepared by J. Odour et al. World Bank and UNODC: Stolen Asset Recovery Initiative.

StAR. 2014. *Few and Far: The Hard Facts on Stolen Asset Recovery.* Prepared by Larissa Grey. World Bank and UNODC: Stolen Asset Recovery Initiative.

Stephenson, M. 2015. Corruption and democratic institutions: a review and synthesis. In S. Rose-Ackerman and P. Lagunes (Eds) *Greed, Corruption, and the Modern State: Essays in Political Economy.* Cheltenham, UK, and Northampton, MA: Edward Elgar.

Stiglitz, J. 1987. Principal and agent, *The New Palgrave: A Dictionary of Economics,* v. 3, pp. 966–971.

Svensson, J. 2005. Eight questions about corruption. *Journal of Economic Perspectives,* 19(3): 19–42.

Thatcher, M. 2011. Risks of capture and independent regulatory agencies in network industries in Europe: a political and institutional analysis. In Estache, A. (Ed.) *Emerging Issues in Competition, Collusion, and Regulation of Network Industries.* London: Centre for Economic Policy Research.

Tirole, J. 1986. Hierarchies and bureaucracies: on the role of collusion in organizations. *Journal of Economics and Organization,* 2: 181–214.

Tirole, J. 1996. A theory of collective reputations (with applications to the persistence of corruption and to firm quality). *The Review of Economic Studies,* 1–22.

Tonry, M. H. 2011. *Why Punish? How Much?: A Reader on Punishment.* Oxford University Press.

Torvik, R. 2009. Why do some resource-abundant countries succeed while others do not? *Oxford Review of Economic Policy,* 25(2): 241–256.

Transparency International. 2007. *Global Corruption Report 2007: Corruption in Judicial Systems.* Transparency International and Cambridge University Press.

Transparency International. 2012. *Money, Politics, Power: Corruption Risks in Europe.* Berlin: Transparency International.

Treisman, D. 2007. What have we learned about the causes of corruption from ten years of cross-national empirical research? *Annual Review of Political Science,* 10: 211–244.

Tullock, G. 1967. The welfare costs of tariffs, monopolies, and theft. *Economic Inquiry*, 5(3): 224–232.

Tullock, G. 2005. *The Social Dilemma: Of Autocracy, Revolution, Coup d'état, and War* (Vol. 8). C. K. Rowley (Ed.). C. K. Liberty Fund Inc.

Tyler, T. 2012. The psychology of cooperation: implications for public policy. Chapter 4 in E. Shafir (Ed.) *The Behavioral Foundations for Public Policy*. Princeton, NJ: Princeton University Press.

Ugur, M. and N. Dasgupta. 2011. *Evidence on the Economic Growth Impacts of Corruption in Low-Income Countries and Beyond*. London: EPPI-Centre, University of London.

Underkuffler, L. S. 2013. *Captured by Evil: The Idea of Corruption in Law*. New Haven: Yale University Press.

UNODC. 2009. *Technical Guide to The United Nations Convention Against Corruption*. Vienna: United Nations Office on Drugs and Crime.

Van Aaken, A., L. P. Feld and S. Voigt. 2010. Do independent prosecutors deter political corruption? An empirical evaluation across 78 countries. *American Law and Economics Review*, 12(1): 204–244.

Van Winden, F. and A. Ash. 2009. On the behavioral economics of crime. *Review of Law and Economics*, 8(1): 181–213.

Vannucci, A. 2009. The controversial legacy of 'Mani Pulite': a critical analysis of Italian corruption and anti-corruption policies. *Bulletin of Italian Politics*, 1(2): 233–264.

Vian, T. 2008. Review of corruption in the health sector: theory, methods and interventions. *Health Policy and Planning*, 23(2): 83–94.

Vicente, P. 2010. Does oil corrupt? Evidence from a natural experiment in West Africa. *Journal of Development Economics*, 92(1): 28–38.

Vicente, P. 2011. Oil, corruption and vote-buying: a review of the case of São Tomé and Princípe. In S. Rose-Ackerman and T. Søreide (Eds) *International Handbook on the Economics of Corruption*, Vol. 2. Cheltenham, UK, and Northampton, MA: Edward Elgar.

Victor, D. G., D. R. Hults and M. C. Thurber (Eds). 2011. *Oil and Governance: State-Owned Enterprises and the World Energy Supply*. Cambridge University Press.

Vira, V. and T. Ewing. 2014. *The Militarization & Professionalization of Poaching in Africa*. A report prepared for C4ADS and Born Free. Available at: www.cvads.org and http://www.bornfree.org.uk.

Voigt, S. and J. Gutmann. 2014. On the wrong side of the law: causes and consequences of a corrupt judiciary. *International Review of Law and Economics*. (forthcoming/in press).

Wade, R. 1982. The system of administrative and political corruption: canal irrigation in South India. *Journal of Development Studies*, 18(3): 287.

Wiig, A. and I. Kolstad. 2012. If diversification is good, why don't countries diversify more? The political economy of diversification in resource-rich countries. *Energy Policy*, 40: 196–203.

Wingerde, K. and G. Gerben Smid. 2015. Negotiated settlements for corruption offences: position in the Netherlands. In A. O. Makinwa (Ed.) *Negotiated Settlements for Corruption Offences: A European Perspective*. The Hague: Eleven Publishing.

World Bank. 2012. *The World Bank: New Directions in Justice Reform*. A Companion Piece to the Updated Strategy and Implementation Plan on Strengthening Governance, Tackling Corruption. Washington, DC: The World Bank.

Yeoh, P. 2015. Whistleblowing laws: before and after Sarbanes–Oxley. *International Journal of Disclosure and Governance*, 12: 254–73.

Index

Aaken, Anne van 199–200
access to information 23–5, 71, 119,
    123, 148, 150, 202–4, 234
Acemoglu, Daron 40, 63
administrative law 19, 27, 158, 184–6,
    203–4
Africa
  elephant poaching 39, 50–51
  see also individual countries
African Union (AU)
  Convention on Preventing and
     Combating Corruption (2003)
     29
agreements, narrow interpretation of
    88–90
aid *see* development loans/lending;
    foreign aid
AIG 10
Albania
  CPI ranking 114
Alderman, Richard 228
Allingham, Michael G. 140–41
Al-Shabab 50
Alt, James 97
André, Michel André 141–2
Andvig, Jens 207–8
Angola
  BP reputation in 218
  condonement of corruption 236
  infrastructure investments 36
anthropological perspective, on
    corruption 18
Anti-Bribery Convention (1997)
    (OECD) 28–30, 86–7, 90, 219–23,
    228
Anti-Bribery Recommendation (2009)
    (OECD) 30
anticorruption approaches and integrity
    systems 22–6

evaluation of integrity systems
    25–6
non-criminal anticorruption
    strategies 23–5
in state administration 53–4
Arab Spring (2010) 7, 79–80
arbitration *see* investment arbitration
Argentina
  CPI ranking 114
Arlen, Jennifer 158
Arthur Andersen 186–8
asset recovery 109–10
Asset Recovery Network of the
    Financial Action Task Force of
    South America against Money
    Laundering 103
attorneys 94–5
Auriol, Emmanuelle 39–40
Australia
  WGB report findings on 94
Austria
  fines for corruption 106
  lack of professional restrictions 108
  WGB report findings on 88, 102
autocratic regimes 7, 209

banking industry, corruption within 10
Bank of China 104–5
bargaining powers 144, 191
basic/essential services 208, 227
Beccaria, Cesare 137
Becker, Gary 21, 137
behavioral economics 126–8, 140–42
Bel, Germà 36–7
Belgium
  CPI ranking 114–15
  WGB report findings on 93, 96–8
Benson, Michael L. 19
Bentham, Jeremy 137

266 *Corruption and criminal justice*

Torny, Michael 138
tort law 27
Total 9
transparency and integrity initiatives 79
Transparency International 9, 10, 29
  Corruption Perceptions Index (CPI)
    36, 66–9, 114–15, 209, 214
  Global Corruption Barometer 73, 80
  National Integrity Studies (NIS) 25
  Philips investigation 104
  recommendations to Italy 84
trust-based vs. threat-based approaches
    178, 209–13
Tullock, Gordon 61, 212, 222, 224–5
Tungodden, Bertil 140–42
Turkey
  CPI ranking 114–15
  Rule of Law Index ranking 96

Uganda
  CPI ranking 114
  Rule of Law Index ranking 96
Ugur, Mehmet 37
Ukraine
  condonement of corruption 236
  CPI ranking 114
Underkuffler, Laura 12
United Kingdom (UK)
  fines for corruption 106
  Public Interest Disclosure Act (1998)
    99
  WGB report findings on 94, 99
United Nations
  Crime Victimization surveys 73
United Nations Convention against
    Corruption (UNCAC) 28, 78,
    86–7, 89–90, 92, 97, 103–4, 222,
    226, 228
United Nations Human Development
    Index 9
United States (US)
  CPI ranking 68, 114–15
  Dodd-Frank Wall Street Reform and
    Consumer Protection Act (2010)
    99
  Enron scandal (2001) 158
  fines for corruption 106
  Foreign Corrupt Practices Act 29, 102

law and economics discourse 21
prosecutorial resources impact
    convictions 97
respondent superior principle 93–4,
    181–2
sanctions as deterrence 31
StAR report on victim compensation
    109–10
strict residual liability 188–9
WGB report findings on 91–2
Uruguay
  CPI ranking 114–15
utility function 129
Uzbekistan
  CPI ranking 114

value chain, of criminal justice/law
    enforcement 27, 111–13
value for money 175–7
Vannucci, Alberto 200
Van Wingerde, Karin 190–91
Venezuela
  condonement of corruption 236
  CPI ranking 114
verdicts 78, 107–8, 110, 122, 124–5,
    145, 168–9, 201, 223
vicarious liability 181–6
victim compensation 109–10, 193
Vietnam
  CPI ranking 114
Vira, Varun 50
Voigt, Stefan 199–200

Wade, Robert 82
wealth registries of parliamentarians
    87–8
whistle-blowers 24, 30, 98–100, 136,
    159, 164, 192, 196, 199, 207
white-collar crime 18–19
Wikileaks 234
William of Ockham 174
Willumsen, Fredrik 67–9
witnesses 27, 83, 98–9, 112–13, 136,
    195
Wolfensohn, James 235
Working Group on Bribery (WGB)
    (OECD) 9, 24–5, 65, 76–8, 84–6,
    88–94, 96–9, 101, 106, 108, 224